Doing Statistics with SPSS

Alistair W. Kerr
Howard K. Hall
Stephen A. Kozub

SAGE Publications
London ● Thousand Oaks ● New Delhi

ISBN 0-7619-7384-2 (hbk)
ISBN 0-7619-7385-0 (pbk)
© Alistair W. Kerr, Howard K. Hall and Stephen A. Kozub 2002
First published 2002
Reprinted 2002, 2004

SAGE Publications Ltd
1 Oliver's Yard
55 City Road
London EC1Y 1SP

SAGE Publications Inc
2455 Teller Road
Thousand Oaks
California 91320

SAGE Publications India Pvt Ltd
B–42 Panchsheel Enclave
PO Box 4109
New Delhi 110 017

British Library Cataloguing in Publication data
A catalogue record for this book is available from the British Library

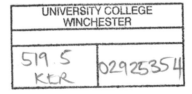
Typeset by SIVA Math Setters, Chennai, India
Printed and bound in Great Britain by
Cromwell Press Limited, Trowbridge, Wiltshire

CONTENTS

1 THE NEED FOR STATISTICS

When you enrolled for a degree course, you were probably under the impression that much of your time would be spent playing sport, participating in outdoor pursuits, meeting new friends, enjoying your leisure activities in the many local hostelries, and even attending the odd lecture, seminar or workshop to learn about important phenomena in your field of interest. To discover that you had to register for a course in data handling is likely to have generated little enthusiasm, and more likely caused you some concern. So, why is it that many degree programmes require students to undertake a statistics course?

The answer to this question lies in the fact that statistics play a vitally important role in research. They help answer important research questions and it is the answers to such questions that further our understanding of the field and provide a knowledge base for academic study. This body of knowledge resides, for the most part, in the textbooks and academic research journals that grace the shelves of university libraries. In the future this knowledge base will continue to expand as many more answers to important research questions are provided.

At this point you may be thinking that you have no interest in research or in becoming a researcher. Although this may be true it is also a fact that during the next few years you will be asked to read a considerable amount of information as part of your academic programme of study. This activity will require you to interpret the results of research employing many different research methods. Consequently, it is imperative that you become familiar with the research process so that you become an informed consumer of the literature in the field, and can think critically about everything you read. An awareness of how to answer research questions and read research articles will enable you to discern valuable information that forms part of the knowledge base in academic study, from unsubstantiated speculation that adds little to our understanding of important issues in the field. Therefore, not only will this book help you understand the research process, but it will help you reflect critically on the research literature.

It is not uncommon for students who are just beginning their university careers to be directed towards the library by academic staff and asked to read selected articles in preparation for a lecture or seminar. However, most undergraduate students find the task of reading a research article to be quite intimidating. If the task can be avoided, the article will rarely be read. If it cannot be avoided, the following strategy appears common. There is a tendency to read the abstract in minute detail, because it is short and concise. Once this task has been completed attention is turned towards the introduction and discussion sections because they appear to be most understandable and contain what most neophyte researchers believe to be the relevant information. Next, the methods section is typically given a cursory glance, or at best it is skimmed because it tends to be dull and boring and simply describes what the researchers did. Then the results section is ignored completely because the statistics appear incomprehensible. Finally the discussion section is read because, like the introduction, it is partially comprehensible. Although this is an understandable strategy when one first encounters research articles, it is not one that is going to produce either informed consumers of research, or university graduates who are independent critical thinkers. Worse still, it can lead to the acceptance of conclusions that a critical examination of the methods and results sections would have shown to be at best speculative and at worst incorrect. Changing this strategy so that you are able to feel confident about reading the results section of a research article is a central aim of this text. However, simplifying the task of understanding the statistics section in a research article is not easy. Even the most dedicated knowledge seeker can be turned off by terms such as canonical correlation, factorial analysis of variance, or discriminant function analysis. However, to avoid getting bogged down with statistical terminology it would be especially wise at this point to keep in mind that statistics are simply tools that researchers employ to help answer research questions.

Using the Appropriate Tools

The selection of the most appropriate tool to perform a job is a crucial issue whether you are a carpenter, a surgeon, a motor mechanic or a research scientist. The tool selected by a carpenter obviously depends upon the job that is being done at the time. Similarly, which statistical tool a research scientist selects depends upon the question being asked. Unfortunately, it is all too noticeable that when students are asked to conduct research they often base the selection of their statistical analysis upon tests which they might have heard mentioned once or twice, rather than upon their suitability for the job. This is analogous to a homeowner who attempts to perform all the major home improvement projects with the first tool that is pulled from a toolbox.

Let us suppose that our homeowner had chosen to work on a project that involved installing a new door on a shed. To complete the job correctly requires the door frame to be rebuilt, a little material to be removed from the bottom of the new door, the door to be rehung on its new hinges, and a new lock attached. All these jobs could be performed efficiently if the homeowner possessed the correct tools for each job. However, the only tool that our homeowner possessed was a hammer. Unfortunately, rather than making an expensive trip to the local 'DIY' store to purchase the appropriate tools, the homeowner attempted to get by with the aid of this one trusty implement. Some early success was met because the door frame only required nailing into position. For this task the hammer proved to be the correct tool for the job. Taking a little off the bottom of the new door with a hammer was more difficult, but it was achieved with a few hefty whacks. The wood splintered and cracked around the bottom of the door, but it was only a shed so it didn't really matter that the job wasn't well done. Next, our homeowner attached the door to the new frame by bashing all the screws into place, again splintering the wood, and bending the screws. This meant the door hinges didn't hold the door in place well but it looked fine from a distance, and it was better than the old door that suffered from dry rot. Finally, the homeowner forced a new lock into place with the aid of the trusty hammer. Unfortunately, the lock no longer worked after the homeowner's efforts with the hammer. The homeowner thought that if the new door was tied to the frame with a piece of string it would look just fine – that is, until it needed opening.

Fortunately, most property owners do not go about making home improvements in this fashion. They attempt to utilise the correct tools for each job. However, the point to be considered here is that it *was* possible for our homeowner to complete the job on the shed door with only the use of the hammer. Upon closer inspection, however, the results indicated that the job was a complete disaster. Similarly, it would be possible for a researcher to select the wrong statistical techniques to analyse data and still be able to draw conclusions from the analyses. Only upon close scrutiny of the results by someone versed in research methods would they be found to be meaningless. Consequently, whether you are a homeowner or a novice researcher, it is recommended that you have an understanding of what tools are suitable for the particular jobs you are likely to undertake. This involves knowing how to use each tool, and recognising when each should be used. Knowledge such as this will allow you to avoid the drawbacks of selecting the wrong tools for the job. That is, picking up your hammer and treating everything as if it were a nail.

Numerophobia

Even when students become aware of the importance of using statistics to help answer research questions, many feel anxious about their mathematical expertise. This is not an uncommon phenomenon. Many intelligent people who are capable of competent performance in other areas experience 'numerophobia' (i.e. a fear of numbers) at the thought of having to solve more than the most basic mathematical problems. Fortunately, the subject of statistics is not mathematics, although it does involve the use of some simple mathematical operations. In using this manual you will need to know how to add, subtract, multiply, use brackets, and understand the principle of squaring and taking the square root of numbers. Beyond this you will not find yourself encountering any mind-blowing mathematics. What might cause a few problems are the symbols and notation that are used to describe particular operations or specify particular statistics. However, just as when learning a foreign language one has to become familiar with new words and symbols in order that the language makes sense, the learning of unfamiliar statistical symbols and notation will take time, patience and some considerable thought before they become second nature to you. The meaning of these symbols and notation *will* be explained to you as you progress through the manual. You can also find a brief description of symbols and notation in Appendix 1. However, if you still find that you do not understand something, consider the alternative strategies that might be available to you to help overcome this barrier. It is important to remember that if you continue to invest effort into understanding the principles covered in this manual you will begin to develop some confidence in the subject and overcome many potential barriers to understanding. In contrast, if you adhere to a view that your lack of understanding cannot be changed, no matter how hard you try, then it is unlikely that you will develop any confidence in the subject matter and this may simply reinforce the numerophobic condition.

The importance of this fact is illustrated by the following story. It describes an incident that took place at the end of the third or fourth lecture of an introductory statistics course being taught by one of the authors of this text. A disgruntled student approached the lecturer and announced angrily: 'I hate this course! I don't understand any of it.' When the lecturer enquired about which aspects in particular were causing the problem, the student looked vacantly at him and replied, 'All of it. I just don't have a clue about anything!' At this point, the lecturer thought for a while and asked why the student hadn't communicated this lack of understanding during the lecture when he had attempted to solicit feedback by asking if everyone understood what was said. Back came the reply: 'Do you think I'm stupid? I'm not going to put up my hand in front of the class and say that I don't understand. You've got to realise that just because there's silence when you ask if we understand, doesn't mean that we do. Anyway, I don't want everyone thinking I'm a half-wit, so I'm not going to give them the opportunity, and publicly embarrass myself in the process.' When quizzed as to why one might perceive others in the class to be so judgemental, the student responded by saying 'Everyone else seems to understand the subject, and I don't.' 'But why does it matter if others really do know more than you?', said the lecturer. 'Surely, what is important is that you feel you've learned something in the course.' This response was met by a torrent of verbal abuse and a diatribe on why it would probably be better to give up on the course rather than to suffer the indignity of realising that others might be more competent and to experience the humility of publicly displaying this lack of understanding.

Realising he was inflaming an emotionally charged situation, the lecturer tried another strategy. He enquired if there were parts of the lecture that made any sense that day. At this point, the student began to describe the different measures of central tendency and their properties. 'You see', said the lecturer, 'You *do* understand something.' The lecturer then stepped up to the whiteboard and drew a long horizontal line, representing the continuum of student understanding. The continuum ranged from no knowledge of statistics to a sound understanding of the subject. He then asked the student to mark a cross at some point on this line which signified the level of understanding of statistics at the start of the course. The student marked the board at the extreme left above the words 'no understanding'. Then the lecturer asked the student to repeat the process by marking a cross on the line to signify current understanding. The student responded by inserting the cross a couple of centimetres to the right of the first mark. At this point, the lecturer looked at the student, and noting that there didn't seem to have been much progress made in understanding, said: 'As I see it, my job is to help you move along this continuum. How far you get in this class depends on how willing you are to invest in reading the assigned material, completing the practical exercises, and asking questions to help you comprehend what it is you've read. Everyone is likely to end up at a different point on the continuum by the semester's end, but that's OK. What is important is that *you* begin to develop a clearer understanding of the subject.' Realising that it was more important to focus upon personal improvement and understanding than on how one's performance compared with that of others in the class, the student departed with a little more reassurance that continued investment could bring rewards.

We would like to be able to recount that this student is now a statistical consultant for a nationally known research organisation, but you would probably not believe this. However, the point of this true story is very simple. Your understanding of statistics will be a direct function of your personal investment in the subject matter. Therefore spend time reading around the subject and asking questions about issues of concern. You will reap the benefits in the future as you read and learn more about the research process and the role it plays in your field of interest.

Stages of the Research Process

Identifying the Research Question

Whether you are reading published research, or attempting to conduct a research project, the first stage is to identify the research question being asked. It is sometimes difficult to identify the research question in a published article, particularly if the author has not made it explicit. However, it can usually be found in the introduction of the article where it is framed within the context of current literature. This literature aims to outline the importance of research on the topic, and explain why an answer to the question is being sought.

The awareness of current research is extremely important, as research questions do not arise in a vacuum. While questions may occasionally arise from personal intuition, personal observation of the environment or personal beliefs, the ideas are more often developed through interaction with others. Similarly, research questions tend to arise from an examination of other people's work which can be found in the research journals and textbooks of different scientific disciplines. Therefore, in order to progress successfully through the first stage of a research investigation, a researcher must become familiar with the current literature on a topic and be able to frame the research question of interest within the context of that literature.

Generating Hypotheses

Once the question has been determined, it will be possible to develop specific, testable hypotheses. Hypotheses outline the propositions to be investigated and state the expected relationships between the variables of interest in the investigation. In other words, they are the researcher's best estimation of the expected results. This will be explored further in Chapter 4.

Conducting the Research

Deciding upon the most appropriate methodology for an investigation depends upon the question being asked. The research question and the hypotheses provide guidelines to the researcher about how to go about collecting data. As data collection is one of the basic foundations upon which scientific enquiry is built, it is necessary for the researcher to design a methodological approach which will allow him/her to obtain an answer to the specific research question. The methods used to answer important research questions take many different forms. These include experimental methods, survey methods, observational methods, historical methods and qualitative methods, to name but a few. The important fact to remember is that the selection of the most appropriate method will be determined by the question being asked by the researcher.

Statistical Analyses

Once data have been collected, statistical analyses can be performed so that the hypotheses put forward by the researcher can be objectively tested. Two types of statistics are used in most research investigations:

1. descriptive statistics
2. inferential statistics.

Descriptive statistics describe or summarise the characteristics of the data set. For example, let's say we are interested in the effects of three different training techniques upon aerobic endurance in college athletes. Rather than describe the scores of every participant training under each condition, we might describe the average scores of participants in each condition by reporting the mean. Then we might describe how much variability existed around the mean in each set of scores by reporting the standard deviation. Descriptive statistics do not allow us to test too many hypotheses, but they provide useful descriptive information to the researcher and should always be reported in any research article. This will become apparent in Chapters 2 and 3.

Inferential statistics are much more complex and coverage of this topic begins in Chapter 4. They are used to test hypotheses, and make inferences about a sample to a larger population. Using the previous example, I could determine which is the most effective training technique to improve aerobic endurance in a sample of college athletes by using a test known as an analysis of variance test. Because the athlete sample is assumed to be representative of a larger population, the results of this test could then be generalised to a larger population containing all college athletes.

The results obtained from the application of inferential statistical tests will either support or refute research hypotheses. When students first utilise statistical analyses to test their hypotheses, it is often tempting for them to suggest that the results of their analysis prove their hypotheses to be correct. However, scientific explanations are always tentative. They are frequently changed and updated. Indeed, one of the beauties of science is that it is open to self-correction. Because of this quality, it is advisable to be cautious and merely suggest support for a hypothesis if the results are in the expected direction. Similarly, if the results are not in the expected direction a hypothesis may be refuted though the results would not be sufficient to establish proof. Coverage of different types of inferential statistics begins in Chapter 5 and various tests are discussed throughout the remainder of the book.

Drawing Conclusions

The final stage of the research process involves relating the results back to the literature from where the question was generated and attempting to offer a clear explanation for what happened in the investigation. While it is a relatively straightforward task to explain research findings that support a hypothesis, it is a little more challenging to explain unexpected results. Regardless of whether the results support or refute a research hypothesis, explaining the results requires a sound knowledge of the subject matter. This is because researchers must often consider alternative explanations for the findings, thereby remaining cautious that their explanation is not the only possibility. This stage, as well as the question-generation stage, is where the researcher's detailed knowledge and creativity are most often demanded.

Before proceeding with the contents of this book you may find it useful to familiarise yourself with the role of statistics in your field of interest. To assist you in this respect it is suggested that you complete the following exercise.

EXERCISE 1.1 EXPLORING THE STATISTICAL CONTENT OF RESEARCH ARTICLES

Understanding how and why statistics are used will only become apparent if you become familiar with current research in your area. The purpose of this exercise is to enable you to become more familiar with this research, and to recognise the range of different statistics that are being used to answer research questions.

1. Find a research journal that focuses on some aspect of your field of interest.
2. Select a research article from the journal. Read through the abstract, and skim read the article.
3. Write down the title of the article and the journal from which it came. Then, based upon your understanding of the abstract, write down the research question that you think the researchers were interested in answering. If you cannot

determine the question from the title or by reading the abstract, examine the last paragraph of the introduction, just preceding the methods section, to see if the authors state the purpose of the investigation.

4. Examine the results section, and make a list of as many different statistics as you can identify. For example:

Descriptive statistics	Inferential statistics
Mean	t-test
Median	Analysis of variance (ANOVA)
Mode	Correlation
Standard deviation	Multiple regression
Variance	Factor analysis
Range	Discriminant analysis
	Chi square
	Repeated measures ANOVA

5. To help you with this task, consult the later chapters of this text, a dictionary of statistical tests or an introductory statistics textbook for your specific discipline. Write a sentence to describe the purpose of each statistical test employed in the research article; that is, explain what the statistical test is designed to do.

6. Explain why it was necessary to use the statistical test to answer the research question posed in the article.

2

DESCRIPTIVE STATISTICS

Introduction to Descriptive Statistics

In attempting to answer most research questions, it is common to collect large amounts of data that often represent individual participant's scores on variables of interest. For example, in order to be able to help in the recovery of patients who have undergone heart surgery, exercise researchers might be interested in knowing how important factors such as age, previous exercise habits and self-confidence on adherence to a cardiac rehabilitation programme. To study the influence of these variables on adherence we would first have to obtain a measurement of each participant's age, previous exercise habits and self-confidence, along with measurements of adherence to the rehabilitation programme. But rather than deal with every individual score on the variables of interest, data reduction techniques would be utilised to refine the data and reduce it to a manageable form. This allows us to make summary statements about the sample as a whole, rather than refer to each participant's scores. We can therefore see that descriptive statistics aim to provide a shorthand description of large amounts of data.

To illustrate what this means let's consider a rather less complex exercise-related example. A researcher who was interested in the exercise behaviour of students at a local university distributed a questionnaire to a sample of students who regularly used the university health club to determine their patterns of use.

The data in Table 2.1 represents part of the information collected by the researcher and it illustrates the number of times per month that a sample of students participated in aerobic exercise classes at the student health club. A sample of 19 students provided the researcher with information on their exercise behaviour.

In statistics the number of observations is denoted by the letter n. Therefore in this case,

$$n = 19$$

As it is displayed in this raw form, it is difficult to comprehend any features of the data and answer any questions about how often people engage in aerobic exercise. One useful process is to arrange the observations in order from the smallest to the largest. This process will produce what is termed an **array** (Table 2.2).

It can now readily be seen from this arrangement that the scores in this data set range between 1 and 13. Therefore, it can be concluded that the minimum amount

Table 2.1 **Raw data**

7	4	5	13	8	10	8
7	3	5	9	8	10	
6	1	6	12	11	9	

Table 2.2 **Array of data**

1	5	6	8	9	10	13
3	5	7	8	9	11	
4	6	7	8	10	12	

of exercise a student engages in is one aerobic session per month, and the maximum number of sessions undertaken is 13. This range equals the highest score minus the lowest score plus one. The reason for the plus one is because this range is inclusive of both the highest and lowest scores:

$$\text{Range of data} = 13 - 1 + 1$$
$$= 13$$

Knowing the number of observations ($n = 19$) and having a rough measure of the dispersion of these scores (range $= 13$) are useful but they are not enough to provide an accurate shorthand description of the data. For example, they do not provide any indication of how the 19 scores are distributed across this range of 13. Furthermore, it is not known whether most students exercise once or twice a month with only an odd few exercising 12 or 13 times a month, or whether most exercise 12 or 13 times a month with only an indolent few exercising once or twice per month. To find out how the frequency of exercise is distributed across this range of 13 the data needs to be classified into what is known as a **frequency distribution**.

To undertake this task the range of scores must be divided into a number of different classes ranging from low attendance to high attendance. Then, the frequency of scores falling within each specific level of attendance can be counted in order to produce a frequency distribution.

Frequency Distribution

If data are to be divided into a number of classes then the first thing to do is to decide how many classes there should be. There is in fact no rule to guide this process. However, it ought to be clear that the more classes there are, the narrower the width of each class. In this example we have decided that the number of classes is to be 7. The number of classes is denoted by the letter k:

$$k = 7$$

$$\text{Range of data} = 13$$

$$\text{Therefore the width of each class} = \frac{13}{7}$$

$$= 1.86$$

The resulting class width of 1.86 is an awkward number to deal with if the frequency distribution is to be worked out by hand. Fortunately, just as the number of classes is arbitrary, so also is the point at which to begin the lowest class and the point at which to end the last class. For example, instead of starting at 1, the lowest score, and ending at 13, the largest score, we could alter this so that the starting point is 1 and the end point is 14. This would ensure the class width becomes a whole number. To see the consequences of this decision, let us repeat the above process:

$$k = 7$$

$$\text{Range of data} = 14 - 1 + 1$$

$$= 14$$

$$\text{Therefore width of each class} = \frac{14}{7}$$

$$= 2$$

As you can see, the effect has been to increase the class width from 1.86 to 2. A class width of 2 is much easier to work with if this exercise is to be calculated by hand.

In the above example seven classes have been created, each with an equal width of two participating points. The first class starts at 1, known as the lower class limit, and ends at 2, known as the upper class limit. If you now consider the array of data in Table 2.2 only one score, which in this case is 1, falls into this first class. Let's now consider the second class. This will have a lower class limit of 3 and an upper class limit of 4. Looking once again at the array of data in Table 2.2 it can be seen that two scores, in this case 3 and 4, fall into this class. This process can be repeated for all seven classes and tabulated in the form of the frequency distribution given in Table 2.3.

Table 2.3 **Frequency distribution of student participation in aerobic exercises per month**

Class	Class limits	Class frequency (f)
1	1–2	1
2	3–4	2
3	5–6	4
4	7–8	5
5	9–10	4
6	11–12	2
7	13–14	1
		Total (Σ) = 19

If the only information available to the reader was this table, then it would be possible to conclude that one student attended one or two aerobic classes per month, two students attended three or four classes per month and so on.

The term **class limits** in the table refers to the smallest and largest value that are permitted in each class. The point half-way between the class limits is termed the **class mark**. So, for example, the class mark of the first class would be 1.5 and of the seventh class 13.5.

Sometimes it is more convenient to define a class not by its upper and lower limits but by its boundaries, that is where it begins and ends. Looking back at our frequency distribution we can see that the first class's upper limit is 2 and the second class's lower limit is 3. Therefore, the boundary between these classes must be between 2 and 3. The definition of where this boundary is does not matter as long as we are consistent. The easiest thing would be to put it half-way between the two, that is at 2.5. This point is known as the **class boundary**.

Graphical Representations

The distribution of the data across the classes can often be more clearly seen from a graphical presentation. A graphical representation of a frequency distribution is known as a **histogram**. A histogram of the above frequency distribution is shown in Figure 2.1.

If a line is drawn that joins all the class marks a **frequency polygon** will be constructed.

As with the frequency distribution this histogram illustrates that one student attended between one and two aerobic classes per month, two students attended between three and four classes per month and so on.

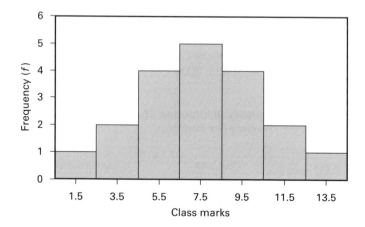

Figure 2.1 **Histogram of student participation in aerobic classes**

Cumulative Frequency Curves

Sometimes it is useful to illustrate the number of observations that are less than certain specified values. For example, it might be useful for the management of the student health club to know how many members attended less than 11 classes per month so that information on exercise adherence could be mailed to them, thereby encouraging them to continue with a regular exercise programme. The cumulative frequency values are the number of scores falling below the lower class limits, beginning with the second class. To see how this works let's use our previous array of data on attendance at aerobic classes shown in Table 2.2.

Table 2.4 shows that only one student attended fewer than three sessions per month, three students attended less than five times a month and so on.

Table 2.4 **Cumulative frequency distribution**

Lower class limit	Cumulative frequency (F)
<3	1
<5	3
<7	7
<9	12
<11	16
<13	18
<15	19

Just as a frequency distribution can be represented graphically by a histogram so the cumulative frequency distribution shown in Table 2.2 can be illustrated by a cumulative frequency curve (Figure 2.2). Note that the cumulative frequency (denoted by F) is on the vertical axis and the lower class limits are on the horizontal axis.

From this graph it can be seen that approximately 16 students attended less than 11 classes per month. This may indicate to the management of the student health club that advice on exercise behaviour and adherence should be mailed to 16 of the 19 students.

Cumulative frequency curves can also be used to illustrate rates of change. For example, imagine you were interested in comparing how effective two training schedules were at promoting skill development. If the frequency with which participants successfully displayed the activity was recorded and plotted against time, a cumulative record of their behaviour would be established. In this case, the slope of the two lines on the graph would show how rapidly the skill was developed by each of the techniques. This approach has often been adopted in learning in animals where the behaviour is automatically recorded on what is known as a cumulative frequency recorder.

A related approach is employed in leisure studies to create a graph that is similar in principle to what economists call a demand curve. For example, imagine you were interested in developing a health centre. After explaining the plan to members of the public, you then ask them whether they would use the facility and how much they would be prepared to pay to use it. If you then construct a frequency distribution and plot a cumulative frequency curve based on the percentage values of each class frequency you will get something similar to the graph in Figure 2.3.

From this graph it can be seen how the percentage of the public who claim they will use the health centre decreases as the entry fee is increased. Multiplying the percentage who claim they will use the facility by the charge at various points would provide a calculation of the entrance fee that would maximise income for the facility.

Figure 2.2 **Cumulative frequency curve**

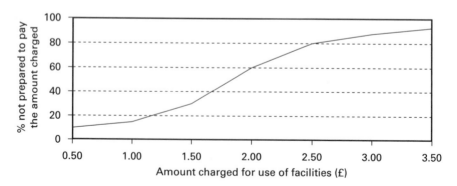

Figure 2.3 **Graph showing the percentage of a sample not prepared to pay various amounts for the use of health centre facilities**

Note: The area above the curved line represents the decreasing proportion of people who will use the health centre as the charge increases.

Measures of Central Tendency

In addition to knowing how the data is distributed, it is also extremely useful to be able to identify the typical score. Using the data in our student aerobic exercise example we might want to know the typical number of aerobic exercise sessions that students attend each month. To find such a value we refer to what are known as **measures of central tendency**, as these aim to provide a typical score around which the other scores are scattered.

Before discussing the student data in detail let's consider an additional data set that the researcher obtained from university staff attending aerobic exercise classes at the student health centre. The data in Table 2.5 represents part of the information that was collected and illustrates the number of times per month that a sample of university staff participated in aerobics classes.

Adopting the same procedure as before, the frequency distribution given in Table 2.6 can be constructed.

Table 2.5 **Array of data of the number of times staff participate in aerobic classes per month**

1	3	4	4	6	9	14
3	4	4	5	7	10	
3	4	4	5	8	12	

Table 2.6 **Frequency distribution of staff participation in aerobic exercises per month**

Class	Class limits	Class frequency (f)
1	1–2	1
2	3–4	9
3	5–6	3
4	7–8	2
5	9–10	2
6	11–12	1
7	13–14	1
		Total (Σ) = 19

The questions we now want to ask are first what is the typical number of times per month that students participate in aerobic classes and second what is the typical number of times per month that staff participate in aerobic classes?

To answer these questions we should note that there are three measures of central tendency that we might employ. These are:

1. the mode
2. the median
3. the mean.

The Mode

This is defined as the observation in the sample that occurs most frequently. If there are two scores that occur most frequently, then the sample is said to be bimodal. If more than two modes exist, then the data set is considered to be multi-modal. In the student data in Table 2.2 there is only one mode and this is the number 8 which occurs three times. Therefore, according to this measure, typically students attend eight classes per month.

For staff, on the other hand, the most frequent observation (from Table 2.5) is 4, which also occurs three times. This suggests that staff typically attend four sessions per month.

The Median

When the data is arranged from the lowest to the highest value, the median is the middle observation in the array. In both our student and staff data we have an odd number of observations ($n = 19$) so the median observation is the 10th observation.

$$\text{Median for student data} = 8$$
$$\text{Median for staff data} = 4$$

Thus for both staff and students, the corresponding modes and medians are the same. That is, both measures suggest that students typically attend eight classes per month and staff four classes per month.

The Mean

This is the sum of all the observations divided by the number of observations made:

$$\text{Mean} = \frac{\sum x}{n}$$

$$\text{Mean for students } (\bar{x}) = \frac{\text{sum of observations}}{n} = \frac{142}{19} = 7.47$$

$$\text{Mean for staff } (\bar{x}) = \frac{\text{sum of observations}}{n} = \frac{111}{19} = 5.84$$

While the mean for the students is very similar to the median and mode, that is 7.47 compared with 8, the corresponding figures for the staff are 5.84 and 4. Given that one measure suggests that staff typically attend nearly six classes per month and the other two measures suggest they attend four classes per month, which measure are we to believe? That is, which provides a truly typical score?

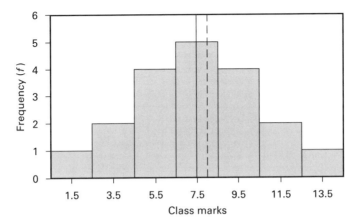

Figure 2.4 **Histogram of student participation displaying the mean, median and mode values**

To answer this question it is important to appreciate that the mean is sensitive to every score in the array, whereas the median and the mode are not. To illustrate this imagine that the score of 14 in the staff data was changed to 140; this would suggest that one faculty member was probably obsessive about exercise. It would also affect the mean of the array so that the mean would become 237/19 = 12.47. However, the median would remain at 4, because it is still the middle score. Therefore, it appears that while the mean becomes distorted by this extreme value, the median remains unaffected.

This example illustrates that how the data is distributed over the range of values will influence the three measures of central tendency in different ways. For this reason an understanding of a concept termed **skewness** is important.

Skewed Distributions

If the mode, median and mean for the student data are drawn on the histogram in Figure 2.1, it can be noted that they almost fall in the same place on the histogram, that is close to 8. If the distribution had been truly **symmetrical**, that is if the scores had been evenly distributed around a mid-point, then the mean, median and mode would all have had exactly the same value and would fall at the mid-point of the distribution.

Note that in Figure 2.4 the mean is represented by the solid vertical line and the median and mode by the dashed line. If this procedure is now repeated for the staff data it can be seen that the measures of central tendency do not fall at the same point because the mean is located to the right of the other two measures. It can also be seen that, whilst the figure representing the student data looks almost symmetrical, the figure representing the staff data (Figure 2.5) is clearly not symmetrical.

Distributions that are not symmetrical are termed **skewed**. They may be skewed to the left (negative) or to the right (positive). The direction of the skewness is determined

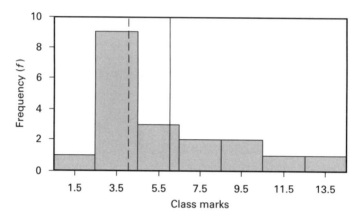

Figure 2.5 **Histogram of staff participation displaying the mean, median and mode values**

by the direction in which the tail of the distribution falls, that is the direction of the most extreme scores.

If a distribution is skewed, its mean will be changed in the direction of these extreme scores. The mean then may not provide us with the most appropriate representation of a typical score. In fact, it can be seen that this is the case for the staff data. Those one or two staff members who are rather more keen on aerobic exercise classes than the others are distorting the mean. However, the median is unaffected by these extreme scores. Therefore, with a skewed distribution, the median will provide a more appropriate indication of the typical score.

The direction of skewness is indicated by the location of the mean relative to the median. As the mean of the staff data is to the right of the median the distribution is skewed to the right or positively skewed. The magnitude of skewness will reflect the difference between the mean and median values.

Boxplots

A useful way of graphically representing the symmetry of data is the boxplot. This type of graph displays the median value by a horizontal bar surrounded by 50% of the scores shown within a box. This 50% of scores falls between the 25th and 75th percentile marks. The 25th percentile is at the bottom of the box and the 75th percentile is at the top. The whiskers extending from both ends of the box show the highest and lowest values that are not outliers. Outliers are scores in the distribution that are more than 1.5 box-lengths from the 25th or 75th percentile, and they are displayed by a circle; those that are more than 4 box-lengths away are shown by an asterisk. Look at the boxplots of the staff and student aerobic participation rates displayed in Figure 2.6.

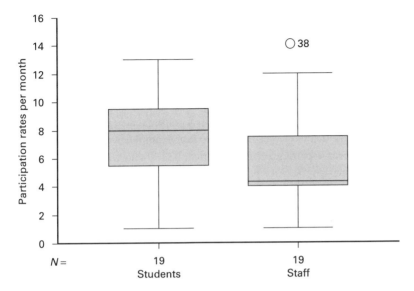

Figure 2.6 **Boxplot of staff and student aerobic class participation rates**

The boxplot for the students looks moderately symmetrical as the box is almost in the middle of the whiskers and the median is only slightly above the middle of the box. This suggests that this data is very slightly negatively skewed and therefore the mean may be employed as the appropriate measure of central tendency.

For the staff data the picture is quite different. The upper whisker is longer than the lower one and has one outlier. The number against this outlier is the case number. This case number identifies which participant had this extreme score. It can also be seen that the median score is at the bottom of the box. This suggests that the data is heavily positively skewed and hence the median may be employed as the appropriate measure of central tendency. Therefore the conclusion is that, on average, students attend 7.47 aerobic classes per month while staff attend only 4 classes per month. Later on you will be instructed in how to generate boxplots using SPSS.

The choice of which measure of central tendency to employ is not restricted to whether the data is skewed or not. In addition, the type of measurement that produced the data needs to be taken into account. Whenever anything is measured, numbers or values are assigned to observations. It is important to remember that how values are assigned determines the arithmetic operations that are permitted on the data. In other words, the type of data that is collected determines the statistical tests that can be used. Thus, different types of measurement result in the production of different types of data.

Levels of Data

Data may be measured in a variety of forms, but there are three specific forms of measurement to which we wish to draw your attention at this point.

First, data may be measured on a **nominal scale** whereby the units used bear no meaningful relationship to one another. For example, the researcher assigned the number 1 to someone who attended aerobic classes, 2 to someone who played field sports, 3 to someone who engaged in track events and so on. Here we can see that the researcher is only nominally (i.e. in name only) assigning these units 1, 2, 3, 4, etc., to participation in these activities and therefore they have no meaningful mathematical relationship to one another. As a consequence of this, it is meaningless to engage in any mathematical operation. For example, we cannot add the units together. Two people participating in aerobic classes who were given the number 1 do not equal one person who participated in field sports and had the number 2 assigned. All we can do is simply determine the frequency with which people participate in the various leisure activities. If the aim is to identify the typical leisure activity then the mode would be the most appropriate measure of central tendency. Because information collected in this way does not fall on any continuous scale it may be less confusing if the term nominal data rather than nominal scale is adopted.

A second form of data is measured on what is termed an **ordinal scale**. For example, children may be asked to rank a list of 10 sports from 1 to 10 in order of preference from most to least enjoyable. In this case the method of ordinal scaling provides no grounds for assuming that the difference in preference between sports listed 2 and 3 is of the same magnitude as that between sports listed 7 and 8. Furthermore, if a leisure researcher had students rank fitness clubs in terms of the facilities each provided for its members, it could not be assumed that the difference in facilities between the first and second ranked clubs was the same as that between the second and third ranked clubs. All that is known is the order in which the clubs were ranked for their facilities, not the magnitude of the distance between them. If a typical score of how these clubs' are ranked is required, then the median (the middle observation) should be employed.

The third distinct form of measurement is that of the **interval scale**. This is like an ordinal scale but with the additional feature that all of the intervals are equal. For example, the data the researcher gathered on participation in aerobic classes might be considered to be measured on an interval scale. The difference between attending three and four classes is the same as the difference between attending 10 and 11 classes, namely one aerobics class.

To obtain a typical measure with interval data the mean is normally employed. However, as described previously, this will only provide a typical score if the distribution is not heavily skewed, that is the distribution is symmetrical. If the data is heavily skewed then the median will render a more typical score. It was for this reason that the median was chosen as the appropriate measure of central tendency for the staff data even though it was measured on an interval scale.

Measures of Dispersion

By itself, a measure of central tendency does not provide an adequate shorthand summary of the data. Whilst it is very useful to know the typical score, it is also important to know how the rest of the data clusters around this mid-point. This requires a measure of the spread of the data. Measures of dispersion provide information on how the data is distributed around the typical score.

For example, if you are told that the mean exam score for a health and fitness class is 55, it tells you the average score that students achieved on the exam, but it does not tell you how the rest of the scores varied around that point. If there was no variability in the exam scores, everyone would have received a grade of 55. If there was a great deal of variability in the scores some students would have performed very poorly on the exam and some would have performed very well. In contrast, if the variability in exam scores had been low then most students would have performed close to the mean score of 55. One simple indication of the variability in exam scores might be provided by the range. Earlier in this chapter it was stated that the range equals the difference between the highest score and the lowest score. It was also noted that sometimes the value 1 is added to this equation to reflect the fact that the range is inclusive of the two extreme scores:

$$\text{Range} = (\text{highest} - \text{lowest}) + 1$$

For example, the range of scores in an exam where the lowest mark is 25 and the highest mark is 75, is 51, not 50. If the smallest value is subtracted from the largest, this would measure the difference between these values, but exclude the values themselves. Another way of expressing this is to recall that each of the scores in the distribution occupies a class interval equal to one unit. Therefore, the mid-points between class intervals extend 0.5 below the lowest score, and 0.5 above the highest score. So 24.5 should be subtracted from 75.5 to produce a range of 51.

Variance

The goal of a measure of dispersion is to produce some metric of how the scores are dispersed around the mean. One obvious solution would seem to be to subtract the mean from each score, and sum the differences to determine the total dispersion:

$$\sum (x - \bar{x})$$

Unfortunately, if the distribution is symmetrical, there will be just as many scores greater than the mean as there are scores smaller than the mean. Therefore, when all the difference scores (i.e. the deviations from the mean) are added together, the answer will always sum to zero. To overcome this problem the differences could be multiplied by themselves; that is, calculate the square of each of the deviation scores. This would have the effect of eliminating all the negative numbers, as a minus multiplied by a minus equals a plus. This sum of the squared deviation from the mean is called the sum of squares:

$$\text{Sum of squares} = \sum(x - \bar{x})^2$$

This process would produce a measure that would increase as the range of the data increased. Unfortunately, the sum of squares would also increase as the number of the observations increased, that is as n increases. To control for the size of n the sum of the squares of the differences can be divided by n. This will calculate what is known as the **variance**, and the formula for this is

$$\text{Variance} = \frac{\text{sum of squares}}{n} = \frac{\sum(x - \bar{x})^2}{n}$$

This formula, translated into words, reads:

1. The mean is subtracted from each score.
2. The results (of step 1) are squared.
3. The squared deviations are summed.
4. The sum total of the squared deviations is divided by the number of observations (n).

In effect, when the variance is calculated, the calculation produces the average of the squared deviations from the mean, that is the mean of the squared deviations from the mean. To illustrate this let's work out the variance for the data concerning student participation in aerobic classes.

Example 2.1 Calculation of the variance of the data set presented in Table 2.2. (The mean of this data set was calculated subsequently to be 7.47.)

x	$x - \bar{x}$	$(x - \bar{x})^2$
1	−6.47	41.86
3	−4.47	19.98
4	−3.47	12.04
5	−2.47	6.10
5	−2.47	6.10
6	−1.47	2.16
6	−1.47	2.16
7	−0.47	0.22
7	−0.47	0.22
8	0.53	0.28
8	0.53	0.28
8	0.53	0.28
9	1.53	2.34

9	1.53	2.34
10	2.53	6.40
10	2.53	6.40
11	3.53	12.46
12	4.53	20.52
13	5.53	30.58
$\Sigma = 142$	0.0	172.72

$$\text{Variance} = \frac{\text{sum of squares}}{n} = \frac{\sum(x - \bar{x})^2}{n}$$

$$= \frac{172.72}{19}$$

$$\cong 9$$

Standard Deviation

In calculating the variance the differences between each observation and the mean were squared. Therefore, the variance reflects the dispersion of scores measured in units that are the square of the original units. For example, if the original units were the number of aerobic classes attended per month then the variance would be these units squared. To get back to our original units, the simplest solution is to take the square root of the variance. This will produce what is known as the **standard deviation**. This is a measure of the average variability in the distribution of scores:

$$\text{Standard deviation } (s) = \sqrt{\text{variance}}$$

If the variance of a data set was equal to 9 then

$$\text{Standard deviation } (s) = \sqrt{9} = 3$$

Standard deviation is a very important concept in statistics but this importance will only become apparent when we consider the normal distribution in the next chapter.

Computational Formulae for Calculating Standard Deviations

The computational formula used above for the variance can be used in calculating the standard deviation. All that needs to be done is to calculate the square root of the variance:

$$s = \sqrt{\frac{\text{SS}}{n}} = \sqrt{\frac{\sum(x - \bar{x})^2}{n}}$$

Usually this statistic is calculated for a sample of scores rather than for the whole population, so the value produced is only an estimate of the standard deviation in the population. Because it is only an estimate an error could have been made, and the statistic may not reflect the true variability in the whole population. In order to over-come this problem and offer a more conservative estimate of variability, $n-1$ is used in the denominator instead of n, thereby increasing the size of the standard deviation slightly.

The formula now reads

$$s = \sqrt{\frac{SS}{n-1}} = \sqrt{\frac{\sum(x-\bar{x})^2}{n-1}}$$

When there are whole numbers in the calculation, this formula is easy to use. However, when the mean involves decimal places, the calculation can become cum-bersome. In this case an easier formula is available:

$$s = \sqrt{\frac{\sum x^2}{(n-1)} - \bar{x}^2}$$

A Simple Example

In case the previous discussion on variance seems a little obscure to you and the for-mulae a little abstract let's consider some simple data sets. In arrays of data that are based on small samples and whole numbers it is easy to visualise what the average variability in the data set might be. Consider the following example where there are three sets of data labelled A, B and C.

A	B	C
3	2	1
3	3	3
3	4	5

For each data set, the mean score is 3. As all the values in data set A are the same there is no variability at all in this data set. There is clearly greater variability in data set B, where the scores range from 2 to 4, and even greater variability in data set C where the scores range from 1 to 5. In data set B, the two scores that deviate from the mean appear to vary by an average of one unit. For data set C, however, the two scores that deviate from the mean appear to vary by an average of two units.

If we were to use the formula below to calculate the standard deviations for data sets B and C we would confirm our speculation:

$$s = \sqrt{\frac{SS}{n-1}} = \sqrt{\frac{\sum(x - \bar{x})^2}{n-1}}$$

Consider data set B in Table 2.7.

Table 2.7 **Data set B**

x	$x - \bar{x}$	$(x - \bar{x})^2$
2	−1	1
3	0	0
4	1	1
		$\Sigma = 2$

$$s = \sqrt{\frac{SS}{n-1}} = \sqrt{\frac{2}{2}} = \sqrt{1}$$

$$s = \sqrt{1} = 1$$

Now consider data set C in Table 2.8.

Table 2.8 **Data set C**

x	$x - \bar{x}$	$(x - \bar{x})^2$
1	−2	4
3	0	0
5	2	4
		$\Sigma = 8$

$$s = \sqrt{\frac{SS}{n-1}} = \sqrt{\frac{8}{2}} = \sqrt{4}$$

$$s = \sqrt{4} = 2$$

These calculations confirm the previous estimates of the average deviation based on a simple inspection of each of the two data sets, for they show that the average deviation for set B is 1 and for set C is 2. However, they also confirm the legitimacy of the formulae as they produce the same values that our quick visual inspection of the two data sets suggested.

Summary

Descriptive statistics aim to provide a shorthand description of large amounts of data by making summary statements about the sample as a whole, rather than making reference to each participant's scores. These statistics include the sample size (n), the typical score (mean, median and mode) and how the scores are dispersed around the typical score (standard deviation).

Which measure of central tendency will provide a typical score depends upon the type of scale on which the data was measured upon (interval, ordinal or nominal) and whether the distribution is symmetrical or skewed. If the data is symmetrical all three measures will have the same value but if the data is skewed the mean will be distorted in the direction of the extreme scores. Hence, the direction of skewness is indicated by the location of the mean relative to the median.

The distribution of the data can be graphically represented in the form of a histogram or a boxplot, or statistically represented through the concepts of variance and standard deviation. The variance is the average of the squared deviations from the mean whilst the standard deviaition is the square root of the variance.

EXERCISE 2.1 DESCRIPTIVE STATISTICS

A student researcher was interested in the importance of sound effects on computer games. He first of all noted the frequency with which a particular computer game was played. Then, using two identical computer games, he arranged for the sound effects on one computer game to be almost inaudible while the other was set at a high level. Observers then noted how often individuals would play the two computer games between midday and one o'clock on two consecutive days. The results of his observations were as follows:

> Data list showing the number of times different individuals played the computer game with the high sound volume:
>
> 8, 7, 2, 3, 5, 3, 4, 6, 4, 4, 5, 3, 6, 7, 5, 6, 4, 5, 6, 2, 7, 5, 8, 1, 9

Data list showing the number of times different individuals played the computer game with the low sound volume:

1, 7, 2, 5, 3, 6, 4, 5, 3, 1, 4, 6, 5, 7

For each of the two groups of data:

1. Construct a frequency distribution.
2. Draw a histogram of the frequency distribution.
3. Compute:
   (a) the mode
   (b) the median
   (c) the mean
   (d) the variance
   (e) the standard deviation.

If you are not sure how to work out the variances then look at the example on page 22.

From your examination of both sets of descriptive statistics does it appear as if there is any difference in the frequency with which the computer game was played when the sound was high and when it was low?

EXERCISE 2.2 IDENTIFYING TYPES OF DATA USED IN RESEARCH

Below are listed a number of scenarios in which you are asked to identify the type of data collected *and* explain the reason for your choice. In carrying out this task you might find it helpful to consider how the researcher records the data and how it could be represented graphically.

1. A woman with a clipboard accosts you outside a shopping centre, and asks you which one of five laundry detergents you use most often.

   Data = Laundry detergents: ....

2. An exercise physiologist is looking at the effects of exercise on the core temperature of the body, and uses a rectal thermometer to measure body temperature.

   Data = Temperature: ....

3. A sports sociologist investigating the effects of socio-economic status (SES) on children's participation in leisure activities measures SES by recording the father's occupation.

Data = SES: ....

4. A researcher interested in comparing the attacking capabilities of each football team in the Premiership assigns the value 1 to the team which has scored the most goals, 2 to the next top scorers, 3 to the third top scorers and so on.

    Data = Attacking capability: ....

5. A researcher measuring how successful marathon runners felt after completing the London Marathon asked participants to rate themselves on a 1 to 10 scale, with 1 being unsuccessful, and 10 being successful.

    Data = Perceived success: ....

6. A physiotherapist, trying to investigate how different sports influence the type and severity of injuries, collects data from athletes involved in several types of sport, and determines the severity of injury by how many days of practice have been missed.

    Data = Type of sport: ....

    Data = Severity of injury: ....

7. During a drunken conversation in a local pub, a friend of yours asks you to list the 10 best athletes in the world in order of their ability.

    Data = Athletes: ....

3

THE NORMAL DISTRIBUTION

Normal Distribution

Any phenomenon which is produced by a large number of 'chance' factors that are not interrelated will produce what is known as a **normal distribution**. The graphical representation (Figure 3.1) of this distribution generates a bell-shaped curve that is symmetrical.

It is important to note that the normal distribution is a mathematical concept defined by the following intimidating equation:

$$Y = \frac{n}{\sigma\sqrt{2\pi}} e^{-(x-\mu)^2/2\sigma^2}$$

where

Y = frequency n = number of cases
x = a raw score σ = standard deviation
e = 2.7183* μ = mean of scores
π = 3.1416*

and the asterisks indicate that these are mathematical constants.

While it is not necessary to remember or understand this equation, it is included here to emphasise that the origins of the normal distribution reside in human endeavours and not in nature. This is important because the normal distribution is a mathematical concept that is the product of human thinking. There should be no expectation that nature will copy human thought and distribute natural occurrences in the form of a normal distribution. What should be expected is that a wide variety of objects, characteristics and occurrences will be distributed in ways that vary in their approximation to a normal distribution.

The fact that objects and qualities are not distributed in an exactly normal manner does not mean that the qualities of a normal distribution, to be outlined below, cannot be applied to phenomena that are imperfectly distributed. The researcher just has to be aware that the accuracy of the descriptions and predictions made will depend upon how close the observed distribution approximates to a perfectly normal

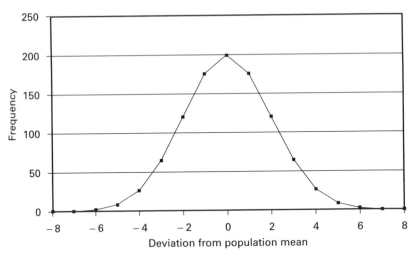

Figure 3.1 **Normal distribution, where *N* = 1000 and *s* = 2**

distribution. For this reason, a researcher should always examine the descriptive statistics relevant to the data before carrying out any statistical analysis.

The Importance of the Normal Distribution

Approximations of normal distributions are not only produced by many things that are of interest to social scientists (e.g. fitness, memory, performance), but they also have a number of unique properties that make them very useful. As in all distributions that are symmetrical, the mean, median and mode are all to be found at the same position at the centre of the distribution. However, normal distributions have one unique characteristic that makes them particularly useful.

This characteristic is that whenever a distance is measured away from the mean in units of standard deviation the same proportion of the area of the curve is always cut off. This fact is illustrated by the graph shown in Figure 3.2. From this graph it can be seen that, as the distribution is symmetrical, the mean is in the middle of the distribution. Therefore, half of the scores in the distribution fall above the mean and half fall below. If a vertical line is now drawn one unit of standard deviation away from the mean then, from Figure 3.2, it can be noted that an area of 15.87% of the distribution is cut off from the end of the distribution. Hence, the area that remains between the mean and this cut-off point of one standard deviation will be equal to 50% of the scores in the distribution less the 15.87% of the scores that are cut off. Therefore the area remaining between the mean and this cut off will be 34.13%. If the distance moved from the mean is increased to two units of standard deviation then Figure 3.2 illustrates that the tail cut-off will have an area of 2.28%. Therefore, the area that now remains between the mean and this point that is two units of standard deviation away from the mean will equal 50% less 2.28%, or 47.72%.

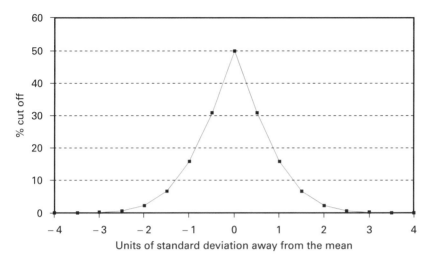

Figure 3.2 **Graph showing area cut off at various distances from the mean, measured in units of standard deviation**

From the above it can be seen that if the area between the mean and one standard deviation away is always 34.13%, then the area between one standard deviation above and one standard deviation below the mean will always be twice this amount, that is 68.27%. Hence, 68.27% of all scores in a normally distributed sample of scores will fall between one standard deviation above the mean and one standard deviation below the mean. For the same reasons the area between two standard deviations above and below the mean will contain 95.45% of all scores in the distribution, and the area between three standard deviations above and below the mean will always include 99.73% of all scores.

These observations concerning the fixed percentage of scores falling, for example, between plus and minus one standard deviation provide a clue as to the importance of this property of normal distributions, for this principle can be extended so that if the mean and standard deviation of a distribution are known then the proportion of scores that fall above, below or between any particular value on the horizontal axis may be determined. Thus the mean and the standard deviation together provide a shorthand description of data that approximates to a normal distribution.

The practical importance of this information can be illustrated through the following example. Understanding the properties of the normal distribution and having knowledge of the mean score and standard deviation of an exam can influence the emotions of students when they discover how they performed. Imagine that your final exam grade for a course that is important to you was 70%. Not surprisingly you begin to glow with pride because at the university 70% is usually considered to be a good grade. Because you are keen to determine how your grade compares with that of others, you ask your lecturer for the mean and standard deviation of the exam. You discover that the mean was 60% and the standard deviation was 5. At this point you become overwhelmed with joy in the knowledge that your score lies two standard deviations above the mean. Therefore, if the scores on the test are normally distributed then only 2.28% of your classmates scored more than you.

However, let's change some of this information slightly and see how your emotions might be affected. Once again you discover you've scored 70% and begin to feel good. Then, however, you discover that the mean of the exam was 80% and the standard deviation was 5. Your initial joy begins to turn to despair as you realise that only 2.28% scores were poorer than your own. If you were then to discover that the standard deviation was not 5, but 3, you could only conclude that despite a grade of 70%, there was a strong probability that your score was perhaps the poorest in the class. This is because your score lies more than three standard deviations below the mean.

It is useful to remember approximately what percentage of scores fall beyond one and two standard deviation points away from the mean. When scores fall at some other point in the distribution then the calculation of the proportion of scores falling above and below that point becomes less straightforward. To illustrate this point, if in the previous example where the mean of the exam was 60% and the standard deviation was 5 you would know that in achieving a grade of 65%, 15.87% of scores in the distribution would fall above yours. However, if you were to score 64% it would be more of a challenge to determine what proportion of scores lay above your own.

To find an exact answer to questions such as 'what proportion of scores fall above, below or between any particular value on the horizontal axis?', it is not necessary to measure the area of the curve cut off. Instead the distance between the mean and the value of interest in units of the standard deviation has to be determined. This is known as the z-**score** and is expressed as

$$z = \frac{x - \overline{x}}{s}$$

In this equation, x is the value of interest and s is the standard deviation of the sample of scores. Note that the numerator determines the distance away from the mean in the original units and the denominator, s, converts this distance to units of standard deviation. Once the value of z is calculated then Table 3.1 may be used to identify the area cut off.

To illustrate this, the distribution of the data set used in the previous chapter concerning aerobic exercise participation by students can be used as it approximates to a normal distribution. On average students went to aerobic classes 7.5 times a month (i.e. the mean = 7.5), and the standard deviation was three classes. To determine what proportion of students participate more than, for example, 10.5 times per month simply substitute these values into the above equation:

$$z = \frac{x - \overline{x}}{s} = \frac{10.5 - 7.5}{3} = 1.0$$

Table 3.1 **The proportion of a normal curve cut off at various distances –
measured in units of standard deviations – away from the mean**

z	0.00	0.01	0.02	0.03	0.04	0.05	0.06	0.07	0.08	0.09
0.0	0.5000	0.4960	0.4920	0.4880	0.4801	0.4801	0.4761	0.4721	0.4681	0.4641
0.1	0.4602	0.4562	0.4522	0.4483	0.4443	0.4404	0.4364	0.4325	0.4286	0.4247
0.2	0.4207	0.4168	0.4129	0.4090	0.4052	0.4013	0.3974	0.3936	0.3897	0.3859
0.3	0.3821	0.3783	0.3745	0.3707	0.3669	0.3632	0.3594	0.3557	0.3520	0.3483
0.4	0.3446	0.3409	0.3372	0.3336	0.3300	0.3264	0.3228	0.3192	0.3156	0.3121
0.5	0.3085	0.3050	0.3015	0.2981	0.2946	0.2912	0.2877	0.2843	0.2810	0.2776
0.6	0.2743	0.2709	0.2676	0.2643	0.2611	0.2578	0.2546	0.2514	0.2483	0.2451
0.7	0.2420	0.2389	0.2358	0.2327	0.2296	0.2266	0.2236	0.2206	0.2177	0.2148
0.8	0.2119	0.2090	0.2061	0.2033	0.2005	0.1977	0.1949	0.1922	0.1894	0.1867
0.9	0.1841	0.1814	0.1788	0.1762	0.1736	0.1711	0.1685	0.1660	0.1635	0.1611
1.0	0.1587	0.1562	0.1539	0.1515	0.1492	0.1469	0.1446	0.1423	0.1401	0.1379
1.1	0.1357	0.1335	0.1314	0.1292	0.1271	0.1251	0.1230	0.1210	0.1190	0.1170
1.2	0.1151	0.1131	0.1112	0.1093	0.1075	0.1056	0.1038	0.1020	0.1003	0.0985
1.3	0.0968	0.0951	0.0934	0.0918	0.0901	0.0885	0.0869	0.0853	0.0838	0.0823
1.4	0.0808	0.0793	0.0778	0.0764	0.0749	0.0735	0.0721	0.0708	0.0694	0.0681
1.5	0.0668	0.0655	0.0643	0.0630	0.0618	0.0606	0.0594	0.0582	0.0571	0.0559
1.6	0.0548	0.0537	0.0526	0.0516	0.0505	0.0495	0.0485	0.0475	0.0465	0.0455
1.7	0.0446	0.0436	0.0427	0.0418	0.0409	0.0401	0.0392	0.0384	0.0375	0.0367
1.8	0.0359	0.0351	0.0344	0.0336	0.0329	0.0322	0.0314	0.0307	0.0301	0.0294
1.9	0.0287	0.0281	0.0274	0.0268	0.0262	0.0256	0.0250	0.0244	0.0239	0.0233
2.0	0.0228	0.0222	0.0217	0.0212	0.0207	0.0202	0.0197	0.0192	0.0188	0.0183
2.1	0.0179	0.0174	0.0170	0.0166	0.0162	0.0158	0.0154	0.0150	0.0146	0.0143
2.2	0.0139	0.0136	0.0132	0.0129	0.0125	0.0122	0.0119	0.0116	0.0113	0.0110
2.3	0.0107	0.0104	0.0102	0.0099	0.0096	0.0094	0.0091	0.0089	0.0087	0.0084
2.4	0.0082	0.0082	0.0078	0.0075	0.0073	0.0071	0.0069	0.0068	0.0066	0.0064
2.5	0.0062	0.0060	0.0059	0.0057	0.0055	0.0054	0.0052	0.0051	0.0049	0.0048
2.6	0.0047	0.0045	0.0044	0.0043	0.0041	0.0040	0.0039	0.0038	0.0037	0.0036
2.7	0.0035	0.0034	0.0033	0.0032	0.0031	0.0030	0.0029	0.0028	0.0027	0.0026
2.8	0.0026	0.0025	0.0024	0.0023	0.0023	0.0022	0.0021	0.0021	0.0020	0.0019
2.9	0.0019	0.0018	0.0018	0.0017	0.0016	0.0016	0.0015	0.0015	0.0014	0.0014
3.0	0.0013	0.0013	0.0013	0.0012	0.0012	0.0011	0.0011	0.0011	0.0010	0.0010
3.1	0.0010	0.0009	0.0009	0.0009	0.0008	0.0008	0.0008	0.0008	0.0007	0.0007
3.2	0.0007									
3.3	0.0005									
3.4	0.0003									
3.5	0.00023									
3.6	0.00016									
3.7	0.00011									
3.8	0.00007									
3.9	0.00005									
4.0	0.00003									

From Table 3.1 it can be noted that a z-value of 1.0 cuts off 15.87% of the area of the curve; that is, 15.87% of the students participated more than 10.5 times per week. As the total area under the curve represents the total number of students it is possible to calculate the actual number of students who would be expected to attend more than 10.5 times a month. To do this, divide the percentage cut off by 100 to convert it to a proportion and then multiply this by the sample size. Therefore, as the sample size was 19 the task is simply to workout 15.87% of 19:

$$\text{Number participating more than 10.5 times per month} = \frac{15.87}{100} \times 19$$

$$= 3.015$$

From an examination of the array of this data in Table 2.2 it can be seen that in fact three students participated more than 10.5 times per month.

To illustrate a more complicated use of Table 3.1 we shall consider what percentage of students achieved a higher exam score than a grade of 64 when the mean for the class was 60 and the standard deviation was 3. This again requires the calculation of z before the table can be used:

$$z = \frac{64 - 60}{3} = \frac{4}{3} = 1.333$$

To use the z-table (Table 3.1) look down the column headed z until the value 1.3 is identified. Now look along that row until the column headed 0.03 is reached. The cell that is identified by the row 1.3 and the column 0.03 contains the value 0.0918. This number represents the area cut off as a proportion when a line is drawn 1.33 standard deviations away from the mean. To convert this proportion to a percentage multiply the value 0.0918 by 100 (i.e. move the decimal place two places to the right). Therefore, a z-score of 1.33 cuts off an area of 9.18%, so it may be concluded that 9.18% of students achieved a grade higher than 64 in the exam.

It should be clear from these examples that a researcher no longer needs the raw data because knowledge of the standard deviation, the mean and the sample size can help to recreate a comprehensive picture of the original data as long as it approximates to a normal distribution. However, the importance of these measures is not restricted to providing a shorthand account of the data, for these statistical measures are also the basic tools that allow for the testing of predictions that are made about the data. It is with the testing of such predictions that the remainder of this book is concerned.

Summary

Normally distributed data is distributed in the form of a bell-shaped curve. Although many phenomena in the real world that are produced by a large number of 'chance' factors that are not interrelated closely approximate to a normal distribution, the distribution itself is a mathematical concept that is defined by a complex equation. Normal distributions have one unique characteristic that makes them particularly useful. This characteristic is that whenever a distance is measured away from the mean in units of standard deviation the same proportion of the area of the curve is always cut off. For example, a vertical line drawn one unit of standard deviation away from the mean will always cut off 15.87% of the distribution. Therefore, if the mean and standard deviation of a distribution are known then the proportion of scores that fall above, below, or between any particular value on the horizontal axis may be determined. Hence, the mean and the standard deviation together provide a shorthand description of data that approximates to a normal distribution.

The distance away from the mean measured in units of standard deviation on a normal distribution is known as the z-score. The proportions of the area that are cut off as the value of z increases from zero are displayed on what are known as z-tables.

EXERCISE 3.1 DESCRIPTIVE STATISTICS

At the end of the academic year, a university professor who was concerned that none of the undergraduate students were being disadvantaged by having a graduate student teaching a class in data handling sat pondering the final grades for the class. She became curious as she noticed that the students in the graduate student's class seemed to perform better overall than students in her own class. Being a good researcher, she did not rely on an inter-ocular test (i.e. eyeballing the data) to draw conclusions. Rather, she set out to test empirically whether there was a difference between the performance of students in her own class and that of the graduate student. The professor reported the data in Table 3.2 that represents the final grades for both her class and the class taught by the graduate student.

Because other pressing matters have prevented the professor from obtaining an answer to her question, you have been selected to act as her research assistant owing to your considerable promise in the area of data handling.

The first step in determining whether there are differences between the student grades is to examine the important descriptive statistics. Your task is to:

1. Calculate the mean, median and mode for both data sets.
2. Construct a frequency distribution for each data set.
3. Calculate the range and standard deviation for each data set.
4. For each data set, describe which measure of central tendency best represents the average score. Provide a brief explanation for your choice.
5. Determine if there is a difference between the grades of the students in the two classes. On what criteria would you base your answer?

Now that you have completed this exercise you will be guided on how to employ SPSS to execute the same analysis. You can use the results from SPSS to check whether your calculations by hand were correct.

Table 3.2

Professor's class		Graduate student's class	
49	55	59	59
51	54	45	59
56	55	51	71
59	58	53	67
91	92	57	61
63	55	56	56
56	55	57	59
10	53	55	61
43	51	49	61
47	56	49	64
52	49	74	65

EXERCISE 3.2 USING DESCRIPTIVE STATISTICS USING SPSS FOR WINDOWS

1. Start SPSS by clicking on the **SPSS** icon. If a window opens with the option **Type in data** then select it and click on **OK**, otherwise just proceed to the next step.

2. Make sure that the **Data View** window is open so that the screen is displaying a series of empty cells in the form of a spreadsheet. If this is not the case then click on the tab **Data View** in the bottom left-hand corner of your screen. In SPSS each participant must have their own row. This means that as there are 44 participants you will require 44 rows. In addition, you will require two columns. The first column is to identify whether the participant is in the professor's class or the graduate student's class and the second column is to contain the participant's final grade. An example of how this should appear is shown below:

Class	Grade
1	49
1	51
1	56
	etc.
2	59
2	45
2	51
	etc.

3. Move the cursor to the first row of the first column and click on it. Type in the number '1' and press the return key. As there are 22 participants in the professor's class, repeat this procedure 21 times, that is until 22 rows have the number 1 in the first column. Now enter the number '2' in the 23rd row and repeat the above procedure until there are number 2s in rows 23 to 44 inclusive.

4. Move the cursor to the first row of the second column and click on it. Now you need to enter the actual final grade. To do this, type in the first value for the professor's class (i.e. 49), and press the return key. Now enter the second value – 51 – and press return. Repeat this procedure until all of the data for both classes is entered.

5. You now need to label the variables. Click on the tab **Variable View** in the bottom left-hand corner of your screen. In the **Name** column double click on the first variable and replace **var00001** with the name 'Class'. Move along to the sixth column which is headed **Values** and click on where the word **None** is written in the first row. A shaded box with three dots will appear at the right-hand end of this cell. Click on this shaded area and a **Variable Labels** window will open. Click on the **Value** box and type in the number 1, then click on the **Value Label** box and type in 'Prof'. Now click on the **Add** box. The cursor will now flash in the **Value** box. Type in the number 2, click on the **Value Label** box and type in 'Grad', then click on the **Add** box. Finally, click on the **Continue** box and then on **OK**.

6. In the **Name** column double click on the second variable and replace **var00002** with the name **Grade**. Click on the tab **Data View** in the bottom left-hand corner of your screen and you should return to the spreadsheet of your data. The names you have written should appear at the top of the two columns of data. In the first column the numbers you entered should now display the labels **Prof** and **Grad**. If they do not then click on the **View** menu at the top of the screen and click on **Value Labels**.

7. You will now make a series of selections from the menus to utilise the SPSS **Explore** option. First of all click on **Analyze** and then on the option **Descriptive Statistics**. Finally select the option **Explore**.

    Select the variable you named 'Grade' by clicking on it once and then clicking on the arrow pointing to the **Dependent List**. Employ a similar process to enter the variable 'Class' in the **Factor List**. Click on the **Plots box** and deselect 'Stem-and-leaf' and select 'Histogram'. Click on **Continue** and then on **OK**.

8. The **Output** window should be displayed. If it is not then click on the **Window** menu at the top of the screen and select **Output1 - SPSS Viewer**. Print out the results by either clicking on the print icon and then click on **OK** in the **Print** window that opens. Alternatively go to the **File** menu and select **Print**.

9. Close down SPSS by selecting **Exit** from the **File** menu. When you are asked if you want to save the output select **No** as you can easily reproduce this. However, when you are asked if you want to save the data select **Yes**, as you will use this again in a later exercise.

10. EXAMINING YOUR PRINTOUT

Descriptive statistics

Professor		Student	
Median	....	Median	....
Mean	....	Mean	....
Standard Deviation	....	Standard Deviation	....

Boxplot

Is the median in the		
middle of the box?	Yes/No	Yes/No
Are the whiskers the		
same length?	Yes/No	Yes/No
Are there any outliers?	Yes/No	Yes/No

What do you conclude about the normality of the distributions of each set of scores from the boxplots?

Professor: ....

Student: ....

Is this interpretation supported by the histograms for the following?

Professor: ....

Student: ....

From comparing the means in the context of the standard deviations and looking at the boxplots, do you think there is a practical difference in the final grades of the students in the two classes?

....

....

....

EXERCISE 3.3 THE NORMAL DISTRIBUTION AND z-SCORES

After your success as a research assistant, you have been approached by Nationwide, the sponsors of the Football Conference, to help it reward the leading goal scorers at each club in the Conference. Nationwide has decided to give £1000 to the top 10% of the leading goal scorers, £900 to the next 10%, £800 to the next 10%, etc. The bottom 10% will receive a reward of £100.

To complete this task you need to know the mean, standard deviation and sample size. These values can be calculated by hand or the data may be entered into SPSS using the instructions from the previous exercise.

1. Using z-scores from Table 3.1 and the data listed below in Table 3.3, calculate what percentage of players scored more than and less than 22 goals, 26 goals, 14 goals. Into which reward band do each of these three scores fall?

2. Calculate how many goal scorers should fall between one standard deviation above and below the mean in the present sample. Does the data confirm this?
3. Because of the current slowdown in the economy and recent reductions in Nationwide profits, the company has decided that it will only reward the top 15% of leading goal scorers in the Conference. How many goals need to be scored in order to receive financial reward? How many goal scorers would you predict to be in the top 15% in the present sample? Does the data confirm this?
4. How many goal scorers would you predict scored between 19 and 31 goals inclusive? Does your data confirm this?

Table 3.3

Goals scored by the leading goalscorer for each team in the Nationwide Conference	
19	34
5	19
11	19
13	31
17	27
16	21
17	16
15	19
9	21
9	21
24	25

1.

	% Scoring more than	% Scoring less than	Reward band
22 goals	......	......	......
26 goals	......	......	......
14 goals	......	......	......

2.

	Predicted	Actual
Goal scorers falling 1 standard deviation above the mean	......	......
Goal scorers falling 1 standard deviation below the mean	......	......

3. How many goals would need to be scored to receive a financial reward? ......
How many goal scorers were predicted to be in the top 15%? ......
Do the data confirm this prediction? Yes/No

4. How many goal scorers were predicted to score between 19 and 31 goals? ......
Do the data confirm this prediction? Yes/No

4   INTRODUCTION TO EXPERIMENTAL RESEARCH

Inferential Statistics

In the previous two chapters we have seen how the sample size, mean and standard deviation provide a shorthand description of data that is normally distributed. These descriptive statistics allow comparisons to be made between different sets of data in terms of their typical scores and how the data is distributed. However, researchers often not only want to describe differences and similarities between sets of data, but also want to make inferences. For example, they may wish to test whether any observed differences reflect the impact of some causal factor or test to see if they can infer a particular sort of relationship between the variables that have been measured. To illustrate this, imagine that it is observed that a group of people who undertake a particular set of exercises have lower mean systolic blood pressure than those who do not. A researcher may want to know if it can be concluded that this observed difference is a product of the exercise training rather than just a product of the variability found in systolic blood pressure within the general population. Or, again, if a researcher observes that there is a tendency for those who are more perfectionist also to be more anxious before examinations, the researcher may want to know if this relationship is due to this personality disposition or just a coincidence. While statistics can aid in this decision making it is the logic that informs how the data is collected in conjunction with the statistics that justifies any claim for there being a causal relationship. This is most simply illustrated in the principles of experimental research.

A Brief Introduction to Experimental Research

To understand what is involved in testing predictions concerning data it is worth remembering that any human enquiry is concerned with gathering information to enhance understanding. An experimental approach is just one method, amongst many, of gathering data. For example, information can also be gathered through surveys, psychometric testing or case studies. However, an understanding of experimental research highlights both the role of statistics in aiding decision making and their limitations.

In an experiment the aim is to test a **hypothesis**. A hypothesis is a testable statement that predicts the relationship between two types of variables. These variables are termed the **independent** and the **dependent** variables. The independent variable is the one that is manipulated and the dependent variable is the one that is measured. For example, if it is predicted that a certain nutritional drink influences performance on an endurance activity, then the consumption of the nutritional drink is the independent variable and the participants' performance is the dependent variable. The experimenter would then measure the dependent variable (i.e. performance) under at least two conditions or levels of the independent variable. These two conditions might comprise a control group (e.g. performing without the nutritional drink), and an experimental group (e.g. performing with the nutritional drink).

Of course, endurance performance is a product of many variables other than the type of drink a participant may have consumed. To rule out the effect of these other variables participants must be tested in a situation where all these other variables, which are known as **irrelevant** or **extraneous variables**, are held constant. These extraneous variables are most often to do with aspects of the situation or the participants that have the potential to influence the dependent variable.

The control of **situational** variables, such as performance conditions, noise and time of day, etc., can generally be achieved with careful experimental design. Advertisements for washing powders provide a simple example of this procedure. Advertisers are usually careful to show that identically soiled clothing is washed in two identical machines and that the only variable that does differ is the washing powder. Sometimes extraneous variables can be a product of the testing procedure itself, for in the above example concerned with a nutritional drink, the testing of the participants has the potential to produce dehydration. If the control group does not have a drink this effect will be larger for this group in comparison with the experimental group. Therefore if the dehydration of the participants in the control group is thought to be a design problem then this group might be given a volume of water equal to that of the nutritional drink.

The other major type of extraneous variables reflect individual differences in participants, consequently they are known as **participant** variables. To illustrate these let us return to the example with the washing machine advertisement. If two articles of clothing are of different levels of cleanliness prior to washing, then any difference in cleanliness after washing may be a product of these original differences rather than the washing powders being tested. In the washing of clothes a soiled garment can be torn in half and one half put in each machine but with human participants individual differences are more difficult to eliminate. The most successful method is to adopt what is known as a **repeated measures design**. In this design the same person is measured on repeated occasions. On each occasion the participant is subjected to a different level of the independent variable. In the context of the previous athletic example concerning the impact of a nutritional drink on endurance performance, this would mean that participants may first perform after consuming a drink of water and then be required to perform again after consuming the nutritional drink. Any differences observed in the dependent variable of performance under the two conditions cannot then be a product of participant variables as the same individuals have been used in both of the different conditions.

Unfortunately this strategy can introduce other **confounding factors** such as **order effects** resulting, for example, from participants being exhausted, bored or having learnt from engaging in the activity in the previous condition. If these effects are symmetrical in that they are the same whichever order the individual is tested in, then counter-balancing may control for them. For example, if there are two conditions then half the participants are tested in one condition first and the other half in the other condition first. In the context of the previous example this would mean that half the participants would first run after consuming the nutritional drink and then run again after the drink of water, whilst the remaining participants would perform in the opposite order.

If the order effects are not symmetrical then they cannot be effectively counterbal-anced and a different strategy has to be adopted to control for individual differences. One such strategy to overcome this problem is to employ a **matched pair design**. In this design different participants are selected to perform under the two or more levels of the independent variable but they are matched in pairs across the conditions on the important individual difference, for example running ability, or body mass. This does not mean that the individuals within each group have to be similar, rather each partici-pant in one condition has to have a matched participant in the other condition. For example, there can be a fast, medium and slow runner in one condition as long as there is a fast, medium and slow runner in the other condition(s). This can be a time-consuming procedure because participants have to be pre-tested on the variables of interest before they can be matched. Of greater importance is the fact that the assump-tion regarding the relevant variable(s) for matching the participants may be incorrect. For example, they may have been matched on skill when physical fitness is the impor-tant factor upon which matching should take place. Unless the assumption in the match-ing forms part of the hypothesis, as it does for example in many studies of intelligence and personality in twins, then the researcher cannot be confident that the correct factor has been chosen. Later on in this chapter the importance of this will be highlighted. It will be noted that the statistical tests that are employed to examine differences between experimental and control groups are exactly the same for data produced by a matched pair design as those that would be employed to data from a repeated measures design. These tests assume that any differences in the groups of data are not a product of indi-vidual differences. Unfortunately, if participants have not been matched on the correct variable(s) then any observed differences could be the product of individual differences.

An alternative solution is to adopt an **independent groups design** in which the participants are **randomly** allocated to the various levels of the independent variable. Random assignment means that each participant has an equal chance of entering any group. The logic of this method accepts that there are individual differences but argues that these differences are distributed across the two or more groups by chance. This random allocation means that it is unlikely that there will be any systematic bias in any group. For example, it is most likely that high- and low-fitness participants will be more or less evenly split across two groups and very unlikely that all high-fitness participants will be in one group and low-fitness participants in the other group. The analysis of data from an independent group design employs different statistical tests to those employed for data collected by means of repeated measures or matched pair designs. These tests recognise that the distribution of individual differences such as fit-ness across the two groups may not be identical and therefore variability within each group is taken into account in the test design. This will be explained in more detail later.

Having hypothesised a relationship between the independent and dependent variables, and chosen a design to control for extraneous factors, the researcher can now collect the data. The data gathered is then subjected to the appropriate statistical analysis. As discussed later in this chapter, this analysis measures the precise probability of getting the observed differences in the dependent variable under the various levels of the independent variable by chance. If there is a relatively small probability that the observed differences occurred by chance, usually less than 5%, then the logic of the experimental design dictates that we attribute the difference to the independent variable. That is, the decision is that there is a **causal** relationship between the independent and dependent variables. To understand this process further the following section explores the logic of statistical inference in more detail.

The Logic of Statistical Inference

In an experiment, a prediction is tested by manipulating the independent variable and measuring changes in the dependent variable while attempting to control extraneous variables. This provides at least two sets of data, one from the control group and one from the experimental group. The decision to be made is whether there is a **significant** difference in the two sets of results that can be attributed to the influence of the independent variable, or whether the difference is due to irrelevant extraneous variables. Thus, statistical testing leads to **inferences** being made from the data as to the **relationship** between the variables.

What is meant by the word 'significant' above? To explain this term, imagine that various weights are put on a mechanical scale and the relationship between the size of these weights and the movement of the pointer is observed. The causal relationship between these two events can be explained by an understanding of the mechanics of the scales. If such an explanation is insufficient the scales can be opened up and the physical relationship between the weights and the pointer movement observed. But in an experiment concerning the effect of a nutritional drink on performance, the human body cannot be 'opened up' in the same way as the scales, nor can a complete explanation of the 'mechanisms' at work be given with the same degree of precision as with the scales. All that can be done is to attempt to keep the irrelevant variables constant and manipulate the independent variable (e.g. the nutritional drink). If a corresponding change in the dependent variable (e.g. performance) is now observed then the logic of the experimental design which has controlled for extraneous variables leads to the inference that a causal relationship exists between the nutritional drink and performance.

Unfortunately, *all* the irrelevant variables can never be kept absolutely constant and thus it can never be proved beyond doubt that chance was not responsible for any changes in the independent variable. Here the word 'chance' is being used as shorthand for irrelevant or extraneous variables. However, by conducting statistical tests on the data, the likelihood that any observed difference is due to chance can be measured. For example, it may be found that the amount of variation in performance between those ingesting the nutritional drink and those who did not ingest the nutritional drink is likely to occur 50 times out of 100 by chance. If this were the case then it would be difficult to credit the nutritional drink as being responsible for the variation. If, on the other hand, the probability of the variation being due to chance was 1 in a 100 then the decision might very well be made to attribute the variation to the independent variable, namely the nutritional drink, for this explanation would be correct 99 times out of 100. The point at which it is decided to reject the chance explanation and attribute responsibility for the difference to the independent variable is called the **significance level**. The significance level is also known as **alpha** (α) for reasons which will become clear later. Most researchers generally choose a significance level of 0.05. That is, as long as the observed differences would only occur by chance 5 times or less out of 100 then the researcher will reject the chance explanation for the observed findings. This is because 95 times out of 100 the observed differences would be due to the experimental manipulation of the independent variable. To some extent the adoption of an α equal to 0.05 (or 5% significance level) is an arbitrary matter and in certain cases one might be far more conservative and choose a level of 0.01 where the probability due to chance is 1 in 100.

Hypothesis Testing

This process of rejecting or accepting the chance explanation is known as hypothesis testing. In the process of statistical inference the researcher is deciding whether:

1. the differences arise because of purely chance fluctuations in the two groups of scores; or
2. the differences are caused, at least in part, by the independent variable.

The first of these is termed the **null hypothesis** and the second is called the **alternate** or **experimental hypothesis**. Thus, in an experiment concerning a nutritional drink and performance, the null hypothesis would be:

> H_0 There will be no significant difference between the mean
>   performance scores of the experimental and control groups.

The alternate hypothesis might state:

> H_1 There will be a significant difference between the mean
>   performance scores of the experimental and control groups.

If, as in the above experimental hypothesis, the direction of the difference is not stated then it is known as a **two-tailed hypothesis**. However, if the alternate hypothesis states the direction of the difference in the two groups of scores, for example the experimental group will score less points for their performance than the control group, then this is known as a **one-tailed hypothesis**.

Unless there are good reasons for doing otherwise, a two-tailed hypothesis should be postulated. One-tailed hypotheses are appropriate when a theoretical perspective based on previous research would suggest that a particular difference is expected or when there is no logical way in which a difference could occur in a direction other than the one predicted.

Type I and Type II Errors

If a significance level of 0.05 is chosen, it is important to realise that on 5% of occasions the observed difference may occur by chance. This means that if the null hypothesis is rejected then the researcher can be 95% confident that the difference found is not the product of chance and there is only a 5% probability of making a mistake. Making the mistake of rejecting the null hypothesis when it is in fact true is known as committing a **Type I error**. The probability of making such a mistake is known as the alpha level and is equal to the significance level adopted.

An obvious solution to the problem of committing a Type I error is to reduce the significance value to, say, 0.01. This would mean that a Type I error would be expected only one time out of a hundred experiments. However, this would result in an increased number of occasions on which the null hypothesis is accepted when it is in fact incorrect. This is known as a **Type II error**. The probability of committing a Type II error is referred to as the beta level (β) and its probability is much more difficult to assess than the alpha level. In spite of this difficulty, it can be seen from the above that a significance level of 0.05 is a compromise that attempts to minimise the probability of committing either of these two types of errors. Another way of expressing the connection between these two errors is in the form of the two scales shown in Figure 4.1.

From these scales it can be seen that in employing a 5% significance level the researcher is accepting that there is a 5% probability that H_0 is correct and a 95%

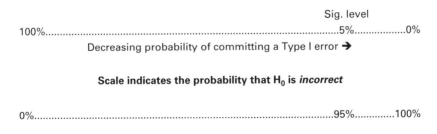

Scale indicates the probability that H_0 is *correct*

Sig. level
100%..5%................0%
Decreasing probability of committing a Type I error →

Scale indicates the probability that H_0 is *incorrect*

0%..95%..............100%

← Decreasing possibility of committing a Type II error

Figure 4.1 **The relationship between significance level, confidence level and Type I and II errors**

probability that H_0 is incorrect. It can also be seen that any attempt to reduce the probability of committing a Type I error by reducing the significance level will result in an increase in the possibility of committing a Type II error.

Statistical versus Practical Significance

When conducting research that involves statistical testing there is a great temptation to suggest that statistical significance automatically implies a practical significance. For example, imagine we found that the mean age at death for those who smoked 30 cigarettes per day was 65 and for those who smoked 40 cigarettes per day it was 63. Also imagine that this difference of two years was statistically significant at the $p < 0.05$ level. However, is this a practically significant finding? To answer this question this difference needs to be examined in the context of the greatly reduced life expectancy of both groups compared with non-smokers whose mean age at death was found to be 78 years. Or, again, imagine that heavy users of digital mobile phones have a 20% increased probability of developing a brain tumour and that this increase is statistically significant. This sounds very worrying. However, if the probability of developing a brain tumour in the wider population is 5 in 100,000 then this research would suggest that the risk for mobile phone users is raised to 6 in 100,000. You may feel that the practical implications of this statistically significant increased risk are not sufficient to deter you from continuing to have the convenience of mobile telephony. The distinction between practical significance and statistical significance is very important and the researcher must be very careful to restrict the term significance to its statistical denotation when writing up experimental reports.

Hypotheses Concerned with Differences and Relationships

Each of the examples of hypotheses given so far has included the word 'difference'. For example, a null hypothesis might state that there will be no significant **difference** between the performance scores of the experimental and control groups. This hypothesis predicts that the means of the two groups will not be significantly different.

Sometimes, however, the focus of interest is not in detecting group differences but rather in identifying relationships between variables. For example, our null hypothesis might predict that there will be no significant **relationship** between the length of the training time and the performance scores. This null hypothesis predicts that knowing how much someone trains will not provide any information about how well they perform.

The distinction between hypotheses concerned with relationships and hypotheses concerned with group differences is very important. This is because they reflect the type of question the researcher asks, which in turn will often influence the way that data is collected. Questions concerned with differences usually employ data collected through experimentation involving the manipulation of one or more independent variables. If through the use of the appropriate statistical tests a significant difference is found then the conclusion may be drawn that there is a causal relationship between the independent and dependent variables.

In contrast, research focusing on relationships often involves data collection through survey methods in which no manipulation of independent variables and limited control of extraneous variables have taken place. Attempts to answer questions concerned with relationships employ different statistical tests to questions focusing on differences. If through the use of the appropriate statistical tests a significant relationship is found then the conclusion that there is a causal relationship between the variables concerned may not automatically be drawn, for the lack of control and manipulations of extraneous and independent variables make it difficult for the researcher to rule out the possibility that some other variable caused the observed significant relationships. The distinction between questions that focus on differences and questions that focus on relationships is one very important factor in determining the type of statistical analysis to be employed and the types of conclusion that can be drawn.

An introduction to statistical tests concerned with relationships between variables will not be presented until Chapter 10. However, it is important to appreciate that whenever a significant difference between two variables exists there will always be a relationship between the two variables.

Samples and Populations

It was stated earlier that the problem facing the researcher when analysing data was one of deciding whether there is any significant difference in the results that can be attributed to the influence of the independent variable, or whether any difference is due to irrelevant variables. Before examining the statistical techniques used to make these decisions it is necessary to understand some of the constraints within research.

When experiments or surveys are undertaken it is not usually possible to employ the total **population** as participants and therefore the researcher relies on data collected from a **sample** of this population. These two words, population and sample, represent very important ideas in statistics. The term population refers to all possible objects of a particular type. Such types might be tennis players, cricket bats or characteristics such as fitness levels. Populations are so large, in fact they may be infinite, that a researcher never has access to them and instead often takes a sample of observations from the population. Unless the sample is representative of the population of interest then findings cannot be extrapolated from the sample and applied to the larger population.

To illustrate this imagine that a researcher at a university wanted to understand how first-year undergraduate students perceived and participated in leisure activities. For obvious practical reasons the questionnaire could not be administered to all undergraduate students in the country of interest so instead a sample of those students has to be employed. Unfortunately, were the researcher to take the most convenient course and administer the questionnaire to all students at his/her own university this would not provide a representative sample. This is because students attending any one particular institution are a self-selecting group that are unlikely to represent a cross-section of the student population. If, instead, the researcher took a **random** sample of students from every institution with undergraduates, then as every undergraduate student in the country had an equal chance of being selected, this would usually provide a representative sample. If the researcher found that the mean time spent on leisure activities was 32 hours per month, then he/she would be justified in inferring that this was an accurate estimate of the average amount of leisure time per month engaged in by the student population. If this process was repeated several times the researcher would probably find a slightly different mean value each time as a result of random variations in the process of sample selection. The actual mean of the country's undergraduate population would lie somewhere close to the average of this series of sample means. This is because the means of the samples will be normally distributed around the population mean. Thus, whenever two samples are taken from the same population we would expect the means to be different. This is a very important point whose statistical implications will be explored in more detail in the next chapter.

A clue to this importance can be found by returning to the experiment concerning a nutritional drink and performance. Here, one might have one set of performance scores from a control group who just drank water and another set of performance scores from the experimental group who had taken the nutritional drink. If the means of these two data sets are different what are the possible explanations? From the previous discussion on samples it follows that any observed difference in means could be found because the means from any two samples of a population will often produce different results. This explanation would suggest that the null hypothesis is correct. Alternatively it could be that the means are different because the samples are drawn from two different populations. If this is the case then the experimental hypothesis is correct. The experimental hypothesis implies that one set of performance figures are produced by a population that performs without the nutritional drink and another set by a population that performs with the nutritional drink and these two populations have different performance statistics.

Which of these explanations is correct? The various statistical tests outlined later on in this manual are designed to answer this question. All the tests do this by working out the probability that the results could be obtained from the same population. If this probability is equal to or less than 0.05, then there is less than a 5 out of 100 chance that these results could be obtained from the same population. In this case the researcher would reject the null hypothesis and accept the experimental hypothesis. Before we attempt to understand how these tests calculate this probability we need to know first how to select the appropriate test.

Selecting the Appropriate Statistical Test

There are four major factors that determine the correct test for any particular set of experimental data. These are:

Table 4.1

Type of test	Type of data	Type of design	
		Related samples	Independent design
Parametric	Interval	*t*-test for paired samples	*t*-test for independent samples
Non-parametric	Ordinal	Wilcoxon test	Mann–Whitney test
	Nominal	Sign test	Chi-square test

1. What is the research question?
2. How many dependent and independent variables are there?
3. Was the data gathered by means of an independent, related or mixed design?
4. What type of scale was used to measure the variables?

In Appendix 2 there are two tables that illustrate how these four factors combine to determine the correct choice of test. However, this section concentrates on points 3 and 4 above and their implications for choosing among a limited range of statistical tests. Before examining what this means in detail note that Table 4.1 illustrates how these two factors influence the choice of two categories of statistical tests.

In looking at this table it is important to remember that the term related samples refers to repeated measure and matched pair designs and the term independent samples refers to the independent group design. If you are not clear about these terms you will find a reference to them in the second section of this chapter.

In the table the terms **parametric** and **non-parametric** tests are introduced. These refer to two basic types of statistical tests that make different assumptions about the data being examined. All that can be noted at present is that the choice of tests is determined in part by how the data is collected and what sort of data is collected.

Parametric Tests

Parametric tests make three basic assumptions:

1. It is assumed that each sample of scores has been drawn from a **normally distributed population**.
2. These samples are assumed to have the same **variance**.
3. The dependent variable is assumed to have been measured on an interval scale.

The following section examines each of these assumptions in more detail.

Checking the Assumption of a Normal Distribution

Unfortunately, it is difficult to prove that a particular sample is drawn from a normally distributed population. Previous research can be examined to see if the data previously formed a normal distribution or the existing data could be plotted in the form a histogram to see if it looks like a normal distribution. However, neither of these procedures is very precise. Therefore, to have any measured confidence in our decision we need to look for statistical alternatives. Two measures that are relevant are the concepts of **skewness** and **kurtosis**. You may have noted already from your printout of Exercise 3.2 that the **Explore** option provides a measure of these statistics. Each of these concepts will now be dealt with in turn.

Skewness

Skewness reflects the existence of extreme scores at one end of the distribution. A skewness of zero means that the distribution is symmetrical. Using the z-table (Table 3.1) it is possible to get an exact measure of skewness and to assess the probability that the distribution is symmetrical. Whilst SPSS will produce this value it is important to understand how it was obtained so that its significance can be interpreted.

Skewness is computed by employing the following formula:

$$\text{Skewness} = \frac{\sum z^3}{n}$$

Here z refers to the distance of each score from the mean measured in units of standard deviation. By cubing this value the sign, whether it be positive or negative, will remain the same but the deviation of extreme scores will greatly increase in magnitude. For example, 1 cubed is 1, 2 cubed is 8 and 3 cubed is 27. The reason for dividing by n is to find the average of the cubed deviations and therefore to control for the sample size.

The larger the value obtained from this calculation the greater the skewness. The particular meaning of any value obtained by this calculation is not obvious as theoretically it could be any value between zero and infinity. What is needed is a scale so that the probability that the distribution is skewed or not can be assessed. Without wishing to pre-empt a later discussion on sampling error, the estimate of skewness within the population is based on the sample of data. This sample may not be representative of the population as it may contain some error. To assess the significance of the value of skewness the ratio of the skewness obtained over the error in its measurement is calculated. This error is known as the standard error for skewness. For moderately large samples this standard error for skewness can be computed by the following formula:

$$\text{SE}_{\text{skew}} = \sqrt{\frac{6}{n}}$$

Table 4.2 **Descriptives**

	CLASS		Statistic	Std. Error
Grades	Professor's Class	Skewness	2.276	.491
	Graduate Student's Class	Skewness	.270	.491

If the value of skewness is divided by this error the result is a z-value for skewness that can be interpreted using the standard z-tables:

$$z_{\text{skew}} = \frac{\sum z^3 / n}{\sqrt{(6/n)}}$$

Note from the z-table (Table 3.1) that with a move of 1.96 standard deviations away from the mean an area of 2.5% of the normal distribution curve is cut off. To check that a distribution is neither positively nor negatively significantly skewed ($\alpha = 0.05$) both ends of the normal distribution must be examined. Therefore as long as the value of z_{skew} is less than ± 1.96 there is 95% confidence that the population distribution is not positively or negatively skewed. To illustrate what this means in practice consider an example.

The output from the SPSS exercise in the previous chapter includes the information given in Table 4.2. Note that if the standard error for skewness is calculated according to the previously given formula the value 0.562 will result and not the value 0.491 shown in Table 4.2. This is because that formula can only be applied to moderately large samples. Also note that for 'Professor's Class' if the skewnes statistic is divided by the standard error for skewness the result is 4.64. As this is much larger than ± 1.96 the conclusion is that these 'Professor's Class' scores are significantly skewed and therefore the distribution significantly deviates from normal. Is this also true for the 'Graduate Student's Class'?

Kurtosis

Kurtosis refers to the peakedness of the curve: that is, is it a flat curve or does it have a sharp point? The procedure for working out the kurtosis is very similar to that employed when working out skewness. The formula is as follows:

$$\text{Kurtosis} = \left(\frac{\sum z^4}{n} \right) - 3$$

Note that here z is raised to the power of 4. This means that, once again, extreme scores will be greatly increased, but this time the signs will all be positive. For example, -1 raised to the power of 4 is 1, -2 raised to the power of 4 is 16, and 3 raised to the power of 4 is 81. The -3 is included in the above kurtosis equation because without it, if there were no kurtosis, this formula would produce a value of 3. Therefore, 3 is subtracted so that if there is no kurtosis a value of zero is produced.

The next step is to work out the likely error in estimating the kurtosis within the population from the sample and this is done as follows:

$$SE_{kurt} = \sqrt{\frac{24}{n}}$$

Then to compute a z-value for kurtosis we divide the kurtosis score by the above error term:

$$z_{kurt} = \frac{kurtosis}{\sqrt{24/n}}$$

As with skewness, a value between ±1.96 suggests with at least 95% confidence that the distribution is normal. If the value obtained is positive, then it indicates that the curve is more peaked than normal (i.e. leptokurtic), whilst if it is negative, then the curve is flatter than normal (i.e. platykurtic). Again, looking at the SPSS exercise in the previous chapter may be helpful.

Looking at the output in this exercise, note that it includes the information in Table 4.3. Using the 'Professor's Class' values in the table, the kurtosis statistics divided by the standard error for kurtosis produce the value 5.93. As this is much larger than ±1.96 it would be concluded that these 'Professor's Class' scores are significantly kurtotic, that is the distribution significantly deviates from normal. Is this also true for the 'Graduate Student's Class'? Now look at the two histograms from the output of the previous SPSS exercise and see if this graphical representation concurs with this statistical interpretation.

By using these two measures of skewness and kurtosis the researcher can decide, with a precise level of confidence, whether the data conforms to the required assumption of being normally distributed.

Table 4.3   **Descriptives**

	CLASS		Statistic	Std. Error
Grades	Professor's Class	Kurtosis	5.644	.953
	Graduate Student's Class	Kurtosis	.236	.953

Checking the Assumption of Equal Variance

The assumption of equal variance is also known as the homogeneity of variance assumption. Some indication of the equality of the variances of two sets of data can be obtained by looking at a graphical representation such as a boxplot, an example of which was provided in Chapter 2. Although it cannot be proved that two samples have equal variance, it can be determined whether they are significantly different. SPSS employs a variety of procedures to test for equivalence of variance and these tests will be discussed as they become appropriate for particular statistical techniques.

Checking the Assumption of Level of Measurement

In Chapter 2 it was noted that measurement is concerned with assigning numbers to observations. How numbers are assigned to observations determines the arithmetic operations that are permissible. The ways in which numbers are assigned in social research can be classified into three different levels. These are:

1. **Nominal data**. Nominal means in name only. Here numbers are used simply to identify the groups or categories to which various objects belong. For example, the number 1 could be assigned to windsurfing, 2 to dinghy sailing and 3 to land yachting. No numerical operations can be carried out with these numbers beyond noting the frequency with which each occurs. These relative frequencies allow the mode to be identified as an indication of the typical score.
2. **Ordinal scale**. In an ordinal scale objects are not only in different categories, but these categories stand in some relation to each other; for example, students rank their preferences in order for different sorts of leisure activities. However, there is no reason for assuming that the difference between the items ranked first and second is the same as that between those ranked second and third etc. As the data stands in an ordered relationship to one another, the median is used to identify the typical score.
3. **Interval scale**. The relationship between the objects is measured on a scale in which all the intervals are equal. For example, if performance is measured in terms of time then the difference between 28 seconds and 29 seconds is the same as that between 34 and 35 seconds, namely 1 second. This system of measurement allows for the mean to be calculated as the indicator of the typical score.

Because parametric tests are used to examine for significant differences between means, they require that the dependent variable be measured on an interval scale.

Non-parametric Tests

In contrast to parametric tests, non-parametric tests make very few assumptions. In fact they make few assumptions about the distribution of the data and they do not assume homogeneity of variance in the samples. The only assumption that is of concern here is to do with the scale on which the dependent variable is measured. Looking at Table 4.1 above it can be seen that some non-parametric tests require that the dependent variable is measured on an ordinal scale whilst others require nominal data.

As non-parametric tests make so few assumptions compared with the corresponding parametric tests then why use parametric tests? The answer is because parametric tests are more likely to detect a significant difference between two sets of scores than their non-parametric equivalent. This is because more information is available to parametric tests than non-parametric tests. For example, whereas a non-parametric test based on ordinal data takes into account the rankings of the participants' scores, a parametric test would not only have this information but also the magnitude of the intervals between the rankings. It is for this reason that parametric tests are more **powerful** than their non-parametric equivalent. Power in this context is defined as the probability of rejecting the null hypothesis when it is false and is defined in the following way:

$$\text{Power} = 1 - \text{probability of Type II error} = 1 - \beta$$

Although parametric tests make the three assumptions listed above, they will still provide a valid result even when some of these assumptions are not perfectly met. Tests that possess this characteristic are described as **robust** and the reason for this quality will be explained later.

Finally, although non-parametric tests are not as powerful as parametric tests, increasing the sample size can increase their power to that approaching their parametric equivalents.

Summary

Statistics are employed to enable the researcher to draw inferences from samples of a population about whether there are real differences between sets of scores or real relationships between variables. In experimental research, as the design should have controlled for most of the extraneous variables, any observed differences in the dependent variable may be attributed to either changes in the independent variable or error in the measurement due to factors such as individual differences. In deciding whether to attribute these changes to the independent variable statistics are employed to measure the probability of obtaining the differences by chance. This chance explanation is known as the null hypothesis and it postulates either that no relationship exists between the variables or that no differences exist between the sets of scores. If the probability of obtaining the observed differences by chance is equal to or less than the established significance level (e.g. 0.05) then the decision is made to reject the chance explanation and accept the alternative that a true difference exists. If a criterion of 0.05 is employed in rejecting this chance explanation then there is always a 5% probability that the wrong decision has been made. This is known as a

Type I error. Alternatively, if the probability was greater than the criterion and the null hypothesis was accepted by mistake, this is known as a Type II error. Even if the researcher decides that there is a real statistical difference between sets of scores this does not mean that this difference is of any practical significance.

The calculation of this probability for accepting or rejecting the null hypothesis varies depending upon the statistical tests. The appropriate test is determined by the research question, the number of dependent and independent variables, the experimental design and the type of scale used to measure the variables. All of the tests covered in this book are known as parametric tests and these tests make three assumptions. They assume that each sample of scores has been drawn from a normal population, that these samples have the same variance and that the dependent variable is measured on an interval scale. The concepts of skewness and kurtosis were introduced as statistical means of evaluating the normality assumption.

EXERCISE 4.1 TEST SELECTION

Below are listed a series of hypothetical situations. In each case indicate which test the researcher should use and why. While this task is made easier if you are familiar with the tests, it is still not that difficult to make the appropriate choice if you ask yourself two things:

A. What experimental design has been adopted?
B. What sort of data has this research generated?

Having answered these questions use Table 4.1 to identify the appropriate test. To keep matters simple, assume that the homogeneity of variance assumption is met and that the data is normally distributed.

1. Which statistical test could be used to test the hypothesis that there is no difference in the number of goals scored by the top 22 first and second division goal scorers? Explain your choice.
2. A geographer who was interested in the apparent reduction of rainfall in East Anglia compared the rainfall in 1991 with that of 2001.
    Which statistical test should she use and why?
3. An ecologist predicted that humidity would influence the amount of time spent foraging by woodlice. He set up an experiment in which a sample of 100 woodlice was randomly assigned to one of two humidity conditions. He then observed how much time they spent foraging over a 24 hour period. The humidity conditions were then reversed for the two groups and the foraging behaviour was once again observed for 24 hours.
    Which statistical test should he use to test his hypothesis? Explain the reasons for your choice.

4. A sociologist was interested in exploring whether there was any association between political choice and religious affiliations. She set up a survey of a representative sample, noting on a tally chart respondents' religion, and which party they usually voted for.

   Which statistical test should she use and why?

5. A psychologist wished to test the hypothesis that the vigorousness of initiation procedures does not influences the degree of affiliation to a group. He persuaded a local employer to assign applicants randomly to one of two methods in selecting staff. One method lasted 30 minutes and the other lasted one day. Ten staff were selected from each group of applicants, the actual selection being based on 30 minutes of testing which was common to both groups. Later the successful applicants were asked to rate the quality of the organisation's work on a scale of 1 to 10.

   What statistical test would be used to test this hypothesis and why?

6. A sociologist wanted to compare the career aspirations of children from working class and professional backgrounds, so 85 'working class' children and 77 'professional' children were randomly selected from a group of homogeneous intellectual capacity. The aspirations of each child were rated by an independent assessor on a scale of 1 to 10 (1 = unskilled, 10 = high-status profession).

   How would one test the hypothesis that the children of parents from the two occupational groups do not have different career aspirations?

7. A newly discovered apple is delicious in flavour. It was decided to test its yielding capacity by planting the new apple adjacent to a standard apple in eight orchards scattered about a region suitable for the cultivation of both apples.

   How would one test for a significant difference between the yielding capacity of the two varieties of apple trees?

8. An historian was interested in changes in the age distribution of a population as a consequence of the Black Death. Focusing on two villages that were matched for size, population structure, etc., before the plague, she noted that one experienced the plague and other did not. She then examined the appropriate census data to see if there was any difference in the number of people aged over 18.

   What test could she use to see if there was a difference in the structure of the population after the plague? Explain your choice.

9. A film on the hazards of smoking was shown to 800 smokers. One week after seeing the film 28 out of the 300 women smokers and 32 of the 500 men smokers were still not smoking.

   What statistical test could be used to test the association between the sex of the participants and giving up smoking?

10. A researcher was interested in whether a particular film on AIDS would influence attitudes towards 'safer sex'. The attitude of a representative sample of students was assessed on a seven-point scale before and after viewing the film.

   What test could one use to see if there was a difference in their attitudes on these two occasions?

EXERCISE 4.2 USING THE NORMAL DISTRIBUTION

This is another exercise that employs the concepts introduced in Chapters 2 and 3. It is included here because a sound understanding of descriptive statistics and the normal distribution is essential for anyone who wishes to employ statistical tests.

1. If the mean amount of beer drunk by male students is 15 pints per week and the standard deviation is 3 pints, then:
    (a) What percentage of students consume more than 22 pints per week?
    (b) What amount of beer do more than 75% of students consume per week?
    (c) What percentage of students consume less than 7 pints per week?
    (d) What percentage of students consume between 10 and 20 pints per week?
2   If 40% of students spend more than 20 hours per week reading and the standard deviation is 6 hours per week, then:
    (a) What is the average amount of time spent reading?
    (b) If the university expects students to read for 30 hours per week, what percentage of students fulfil this requirement?
3   In a population of 230,000 students, the mean debt that they have accumulated by the time they graduate is £6400 and the standard deviation is £1600.
    (a) How many students graduate with a debt greater than £10,000?
    (b) How many graduate with a debt of less than £1000?
    (c) How many graduate with a debt of between £4000 and £8000?

5 SAMPLING ERROR

In the previous chapter reference was made to parametric and non-parametric tests. You may be wondering why these two sorts of tests have been given these particular labels. The answer to this question becomes obvious once two facts are recalled. Firstly, the descriptive measures of a population, such as the mean and the standard deviation, are known as **parameters**, whereas the same measures of a sample are known as **statistics**. Secondly, **parametric tests** are ones that use the sample statistics to make estimates of the population parameters. For example, they estimate the mean of the population from examining the mean of the sample.

In making these estimations of the population parameters it is assumed, for example, that the population's mean is the same as the sample mean. However, in reality, the sample mean will not always be exactly the same as the population's mean. Any difference between these two reflects the effect of what is termed **sampling error**.

Sources of Sampling Error

With a little reflection, it is not difficult to identify the potential sources of this sampling error. Imagine two researchers were interested in the achievement motivation of first-year psychology undergraduates at their respective universities, A and B. To estimate the population parameters, each researcher took a random sample of undergraduates and administered an inventory that purported to measure achievement motivation. Now add two more facts. The population of undergraduates at A was a very homogeneous body who actually all had the same achievement motivation, while those at B were very heterogeneous and therefore differed widely in achievement motivation.

When the researcher at A estimates the population mean from the sample mean there cannot be any sampling error as there is no variability in the population. It does not matter who is sampled from the population as the same achievement motivation score will be obtained. In contrast the researcher at B is much more likely to have sampling error in the estimation of the population parameters because of the large variance within the population. Extrapolating from these two cases, it may be concluded that as the variance increases so the sampling error increases, that is

Sampling error is proportional to the population variance.

It is not inevitable that the estimated population mean of the researcher at B will suffer from a large sampling error. If the sample is truly representative of the population then the sampling error can be dramatically reduced. To illustrate this, imagine that the researcher at B foolishly took a sample of only one. Now while it is possible that the estimation of the population mean from this sample may provide an accurate estimation of the actual population mean, it is not likely to do so. Furthermore, if this researcher was to take another random sample of one, it is quite probable that the mean of this second sample will be very different from the mean of the first sample. For example, it is quite possible that by chance the researcher may have selected the individual with the strongest achievement motivation in the first sample and the weakest motivation in the second. In both cases the sample is not large enough to be truly representative of the population and therefore a large error will occur in the estimation of the population parameters.

Now imagine that the researcher at B was unnecessarily conscientious and took a sample of 275. On this occasion it is very likely that the mean of the sample is very similar to the mean of the population as the sample includes over 90% of the population. It is therefore very difficult for the sample not to be truly representative of the population. Also, if this researcher was to take another random sample of 275 it is most likely that the mean of this second sample will be very similar to the mean of the first sample. Again, this is because the very size of the sample dictates that some of the participants must be drawn from most sections of the population. Extrapolating from these examples, it may be concluded that as the sample size increases so the sampling error decreases, that is

> Sampling error is inversely proportional to the sample size.

Combining both of the above conclusions together suggests that the size of the error in estimating the population mean from the sampling mean will be directly proportional to the variance of the sample and inversely proportional to the sample size, that is

$$\text{Sampling error will be a function of } \frac{s^2}{n}$$

where

$$s^2 = \text{variance of the sample}$$
$$n = \text{number of observations}$$

Why Is Sampling Error Important?

The notion of error in measurement is at the heart of the rationale for statistical tests. If there were no sampling error there would not be any need for statistical tests. To illustrate this imagine that a researcher wanted to know if there was a difference in the typical achievement motivation scores of sociology and psychology first-year undergraduates at national universities. To answer this question the researcher simply needs to determine what the typical achievement motivation scores are for each group of undergraduates. If the researcher was to measure each of the many thousands of undergraduates then the typical score could be determined without any sampling error and the researcher would have an answer to the question.

In reality both practical and commercial considerations result in the researcher not measuring all of the individuals but instead relying on samples. Because the use of samples introduces the potential for sampling error, any observed difference in the typical achievement motivation score of sociology and psychology undergraduates must be considered within the context of any such error in the measurement. Statistical tests are simply strategies for determining the probabilities that differences or relationships occur given the error in the measurement of the dependent variables.

If this seems rather abstract then consider the following situation. You have been asked to measure the length of two very similar fields to determine which is the larger and hence more suitable for an outdoor concert. Equipped with an electronic measuring device you measure the first field to be 1450 metres long and the second to be 1475 metres long. As you confidently walk back with the conviction that the second field is 25 metres longer than the first you read on the back of the measuring device that it is accurate to ±50 metres. This means that while you have observed a difference of 25 metres it is less than the potential error in your system of measurement and therefore any difference you have observed may be a consequence of your measuring device rather than any true difference in the length of the fields. This process of deciding whether differences between groups' scores are real differences or whether they are just a product of chance caused by error in the system of measurement is most clearly illustrated in the paired samples *t*-test.

Paired Samples *t*-test

Purpose

The purpose of this technique is to test for significant differences between two group means from data that has been gathered by means of a related measures design.

Research Question

t-tests are employed to address research questions that focus on the difference in the means on one dependent variable produced by one independent variable with two levels. For example, imagine a researcher was interested in the question: is there a difference in performance when executing a difficult task alone or with an audience? Adopting the appropriate counterbalancing procedures, the researcher might test a group of participants on their ability to perform this task under the alone and audience conditions.

Null Hypothesis Tested

A *t*-test could be used to test the null hypothesis that there is no significant difference between the performance means in the alone and audience conditions. If there is no significant difference then the two samples are drawn from the same population.

Assumptions

The *t*-test is a parametric test and it makes the following assumptions:

1. The level of measurement of the dependent variable must be at least interval.
2. The dependent variable is normally distributed in the population.
3. The variances of the samples are not significantly different.

When some of these assumptions are not met it is possible to make a statistical correction. The form that these corrections take depends upon the statistical technique being employed. For example, with the *t*-test, when the assumption of homogeneity of variance is not met (assumption 3) then SPSS will provide an alternative test statistic that is not based on this assumption. This will be explained in more detail later in this chapter when discussing the independent *t*-test.

Principle Behind a Paired Samples t-test

If there is no significant difference in the performance scores in the alone and audience conditions then it can be concluded that the two samples are drawn from the same population. Imagine that this is in fact true. Theoretically, if the two sets of mean performance scores from the alone and audience conditions are drawn from the same population then they should have the same value. Therefore the difference between the two sets of scores should equal zero. However, in reality there will always be differences due to sampling error. These differences will vary from sample to sample. To illustrate how the magnitudes of these differences are distributed, two samples of a fixed size may be repeatedly drawn from a population and then the differences between each pair of samples plotted on a frequency distribution. Interestingly, for sample sizes greater than 20, the distribution of mean differences is almost always approximately normal regardless of the population distribution. This is known as the **central limit theorem** and is illustrated by the graph in Figure 5.1.

The horizontal axis of this graph presents the differences between the two means, measured in units of standard deviation. From the graph it can be noted that usually the difference between the two sample means is very small but occasionally, by chance, sampling error will produce some very large differences.

The standard deviation of the sampling distribution of the differences is called the **standard error** and it will decrease as the sample size increases. If the value of this standard error is known then any particular observed difference between a pair of means can be divided by it to produce a *z*-score. This *z*-score indicates how many

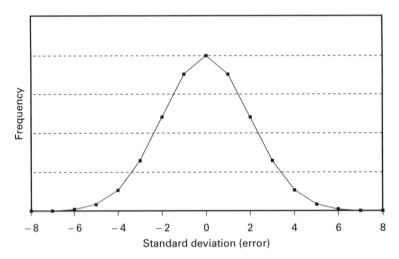

Figure 5.1 **Sampling distribution of difference means**

standard deviations the observed difference between two means is away from the middle of the distribution. Knowing this distance in units of standard deviations allows the z-table to be used to determine the probability of getting the observed difference by chance.

To carry out the procedure of repeatedly extracting pairs of samples and plotting the observed differences would be very time consuming. Fortunately this is unnecessary as an estimation of the standard error can be obtained by taking the square root of s^2/n of the sample. Note once again that a large variance and a small sample will produce a large standard error.

$$\text{Standard error} = \sqrt{\frac{\text{variance}}{n}} = \sqrt{\frac{s^2}{n}} = \frac{s}{\sqrt{n}}$$

If the null hypothesis is incorrect, it would be expected that the difference between the two means would be larger than the standard error. That is, the average difference between the participants' performance scores in the alone and audience conditions would be larger than the error made in accepting that these scores represent the means of two samples drawn from a single population. If the difference between the alone group and audience group means is divided by this standard error then as this value increases, the probability that the observed difference in the two means is a product of chance diminishes. The difference between the means of two groups divided by the standard error produces a t-ratio. Therefore

$$t = \frac{\text{mean of the differences}}{\text{standard error}} = \frac{\overline{d}}{\sqrt{s^2/(n-1)}}$$

Note that in the above formula $(n-1)$ was used instead of (n) as an estimate of the error in the population required.

Summary of the Paired Samples t-test

This technique tests the null hypothesis that the two sample means are not significantly different. It does this by assuming that, if this was the case, the mean difference would be zero, and then:

- It calculates the mean difference between pairs of related values.
- It uses the variance of the differences to estimate the standard deviation of a sampling distribution of similar differences.
- It works out the number of standard deviations that the observed mean difference is from zero. This value is known as t.

Calculating a Paired Samples t-test

Let us return to the hypothetical situation above where the focus of interest was in seeing if individuals' performances are significantly different when performing a difficult task alone or with an audience. Adopting the appropriate counterbalancing procedures the researcher tested a group of participants on their ability to perform this task under the two conditions. The results from this experiment are given in Table 5.1.

Table 5.1 **Performance scores in the alone and audience conditions**

Participant	Alone	Audience	Differences (d)	d^2
1	5	3	2	4
2	8	6	2	4
3	4	5	−1	1
4	7	6	1	1
Totals (Σ)	24	20	4	10
Means	6	5	1	2.5

$$\text{Variance } (s^2) = \frac{\sum d^2}{n} - \bar{d}^2$$

$$= \frac{10}{4} - 1 = 2.5 - 1 = 1.5$$

$$t_{n-1} = \frac{\bar{d}}{\sqrt{s^2/(n-1)}} = \frac{1}{\sqrt{1.5/(4-1)}}$$

$$= \frac{1}{\sqrt{1.5/3}} = \frac{1}{0.71} = 1.41$$

Therefore the observed difference in means is 1.41 standard deviations away from the mean difference of zero as predicted by the null hypothesis in Figure 5.1 above.

Interpreting the Value of *t*

As *t* is simply the ratio of the mean difference divided by the error in the measurement, then the larger the value of *t* the less likely it is that the difference in means is the result of chance and the more likely that it is due to the different levels of the independent variable. However, to know the precise probability of obtaining an observed value of *t* its value has to be interpreted using the *t*-distribution tables. To do this three things must be known:

1. The degrees of freedom.
2. Whether the hypothesis is one or two tailed.
3. The significance level.

A brief review of each of these concepts may be useful.

Degrees of Freedom

Degrees of freedom refer to how the data is free to vary. To illustrate this, imagine you have decided to paint your bedroom. If the room has four walls, you have only three choices to make in terms of which order you paint the walls. By the time you have made your third choice only one wall is left and therefore there are no more choices to be made. In other words, there are no more degrees of freedom. In this example there are three degrees of freedom. In the same way, if three numbers have a mean of 21, then two of them can be any number but the last one has to make the total equal to 63 and therefore there are 2 degrees of freedom. You may have noted that the degrees of freedom in both of these examples are one less than the number in the sample and hence can be expressed as $n - 1$.

Types of Hypotheses

In the process of statistical inference a decision has to be made between two competing explanations of why any observed differences in the means have occurred. One explanation is that the two sets of scores are drawn from the same population and that any observed differences are a product of error in the measurement. If this is the decision then the null hypothesis is accepted. The other explanation is that the two sets of scores are drawn from two distinct populations and that the observed differences are a product of the independent variable. If this is the decision then the null hypothesis is rejected and the alternate, also known as the experimental, hypothesis is accepted.

Table 5.2

Null hypothesis	μ_{Alone}	$=$	$\mu_{Audience}$
Two-tailed experimental hypothesis	μ_{Alone}	$\neq$	$\mu_{Audience}$
One-tailed experimental hypothesis	μ_{Alone}	$<$	$\mu_{Audience}$
One-tailed experimental hypothesis	μ_{Alone}	$>$	$\mu_{Audience}$

Note: The Greek letter μ stands for the mean of the population. Whenever Greek letters are used they are referring to some parameter of the population.

In the above example concerning performance in alone and audience conditions, the null hypothesis would predict that there would be no significant difference in the performance of the two groups. In contrast, the alternate hypothesis might state that there would be a significant difference in the performance of the two groups. If, as in the above example, the direction of the difference is not stated then this is known as a **two-tailed hypothesis**. However, if the alternate hypothesis states the direction of the difference in the two groups of scores, for example the alone group will score less points for their performance than the audience group, then this is known as a **one-tailed hypothesis**. These hypotheses are often expressed as shown in Table 5.2.

Whether an alternate hypothesis is one or two tailed will influence the probability that an observed difference between two means is significant or not. Before considering this implication we need to be clear about what is meant by the term significance.

Significance Level

In an experiment all variables are ideally held constant and then the independent variable is manipulated and changes in the dependent variable are measured. However, it is not possible to keep all of the irrelevant variables, such as sampling error, absolutely constant. This means that there is always a probability that any observed difference in the dependent variable is a product of irrelevant variables and not the independent variable. The usual convention is that as long as this probability is less than 5 in 100, which is normally expressed as 5% or 0.05, the researcher would still accept that any observed difference is not the product of chance. This is known as adopting a 0.05 significance level. Therefore the term significance level refers to the point at which it is decided to reject the chance explanation and accept that the independent variable is responsible for the observed differences. Hence, a researcher adopting a 0.05 significance level wants to be 95% confident that the differences were not the product of chance before the null hypothesis is rejected and the alternate hypothesis accepted.

It is important to recognise that in adopting a 0.05 significance level the researcher is accepting that, if the same experiment were conducted in the future, then on 5% of occasions the observed difference might be expected to occur by chance. This

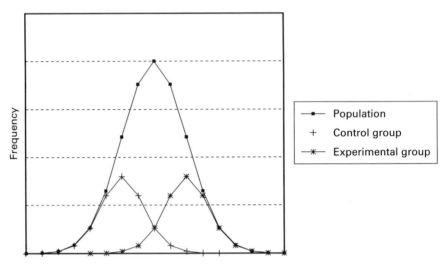

Figure 5.2 **Testing the null hypothesis**

means that if the null hypothesis is rejected, then the researcher can be 95% confident that the difference found is not the product of chance, and therefore that there is only a 5% probability that a mistake is being made. As discussed earlier, this mistake of rejecting the null hypothesis when it is true is known as committing a Type I error and its probability is known as the alpha level.

The opposite of committing a Type I error is to accept the null hypothesis when in fact it is false. That is, the experimental hypothesis should have been accepted but it was not. This mistake is known as a Type II error and its probability is known as the beta level. The probability of committing a Type I error could be reduced by changing the significance level from, say, 0.05 to 0.01, but in so doing we increase the probability of committing a Type II error.

Testing the Null Hypothesis

In testing the null hypothesis the decision has to be made as to whether the two samples are drawn from the same population, in which case the null hypothesis (H_0) is accepted, or whether the two samples are drawn from two different populations, in which case H_0 is rejected. If the null hypothesis is correct then the relationship between the samples and the population can be illustrated in a graph such as that shown in Figure 5.2.

In the figure the control and experimental groups are viewed as two samples of a particular size, mean and standard deviation that are extracted from a population with a particular mean and standard deviation. Testing the null hypothesis involves deciding if this interpretation is correct. This decision as to whether to accept or reject the null hypothesis is based on the probability of getting two samples with

Table 5.3 **Sample of critical values of t**

	Level of significance for one-tailed hypothesis	
	0.05	0.025
	Level of significance for two-tailed hypothesis	
	0.10	0.05
Degrees of freedom (df)		
1	6.3	12.7
3	2.3	3.2
10	1.8	2.2
∞	1.6	1.9

these statistics from a population with the above parameters. These probabilities are contained in what are known as *t*-tables.

SPSS 'Sig.' Values

When using SPSS it is not necessary to look up probabilities in any *t*-tables as the exact probabilities associated with observed values of *t* are printed in the output. In SPSS these probabilities are labelled as 'Sig.' values but they should be interpreted as the probability that the null hypothesis is correct. For example, if SPSS calculates a 'Sig.' value associated with a particular value of *t* as 0.04, this means that 4 times out of 100 the observed mean difference would be obtained by chance from two samples drawn from the same population. Therefore if the alpha level employed is 0.05 then the null hypothesis would be rejected and the alternate hypothesis accepted. The conclusion is that the two samples are drawn from two different populations.

Looking up Critical Values from the *t*-tables

Although SPSS provides the exact probabilities for observed values of *t* an understanding of how to use *t*-tables is important because it illustrates a number of points concerned with the process of significance testing (Table 5.3).

There are two important points to note from Table 5.3. Firstly, as the degrees of freedom increase so the critical value of *t* decreases. For example, the critical value of *t* for a two-tailed hypothesis at 0.05 significance is 12.7 when there is 1 degree of freedom and 3.2 when there are 3 degrees of freedom. The second point to note is that the critical value of *t* at 0.10 significance for a two-tailed hypothesis is the same as the critical value required for 0.05 significance with a one-tailed hypothesis.

To see how this works in practice consider the previous example concerning performance under alone and audience conditions. By looking back at page 63 it can be noted that the observed value of $t = 1.41$, the number of degrees of freedom was 3 and the mean difference was 1. From Table 5.3 above it can be noted that the critical value at 0.05 significance for a two-tailed hypothesis with 3 degrees of freedom is 3.2. Note that the observed value of t is less than the critical value of t. Therefore, a mean difference as large as 1 from two samples of four drawn from the same population would occur more than 5 times out of 100 by chance. As this probability is greater than the criterion of 0.05 it is not possible to be 95% confident that the observed differences were not a product of error in the measurement of the dependent variable. That is, there is more than a 5% probability that the observed differences could have been obtained from two samples drawn from the same population. Therefore the null hypothesis is accepted and consequently the alternate hypothesis has to be rejected. Finally, it is concluded that there is no significant difference in the performance of participants in the alone and audience conditions.

Why Does the Critical Value of t Decrease as the Sample Size Increases?

Looking at Table 5.3 it can be noted that the level of significance decreases as the sample size increases. To understand the reason why this occurs imagine that repeated pairs of samples of four people have been drawn from a population, their heights measured and the mean difference between each pair of samples calculated. If this is done hundreds of times then a frequency distribution of the mean differences similar to the one in Figure 5.3 could be produced.

This graph is quite tall and thin compared with the previous examples of a normal distribution. This is because, as the sample size decreases, it is more likely that a sample will contain extreme scores. More extreme scores will result in the curve having fatter tails and consequently it must have a thinner middle section. In testing the null hypothesis with a 0.05 significance level the critical t-value is the distance away from the mean measured in units of standard deviation that cuts off the last 5% of the distribution. If the distribution has fat tails then to cut off the last 5% the line has to be drawn further away from the mean than on a distribution produced by larger samples which will have relatively thin tails. It is for this reason that the critical value of t decreases as the sample size increases.

As the sample size becomes larger so the t-distribution more closely approximates a z-distribution and the critical value of t will be the same as the z-value required to cut off the appropriate percentage. This can be illustrated by comparing values from both t-tables and z-tables with relatively large degrees of freedom as shown in Table 5.4.

From this table it can be noted that the critical value of t at 5% significance with a one-tailed hypothesis when the degrees of freedom are 120 is 1.658. This value is almost identical to the z-value of 1.645 that is required to cut off the last 5% of a normal distribution.

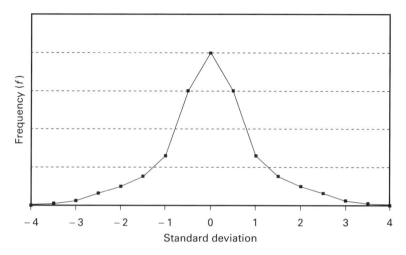

Figure 5.3 **Graph showing hypothetical frequency distribution of means (*t*-curve) when sample size is small**

Table 5.4 **A sample of *t*- and *z*-values**

Significance level (3 df)	5%	2.5%
Critical values of *t* (one tailed)	2.35	3.18
Critical values of *t* (two tailed)	3.18	
Significance level (120 df)	**5%**	**2.5%**
Critical values of *t* (one tailed)	1.658	1.98
Critical values of *t* (two tailed)	1.98	
Area under a normal curve (*z*-tables)	**5%**	**2.5%**
Units of standard deviation from (*z*-tables)	1.645	1.96

Why Is the Significance Level for a Two-tailed Hypothesis Half that for a One-tailed Hypothesis?

Looking back to Table 5.3 it can be noted that the significance level for a two-tailed hypothesis is twice as large as that for a one-tailed hypothesis. For example, with 10 degrees of freedom a *t*-value of 1.8 has a significance value of 0.05 for a one-tailed hypothesis and 0.10 for a two-tailed hypothesis. The reason for this can also be gleaned from Table 5.4. From this table it can be noted that with 120 degrees of free-dom the critical value of *t* for a two-tailed hypothesis at 5% significance is 1.98. This is almost the same value as the *z*-value of 1.96 that is required to cut off the last 2.5% of a normal distribution. This similarity in value provides a clue as to why the signi-ficance level for a two-tailed hypothesis is half that for a one-tailed hypothesis.

In a two-tailed hypothesis it is not specified whether one group is going to score more or less than the other; therefore the 5% area to be cut off has to be divided between both extremes of the distribution. Hence, if a 5% significance level with a two-tailed hypothesis is employed then the statistics must test to see if it lies in the last 2.5% at each end of the distribution. As the last 2.5% is further from the mean than the last 5%, so the critical value is greater for a two-tailed hypothesis than its one-tailed equivalent. This can be confirmed by an examination of Table 3.1 where it can be seen that to cut off 5% the distance in units of standard deviation is 1.645, whilst to cut off 2.5% this distance increases to 1.96 units of standard deviation.

Independent *t*-test

In the previous example the same participants were employed in both the alone and audience conditions. This is known as a repeated measures design. If the participants had been randomly assigned to the two conditions then this would be an independent group design. If an independent group design is employed rather than a repeated measures design the logic behind the *t*-test remains the same in that *t* is still the ratio of the mean differences divided by the error in the measurement. However, as there are two groups of different individuals with possibly different variances and sample sizes, the standard error has to take into account the sampling error from both these groups. As a consequence, the formula is slightly different:

$$t_{(n_1-1)+(n_2-1)} = \frac{(\bar{x}_1 - \bar{x}_2)}{\sqrt{(s_1^2/n_1 - 1) + (s_2^2/n_2 - 1)}}$$

Although this formula looks complicated it contains nothing that has not been introduced before. The numerator is concerned with the mean differences between groups 1 and 2 and the denominator is concerned with the standard error. On page 62 it was noted that the standard error was simply the square root of the variance over the degrees of freedom. In an independent *t*-test the variances and samples sizes of both groups have to be taken into account in calculating the standard error.

From this formula it can be deduced that this test examines the differences between two means from two sets of unrelated values. It estimates, using the variance of both sets, the likely standard error of a sampling distribution of differences between two means drawn from the hypothetical single distribution. The null hypothesis predicts that the mean of this distribution is zero. It is the number of standard errors away from zero that provides the value of *t*.

While this sounds complex it makes no practical difference, as our task is simply to choose which test to employ and then have the computer carry out the analysis. Our interpretation of this analysis is exactly the same as for the related *t*-test with the exception of one small complication.

As a parametric test, the *t*-test assumes that the variances of the samples are not significantly different. In a paired samples *t*-test there is only one set of differences

Table 5.5 **Part of the independent samples t-test output from SPSS**

	Levene´s Test for Equality of Variances		t-test for Equality of Means				
	F	Sig.	t	df	Sig. (2-tailed)	Mean Difference	Std. Error Difference
Equal variances assumed	.370	.546	-.797	42	.430	-2.1818	2.7392
Equal variances not assumed			-.797	36.20	.431	-2.1818	2.7392

and hence only one value for the variance. Therefore the assumption of homogeneity of variance is not relevant to a paired samples *t*-test. However, when employing an independent *t*-test there are two sets of variances and the assumption is that these are not significantly different. When SPSS executes an independent samples *t*-test it will display the results from Levene's test of equality of variance. This technique is used to test the null hypothesis that there is no significant difference in the two variances. If the value in the 'Sig.' column, third column from left, is greater than 0.05 then the null hypothesis is accepted and the conclusion is that the homogeneity of variance assumption is met. In this case the results of the *t*-test displayed in the 'Equal variances assumed' row as shown in Table 5.5 should be examined. If, on the other hand the result is significant as the 'Sig.' value is 0.05 or less, then the conclusion is that the variances are significantly different. Thus, the *t*-test results displayed in the 'Equal variances not assumed' row should be examined.

In this particular example although the *t*-values and their associated probabilities, shown in the column headed 'Sig. (2-tailed)', are identical in both rows, this will not always be the case. The value of *t* in the table is calculated by dividing the mean difference by the standard error value. Hence

$$t = \frac{\text{mean of the differences}}{\text{standard error}} = \frac{-2.1818}{2.7392} = -0.797$$

The fact that the *t*-value is negative is ignored as it simply means that the larger mean was subtracted from the smaller mean. The observation that this *t*-value is less than 1 immediately points to the fact that the observed difference in means is smaller than the error in the measurement. The two-tailed probability associated with this value of *t* is 0.430. This indicates that 43 times out of 100 a mean difference as large as 2.1818 would be obtained by chance from two groups drawn from the same population. Therefore, the null hypothesis that there is no significant difference in the means of the two groups is accepted.

Had the researcher postulated a one-tailed hypothesis then the significance value of 0.43 would be divided by 2 to produce a new significance of 0.215. In this case the interpretation is that 21.5 times out of 100 two samples would produce a mean difference of 2.1818 by chance. The conclusion again is that chance brought about the observed differences in means and the null hypothesis is accepted.

Example 5.1 A Paired Samples *t*-test Using SPSS

To illustrate parts of the output from SPSS and to allow a comparison of the results with the calculations by hand on page 63 the same data has been analysed using SPSS. Remember that in this example the experimental hypothesis is that there will be a difference in the scores obtained by participants in the alone and audience conditions.

The first part of the output (Table 5.6) provides the descriptive statistics for the two groups.

Table 5.6 **Paired samples statistics**

		Mean	N	Std. Deviation	Std. Error Mean
Pair 1	ALONE	6.0000	4	1.8257	.9129
	AUDIENCE	5.0000	4	1.4142	.7071

Earlier it was noted that

$$\text{Standard error} = \sqrt{\text{Variance}/n} = \sqrt{s^2/n} = s/\sqrt{n}$$

Therefore for the alone group

$$\text{Standard error} = 1.8257/2 = 0.9129$$

and for the audience group

$$\text{Standard error} = 1.4142/2 = 0.7071$$

The next part of the output (Table 5.7) presents the *t*-value and its associated significance.

From this table note that the *t*-value, printed in the third column from the right, is obtained by dividing the difference between the two means (1.0000) by the standard error (0.707). SPSS defaults to provide a two-tailed probability. In this case the value 0.252 indicates that there is a 25.2% probability that a difference as large as 1.0000 would be obtained by chance if two samples of four were taken from a single population. The null hypothesis that there is no significant difference between the two means is therefore accepted.

Table 5.7 **Paired samples test**

Paired Differences					t	df	Sig. (2-tailed)
Mean	Std. Deviation	Std. Error Mean	95% Confidence Interval of the Difference				
			Lower	Upper			
1.0000	1.4142	.7071	-1.2503	3.2503	1.414	3	.252

Summary

Parametric tests use the sample statistics to make estimates of the population's para-meters. Any difference between the statistics and parameters is due to sampling error, which is a function of the sample size and variability in the population. This concept of error is used in statistical testing to measure the probability that any observed differences or relationships between sets of scores reflect real differences or relationships in the population(s).

This is illustrated in the paired samples *t*-test which tests for significant differ-ences between two group means from data that has been gathered by way of a related measures design. The test statistic *t* is the ratio of the differences between the sam-ple means divided by the standard error in the measurement. Taking into account the degress of freedom, SPSS calculates the probability that a real difference exists. How the researcher interprets this will depend upon whether the hypothesis is one or two tailed and the significance level being employed.

If an independent group design is used to collect the data then an independent samples *t*-test is employed. Although the formula is different to that for a paired sam-ples *t*-test the resulting *t*-value is still the ratio of the mean differences divided by the error in the measurement. SPSS will provide probabilities based on both the homo-geneity of variance assumption being met and not met (i.e. 'Equal variance assumed' and 'Equal variance not assumed'). To determine which probability to employ the results of Levene's test of equality of variance should be examined.

EXERCISE 5.1 INDEPENDENT *t*-TESTS USING SPSS FOR WINDOWS

As part of a research project in sports psychology you have decided to investigate the sources of pre-performance anxiety in scuba diving. After reading the extant literature on this topic, you feel that one factor which may affect cognitive anxiety prior to performance is the level of experience of the diver. Your research question becomes

What is the effect of experience on pre-performance anxiety in scuba diving?

Through your local scuba club, you are able to identify two groups of divers: those with less than one year of experience (Beginners) and those with more than three years of experience (Intermediates).
   Write a research hypothesis that relates to the research question stated above.

Prior to their next dive, you assess the divers' cognitive state anxiety using the Competitive State Anxiety Inventory (CSAI-2), and obtain the following data:

Beginners	Intermediate
10	09
18	10
22	25
19	25
16	17
14	21
16	11
19	12
18	27
12	16
17	14
22	22
26	26
18	16
27	17
10	22
24	15
21	11
11	09
23	09

Table to show how the data should appear in SPSS, after following the instructions below.

Exp	Anxiety
1	10
1	18
1	22
etc.	etc.
2	9
2	10
2	25
etc.	etc.

1. Start SPSS by clicking on the **SPSS** icon. If a window opens with the option **Type in data** then select it and click on **OK**, otherwise just proceed to the next step.
2. Make sure that the **Data View** window is open so that the screen is displaying a series of empty cells in the form of a spreadsheet. If this is not the case then click on the tab **Data View** in the bottom left-hand corner of your screen. Enter the data in exactly the same manner as for the previous descriptive statistics exercise. Remember that in SPSS each participant must have their own row. As there are 40 participants you will require 40 rows. In addition, you will require two columns. Use the first column to identify whether the participant is a beginner or intermediate scuba diver and the second column to enter the participant's anxiety score. An example of how this should appear is shown above.

You now need to label the variables. Click on the tab **Variable View** in the bottom left-hand corner of your screen. In the **Name** column double click on the first variable and replace **var00001** with the name **Exp**. Move along to the sixth column which is headed **Values** and click on where the word **None** is written in the first row. A shaded box with three dots will appear at the right-hand end of this cell. Click on this shaded area and a **Variable Labels** window will open. Click on the **Value** box and type in the number 1, then click on the **Value Label** box and type in 'Beginners'. Now click on the **Add** box. The cursor will now flash in the **Value** box. Type in the number 2, click on the **Value Label** box and type in 'Intermediate', then click on the **Add** box. Finally, click on the **Continue** box and then on **OK**.

In the **Name** column double click on the second variable and replace **var00002** with the name **Anxiety**. Click on the tab **Data View** in the bottom left-hand corner of your screen and you should return to the spreadsheet of your data. The names you have written should appear at the top of the two columns of data. In the first column the numbers you entered should now display the labels **Beginners** and **Intermediate**. If they do not then click on the **View** menu at the top of the screen and click on **Value Labels**.

3. Use the instructions from the previous SPSS exercise in Chapter 3 to use the **Explore** option, that is

Analyze
  Descriptive Statistics
    Explore
      Enter 'Anxiety' in the **Dependent List** and 'Exp' in the **Factor List**
        Click on the **Plots** box
        Deselect **Stem-and-leaf** and select **Histogram**
          Continue
          OK

4. Go to the **Analyze** menu and open the sub-menu **Compare Means**. Click on the **independent sample t-test**. The *t*-test will determine whether there are differences between beginning and intermediate divers in pre-performance cognitive state anxiety. Therefore, the test variable is anxiety, and the grouping variable is experience (**Exp**). Before you can proceed, you must indicate how many groups you have by clicking on the **define groups** dialogue box and inserting the numerical code that identifies beginning and intermediate divers. Once you have done this, run the analysis by clicking on **OK**.

5. The **Output** window should be displayed. If it is not then click on the **Window** menu at the top of the screen and select **Output1 - SPSS Viewer**. Print out the results by either clicking on the print icon and then click on **OK** in the **Print** window that opens. Alternatively go to the **File** menu and select **Print**.

6. Close down SPSS by selecting **Exit** from the **File** menu. When you are asked if you want to save the output select **No** as you can easily reproduce this. However, when you are asked if you want to save the data select **Yes**, as you will use this again in a later exercise.

7. Examine the descriptive statistics output and enter the appropriate values in the spaces below.

Descriptive Statistics

Beginners		**Intermediate**	
Median	....	Median	....
Mean	....	Mean	....
Standard Deviation	....	Standard Deviation	....
Skewness	....	Skewness	....
Std Err. Skewness	....	Std Err. Skewness	....
Skewness/Std Err	....	Skewness/Std Err	....
Kurtosis	....	Kurtosis	....
Std Err. Kurtosis	....	Std Err. Kurtosis	....
Kurtosis/Std Err	....	Kurtosis/Std Err	....

What do you conclude about the normality of the distributions of each set of scores from the skewness and kurtosis statistics?

Beginners: ....

Intermediate: ....

Boxplot

	Beginners	Intermediate
Is the median in the middle of the box?	Yes/No	Yes/No
Are the whiskers the same length?	Yes/No	Yes/No
Are there any outliers?	Yes/No	Yes/No

What do you conclude about the normality of the distributions of each set of scores from the boxplots?

Beginners: ....

Intermediate: ....

Is this interpretation supported by the histograms for the following?

Beginners: ....

Intermediate: ....

8. From comparing the means in the context of the standard deviations and looking at the boxplots, do you think there is a practical difference in the anxiety levels of beginners and intermediate scuba divers?

....

....

....

9. Next look at the 'Independent Samples Test' table and explain the results of Levene's test and then the *t*-test.

    ....

    ....

    ....

10. State whether your experimental hypothesis was supported or refuted. What conclusions would you draw from the results of this analysis?

    ....

    ....

    ....

REVISION EXERCISE

The concepts introduced so far underpin all the subsequent chapters in this book. To ensure that you have a sound understanding of the terms and what they mean make sure you can answer the following questions.

What is meant by:

- Descriptive statistics?
- Parameters of a population?

What do the following symbols denote?

K f n F Σ s s^2 σ

What is the difference between a histogram and a barchart?

What does a measure of central tendency aim to provide?

Define three measures of central tendency.
Where does each measure fall on a symmetrical distribution?
What does the term skewed refer to?
On a positively skewed distribution where does each measure of central tendency fall?

What is meant by 'levels of data'?
Give an example of each level of data.

What is meant by measure of dispersion?
What does the term sum of squares (SS) refer to?
What is meant by the terms variance and standard deviation?
What is the relationship between the variance and the standard deviation?

What shape is a normal distribution?
What phenomena are normally distributed?
What are the properties of a normal distribution?
What does the term z-score refer to?

What is a hypothesis?
What do the terms independent and dependent variable refer to?
What is meant by irrelevant and extraneous variables?

What is meant by the term related design?
What is meant by confounding factors?
What are order effects?
What is an independent group design?

What factors does one have to take into account in selecting a statistical test?

What is:

- a null hypothesis?
- an alternate hypothesis?
- a one-tailed hypothesis?
- a two-tailed hypothesis?

What is meant by:

- significance?
- Type I and Type II errors?
- samples and populations?
- representative and random samples?
- sampling error and standard error?
- degrees of freedom?

When we employ a statistical test, which type of hypothesis do we test?
What is meant by the terms parametric and non-parametric?
In the context of statistical tests what is meant by the terms robust and powerful?

When is it appropriate to use a t-test?
What is t a ratio of?

6

BETWEEN-GROUPS ONE-WAY ANALYSIS OF VARIANCE

Purpose

The purpose of this technique is similar to that of an independent t-test in that it tests for significant differences between group means from data that has been gathered by an independent group design. It is different from a t-test in that instead of being restricted to an examination of the difference between two means a between-groups one-way ANOVA can examine the difference between two or more group means.

Research Question

One-way ANOVAs are employed to address research questions that focus on the difference in the means of one dependent variable and one independent variable with two or more levels. For example, the independent variable gender has two levels: male and female. To illustrate the point about levels let us imagine that a researcher was interested in the research question: is there a difference in the performance of three groups of athletes who have each undergone one of three distinct training schedules? In this case there is one dependent variable (i.e. performance), and three levels of the independent variable (i.e. the three training schedules). This experiment used three groups of three participants; therefore $N = 9$ (Table 6.1).

Table 6.1 **Performance scores obtained from three training schedules ($N = 9$)**

	A	B	C
	1	3	7
	0	5	8
	2	4	6
$\bar{x}$	1	4	7

Null Hypothesis

In a one-way ANOVA the null hypothesis that is tested predicts that the means of the dependent variable scores for each level of the independent variable will not be significantly different. So in the above example the appropriate null hypothesis would predict that the performance scores of groups A, B and C would not be significantly different from each other. If these three sample means are not significantly different then the three samples are drawn from populations that have the same mean, namely $\mu_A = \mu_B = \mu_C$, and therefore the three samples are drawn from the same population.

Why Not Use Multiple t-tests?

To test the null hypothesis that $\mu_A = \mu_B = \mu_C$, multiple t-tests could be employed. This would involve testing that $\mu_A = \mu_B$, that $\mu_A = \mu_C$ and that $\mu_B = \mu_C$. Unfortunately carrying out three t-tests would involve reanalysing the same data three times and this would increase the probability of committing a Type I error, that is the null hypothesis is rejected when it is in fact true.

To understand why the use of multiple t-tests increases the risk of committing a Type I error it is useful to recall that the probability of committing a Type I error is equal to the significance level. So, if a significance level of 0.05 is employed, then each time a t-test is carried out there is a 1 in 20 chance that a Type I error will be committed. It follows that the more t-tests are carried out on the same data, the more likely it is that a Type I error will be committed. Employing a single one-way ANOVA circumvents this problem as it analyses the data only once.

Assumptions

As a one-way ANOVA is a parametric test it shares similar assumptions to a t-test. These are that the dependent variable has been measured on an interval scale, that the variances of the groups based on the levels of the independent variable are equal and that the distribution of scores in each group does not significantly deviate from normal. These assumptions will be discussed in more detail later on in this chapter.

Principles Behind a One-way ANOVA

ANOVA, as its name implies, is concerned with the analysis of variance. In a between-groups ANOVA the focus of interest is on the variance between the groups. However, this between-groups variance can only be understood in the context of the variance that occurs within each of the three groups.

To illustrate the principles behind a one-way ANOVA the data shown in Table 6.1 will be used. Table 6.1 displays the performance data from nine participants who have been randomly assigned to one of three training schedules A, B and C.

Within-groups Variance

Consider the dispersion of scores within group A in Table 6.1. The values 1, 0, 2 are a product of three factors. These factors are:

1. **Inter-individual variability**. The three scores, 1, 0, 2, are different in part because they are produced by three different people and therefore they reflect individual differences.
2. **Intra-individual variability**. This refers to the potential variability within each person's score. Whenever an individual does something twice there will always be some difference in their behaviour on the two occasions. This difference reflects the variability in the behaviour of individuals. For example, the individual in group A who scored zero on this particular occasion might not score zero if they were to be tested on some other occasion.
3. **Random fluctuations**. By this is meant the extraneous variables, such as situational variables, that cannot be controlled. These variables were discussed at the beginning of Chapter 4.

These three sources of variance in group A also apply to the dispersion of scores within groups B and C. Now consider the dispersion that exists not within any one group but across the groups.

Between-groups Variance

The dispersion of scores between the groups A, B and C, for example 2, 4 and 6, is due to all of the above three sources of variance plus one other which is the different levels of the independent variable. This source of dispersion is:

4. **Treatment variability**. This refers to the effect of the independent variable, for example training schedule, on each of the participants.

Error

All of the three sources of within-groups variance, that is inter-individual variability, intra-individual variability and random fluctuations, are considered to represent errors in the measurement of the dependent variable. As these errors occur within all three groups A, B and C then the total error in the measurement will be the variance within group A plus the variance within group B plus the variance within group C. This product will reflect the overall error in the measurement of the dependent variable.

You might be wondering why these sources of within-groups variance are termed error. This is not difficult to understand if one imagines that these sources of variability could be controlled. This would mean that there would be no variability *within* each of the three groups A, B and C, hence all of the scores within each of the groups would be the same. Now consider the between-groups variance. Any variance that occurs between the groups A, B and C can only be a product of one factor, the treatment variable. If the sources of within-groups variance could be removed then there would be no need for any inferential statistics, as any observed differences between the groups would not be confounded by error and could only be attributed to the treatment effect. In one sense all inferential statistics are strategies for dealing with errors in measurement and because the social sciences have lots of errors in their data so they have to employ sophisticated statistics in an attempt to control for their effects.

F-ratio

Unfortunately the three sources of error cannot be completely controlled. Therefore the within-groups variance reflects these sources of error in the measurement and a between-groups variance reflects both these errors and any treatment effects due to the different levels of the independent variable. It follows that if the independent variable, for example the training schedule, has any effect on the dependent variable, for example the performance, then it would be expected that the dispersion of scores between the groups would be greater than the dispersion of scores within the groups. That is, the effect of error and treatment would result in a greater variance than error alone. The test statistic F for ANOVA is simply the ratio of this between-groups variance to the within-groups variance:

$$F = \frac{\text{between-groups variance}}{\text{within-groups variance}} = \frac{\text{error} + \text{treatment}}{\text{error}}$$

If the independent variable has no effect then the dispersion of scores between the groups will be very similar to the dispersion of scores within the groups and hence F will tend towards unity. On the other hand, the more the independent variable has an effect, the more the dispersion between the groups will increase and F correspondingly becomes greater than 1.

It is important to note that we do not know what the value of the error component is in the between-groups variance. All we can do is estimate its value based on the within-groups variance. Together these between- and within-groups variances represent the total variance of the whole set of scores. This may be expressed as

Total variance = between-groups variance + within-groups variance

Calculating the Variances

Before the value of F can be calculated the between- and within-groups variances need to be determined. The procedure for calculating variance was discussed in Chapter 2. In that chapter the first stage involved subtracting the mean from each score, squaring the result to get rid of the minus values, and summing the total for all the scores included. This process was expressed in the following formula:

$$\sum (x - \bar{x})^2$$

This procedure produces what is known as the sum of the squares (SS). This label is intuitively meaningful, as the product of this equation is the sum of the squared difference between each score and the mean.

We noted earlier that if the treatment has any effect, then we would expect the dispersion of scores between the groups to be greater than the dispersion of scores within the groups. We can now employ the sum of the squares outlined above as the first step in working out the dispersion within and between the groups.

Working out the Within-groups Sum of Squares

Let's consider the within-groups sum of squares first. Here we are interested in how far each score is dispersed from its group mean.

For groups A, B and C the total sum of the squares within the three groups is

$$
\begin{aligned}
SS_{\text{within-groups}} &= \sum(\text{each score in that group} - \text{mean of each group})^2 \\
&= (1-1)^2 + (0-1)^2 + (2-1)^2 + (3-4)^2 + (5-4)^2 \\
&\quad + (4-4)^2 + (7-7)^2 + (8-7)^2 + (6-7)^2 \\
&= 6
\end{aligned}
$$

Working out the Between-groups Sum of Squares

Now let's consider between-groups sum of squares. Here we are interested in how far the means of each group are dispersed around the grand mean. That is, the mean of the scores contained in all of the groups. To calculate the between-groups sum of squares the grand mean is subtracted from the mean of a group and the result is squared and then multiplied by the number of scores in that group. This process is repeated for each of the groups and the results are summed.

$$
\begin{aligned}
SS_{\text{between-groups}} &= \sum n(\text{mean of each group} - \text{mean of all the scores})^2 \\
SS_{\text{between-groups}} &= \sum n(\bar{x} - \bar{X})^2 \\
&= n(1-4)^2 + n(4-4)^2 + n(7-4)^2 \\
&= 3(-3 \times -3) + 3(0-0) + 3(3 \times 3) \\
&= 3(9) + 3(0) + 3(9) \\
&= 54
\end{aligned}
$$

Working out the Total Sum of Squares

Finally, consider the total sum of squares. Here we are interested in how far the scores are dispersed around the grand mean $\bar{X}$.

$$SS_{\text{total group}} = \sum (\text{each individual score} - \text{mean of all the scores})^2$$

$$\begin{aligned} SS_{\text{total group}} &= (1-4)^2 + (0-4)^2 + (2-4)^2 + (3-4)^2 + (5-4)^2 \\ &\quad + (4-4)^2 + (7-4)^2 + (8-4)^2 + (6-4)^2 \end{aligned}$$

$$= 60$$

You may have noticed that the total sum of the squares is equal to the sum of the between-groups and within-groups sum of squares, that is

$$SS_{\text{total group}} = SS_{\text{between-groups}} + SS_{\text{within-groups}}$$
$$60 \qquad\quad = 54 + 6$$

Calculating F

We previously observed that F can be defined as follows:

$$F = \frac{\text{between-groups variance}}{\text{within-groups variance}} = \frac{\text{error} + \text{treatment}}{\text{error}}$$

But this cannot mean that

$$F = \frac{SS_{\text{between-groups}}}{SS_{\text{within-groups}}}$$

as each sum of the squares is influenced by the number of observations. You may have noticed that this is exactly the same argument as that employed in Chapter 2 when the formula for the variance was developed. If the sum of the squares is divided by the number of observations then the average sum of squares would be calculated. This was how the sample variance was defined in Chapter 2. However, here the interest is in what is termed the **mean square (MS)**, which is the sum of squares divided by the appropriate degrees of freedom. Again this label should seem intuitively meaningful, as the mean square is the mean of the sum of squares.

Degrees of Freedom

$SS_{\text{within-groups}}$ was calculated by taking the square of the deviation of each score in a group from the mean of that group, summing these values together and repeating this process for every group. As each group has a degree of freedom equal to $(n-1)$ and as there were k groups, df $= k(n-1)$. For example, if there are three groups with three subjects in each group then the degrees of freedom will equal $3(3-1)$ which equals 6.

$SS_{\text{between-groups}}$ was calculated by summing the square of the deviation of each group mean from the grand mean. As there were k observations contributing to the final value df $= (k-1)$. Therefore, if there are three groups then the number of degrees of freedom will equal 2.

Therefore to calculate the two variances the sum of the squares must be divided by the appropriate degrees of freedom:

$$F = \frac{SS_{\text{between-groups}}}{(k-1)} \div \frac{SS_{\text{within-groups}}}{k(n-1)}$$

$$= MS_{\text{between-groups}} \div MS_{\text{within-groups}}$$

So in our example

$$F = \frac{54}{2} \div \frac{6}{6} = \frac{27}{1}$$

$$= 27$$

The researcher can now look up the critical value in what are known as F-tables using the appropriate degrees of freedom which are:

$$(k-1) \text{ for the numerator}$$
$$k(n-1) \text{ for the denominator}$$

If the observed value exceeds the critical value then the null hypothesis is rejected. Fortunately, using SPSS makes the use of such tables redundant as it prints out the probability of obtaining the observed value of F by chance.

Being aware of how a one-way ANOVA is calculated by hand is useful because it illustrates, for example, why the particular degrees of freedom are employed in the within- and between-groups variances. To make this manual calculation less tedious a number of shortcuts can be employed. These are shown below. However, if you have a limited interest in the 'nuts and bolts' of ANOVA analysis then jump to the next section.

Calculating a Between-groups One-way ANOVA by Hand

Results of analyses of variance are often set out in the format below.

SOURCE	SUM OF SQUARES	df	MEAN SQ. $= SS/df$	F
BG	$\dfrac{\sum t^2}{n} - \dfrac{T^2}{N}$	$k-1$	$\dfrac{\sum t^2}{n} - \dfrac{T^2}{N} \div (k-1)$	$\dfrac{MS_{BG}}{MS_{WC}}$
WG	$\sum x^2 - \sum(t^2 \div n)$	$k(n-1)$	$\sum x^2 - \sum(t^2 \div n)$ $\div k(n-1)$	
Total variance	$\sum x^2 - \dfrac{T^2}{N}$	$k(N-1)$		

where

$$t = \text{group total}$$
$$T = \text{grand total}$$
$$n = \text{number of scores in a group}$$
$$N = \text{total number of scores}$$

Table 6.2 **Performance scores obtained from three training schedules**

	A	B	C
	1	3	7
	0	5	8
	2	4	6
t	3	12	21
$\Sigma x/n$	1	4	7

$$k = \text{number of groups}$$

To illustrate the validity of the formula in this box let's return to the previous example (Table 6.2).

Here

$$k(\text{number of groups}) = 3$$
$$n(\text{observations per group}) = 3$$
$$SS_{BG} = \frac{\sum t^2}{n} - \frac{T^2}{N} = (3 + 48 + 147) - 1296/9$$
$$= 198 - 144 = 54$$
$$SS_{total} = \sum x^2 - \frac{T^2}{N} = 204 - 144 = 60$$

Therefore

$$SS_{WG} = SS_{total} - SS_{BG} = 60 - 54 = 6$$

Alternatively

$$SS_{WG} = \sum x^2 - \sum(t^2 \div n) = 204 - 198 = 6$$

$$\text{Mean square}_{BG} = \frac{SS_{BG}}{k-1} = \frac{54}{(3-1)} = \frac{54}{2}$$
$$= 27$$

$$\text{Mean square}_{WG} = \frac{SS_{WG}}{k(n-1)} = \frac{6}{3(3-1)} = \frac{6}{6}$$

$$= 1$$

Therefore

$$F = 27 \div 1$$

$$= 27$$

Looking up 'Numerator/Denominator df 2df/6df' in F-tables we find that

Critical value of $F = 5.14$ at 5% significance level

Therefore, as the observed value of F is greater than the critical value the null hypothesis is rejected. That is, the three group means are significantly different from each other and the conclusion is that the type of training schedule influenced performance. However, it is important to note that in rejecting the null hypothesis we cannot conclude that all three means are significantly different; all we can conclude is that at least one mean is significantly different from one of the other two.

Example of How to Use SPSS to Undertake a Between-groups One-way ANOVA

In the following the data used in this chapter has been analysed using SPSS. Work through this example, compare your results with those provided by the manual calculation above and answer the questions that accompany the extracts from SPSS output.

A researcher wanted to test the null hypothesis that there was no difference in the relative effectiveness of three distinct training schedules on performance (Table 6.3). In this case we have one dependent variable, namely performance, and three levels of the independent variable, the training schedules. This experiment used three groups of three participants (i.e. $N = 9$).

Call up SPSS for Windows and enter the above data in the same way as you did for the descriptive statistics exercise. Remember that columns represent variables

Table 6.3 **Performance scores obtained from three training schedules**

A	B	C
1	3	7
0	5	8
2	4	6

and rows represent the participants. Therefore, in addition to the column needed to contain the performance scores, a second column is needed to identify which of the three groups produced the scores. As each participant requires their own row and as there are nine participants, then nine rows are required.

Typically before an ANOVA is executed the **Explore** option ought to be used to check that the data for the three groups does not significantly deviate from normal in terms of skewness and kurtosis. However, as there are only three participants in each group it is not possible to complete this process.

To analyse the data click on **Analyze**, then **Compare Means** and then **One-way ANOVA**.

Enter the dependent variable into the **Dependent list** and then enter the variable that identifies which group the scores come from into the **Factor** list.

Click on the **Options** box and then select **Descriptives** and **Homogeneity of variance**. Both of these options should have an **x** in their boxes; if they do not click on the box. Now click on **Continue** and then on **OK** to execute the analysis.

To get a graphical illustration of the distribution and overlap in the three sets of scores select **Graphs** then **Boxplot**. Make sure **Simple** and **Summaries for groups of cases** are selected and then click on **Define**. Enter the names of three groups into the **Boxes Represent** box and click on **OK**.

Now get a printout of the results by selecting the **File** menu and then selecting **Print**. This should produce something similar to the following.

1. Do the means and standard deviations of the three groups (Table 6.4) suggest support for the null hypothesis? That is, do they suggest significant differences in the outcomes of the three training programmes?

Table 6.4

SCORE   Descriptives

	N	Mean	Std. Deviation	Std. Error	95% Confidence Interval for Mean		Minimum	Maximum
					Lower Bound	Upper Bound		
A	3	1.00	1.00	.58	-1.48	3.48	0	2
B	3	4.00	1.00	.58	1.52	6.48	3	5
C	3	7.00	1.00	.58	4.52	9.48	6	8
Total	9	4.00	2.74	.91	1.89	6.11	0	8

2. What does the boxplot in Figure 6.1 suggest about:

    (a) the normality of the distribution of scores in the three groups?
    (b) differences in the outcomes of the three training programmes?

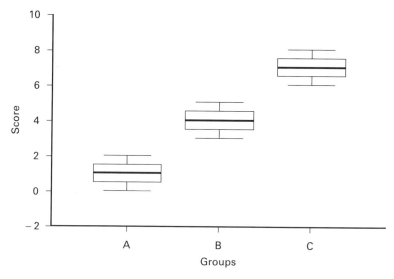

Figure 6.1 **Boxplot showing actual distribution of performance scores obtained from three training schedules**

3. Parametric tests assume that the variances in the groups are homogeneous. The following test is used to test the null hypothesis that there is no significant difference in the variances of the three training schedule groups. If the parametric assumption is to be met then this null hypothesis needs to be accepted. On pages 91–92 you will find a section on checking the assumption of equal variance. You may find it helpful to read that section before answering the following question.

What do you interpret from Table 6.5?

Table 6.5

Test of Homogeneity of Variances

Levene Statistic	df1	df2	Sig.
.000	2	6	1.000

4. In looking at Table 6.6 remember that SS divided by df produces the MS. So, for example, 54/2 results in 27. Also remember that $F = MS_{BG}/MS_{WG}$, so 27/1 produces an F-value of 27.

Does the following table lead you to reject or accept the null hypothesis?

Table 6.6

SCORE   ANOVA

	Sum of Squares	df	Mean Square	F	Sig.
Between Groups	54.000	2	27.000	27.000	.001
Within Groups	6.000	6	1.000		
Total	60.000	8			

Assumptions of ANOVA

In Chapter 4 it was pointed out that parametric tests make three assumptions. These were:

1. That each sample of scores has been drawn from a normal population.
2. These samples have equal variance.
3. The dependent variable is measured on at least an interval scale.

In fact there is a fourth assumption which must also hold true. This is:

4. Independence of observations.

This fourth assumption requires that the scores one individual gives are not influenced by other participants, as might happen if participants are tested in small groups rather than individually. However, it is on the first two assumptions that the next section will focus.

Checking the Assumption of a Normal Distribution

In Chapter 4 it was noted that unfortunately it is not possible to prove that a particular sample is drawn from a normally distributed population. What can be done is to refer to previous research to see if the data has previously been found to form a normal distribution, or to have SPSS construct a histogram of the data to see if it looks like a normal distribution.

It was also noted that neither of these procedures is very precise. Therefore, to have any measured confidence in the decision concerning the normality of the distribution statistical alternatives need to be explored. Two measures that were introduced were the concepts of skewness and kurtosis. Skewness reflects the existence of extreme scores such that a skewness of zero means that the distribution is symmetrical. Kurtosis refers to the peakedness of the curve: that is, is it a flat curve or does it have a sharp point? If you cannot recall these concepts then reread the appropriate section in Chapter 4.

Consequences of Violating Assumption of Normality

It is generally held that ANOVA is not greatly influenced if the distribution is not normal as long as the scores are symmetrically distributed and the sample sizes are equal and greater than 12 (Keppel 1991). If these conditions do not hold true then there is an inflated risk of committing a Type I error. To overcome this problem the significance level should be reduced, for example from 0.05 to 0.025. However, there is no absolute guidance on when a correction is necessary and how much correction is required. Therefore the normality assumption should be checked and any violations that are observed should be reported.

Checking the Assumption of Equal Variance

Again, it cannot be proved that two or more samples have homogeneity of variance. But as with the question of normality, the spread in the two sets of data may be examined to see if they look similar and the magnitude of the variances of the data for each group may be noted. Keppel (1991) reports that it is commonly held that 'the F test was relatively insensitive to the presence of variance heterogeneity, except when unequal sample sizes were involved' (page 98). However, he suggests that work by Wilcox (1987) demonstrates that this is not the case and that the F-test can become seriously biased with heterogeneous variance.

There are a variety of techniques available for testing for homogeneity of variance. One was displayed in the output of the exercise at the end of Chapter 5 in order to test this assumption when employing an independent t-test. The method that was employed was Levene's test for equality of variance. In the one-way ANOVA procedure employed by SPSS this test is also available by selecting the **Options** box in the **One-way ANOVA** window and then selecting the **Homogeneity-of-variance** box. (We also suggest that you select the **Descriptive** box for reasons that will become apparent in a moment.) It is important to remember that in testing the homogeneity of variance assumption researchers hope that the probability will be greater than 0.05 as they want to accept the null hypothesis that the variances are not significantly different, for if the null hypothesis is accepted then the conclusion may be drawn that the homogeneity of variance assumption is met.

Unfortunately a test such as Levene's – and there are at least 56 of them – is influenced by departures from normality as well as inequality between the variances. For this reason amongst others Keppel (1991) is reluctant to recommend any of them and instead suggests that one looks at the ratio of the largest within-groups variance to the smallest. This ratio he calls F_{max}. When this ratio is 9 or greater then the effect is to inflate the alpha level, for example from 0.05 to 0.08. How much the alpha is inflated is inversely related to the sample size and directly related to the degree of heterogeneity. In addition if this heterogeneity is not evenly distributed, for instance there is only one deviant group, then this will again inflate the alpha level. Tabachnick and Fidell (1989) point out that this effect is further complicated because: 'If the group with the smaller n has the larger variance, the F test is too liberal, leading to increased Type I error rate and an inflated α level' (page 48).

To overcome this problem one can reduce the alpha level, but unfortunately, as with the assumption of normality, there is no clear guidance as to how much correction is required. Keppel (1991) demonstrates that if F_{max} is equal to 9 then reducing the alpha to 0.01 would mean that the actual significance would never exceed 0.05. He goes on to note that as this produces an overcorrection then adopting an alpha of 0.025 might be a more valid procedure. He also points out that the influence of heterogeneity on alpha levels reinforces the importance of reporting group standard deviations and that corrections should be introduced once F_{max} is equal to or greater than 3.

Summary

Before we move on to a more detailed examination of the output from SPSS it might be useful to summarise what has been stated so far. A one-way ANOVA is used to test the significance of group differences when there is one dependent variable and one independent variable. This can be seen from the tables in Appendix 2.

Whereas a t-test can only test the differences between the means of two groups, there is no restriction on the number of groups a one-way ANOVA can test. Therefore, when we have more than two groups a one-way ANOVA is used in preference to multiple t-tests because it does not increase the risk of committing a Type I error.

A one-way ANOVA tests the null hypothesis that all the means of the groups are equal. If the probability associated with the value of F is less that the significance level we reject the null hypothesis.

A one-way ANOVA can be applied to almost any situation in which the t-test can be used. In fact the t-test is a special case of the F-test and the two are related in the following manner:

$$F = (t)^2 \quad \text{and hence} \quad t = \sqrt{F}$$

You can convince yourself that this is the case by reanalysing the data on page 74 using a one-way ANOVA, and comparing the value of F obtained with the previously computed value of t.

It is important in ANOVA that the assumptions of normality and heterogeneity are met. To test the former the **Explore** option should be used to see if the z-values for skewness and kurtosis are larger than ± 1.96. To test for heterogeneity of variance, Levene's test should be used. However, if the normality assumption is not met then the values of F_{max} should be established from the descriptive statistics. If any values are equal to or greater than 3 then a reduction in the alpha level should be made to avoid any increase in the risk of committing a Type I error.

To illustrate what this means and to provide a model for you to refer to in the future, an example is provided next. This example displays edited sections of SPSS output and explains what should be interpreted from each section.

Example 6.1 A Between-groups One-way ANOVA

A researcher was interested in the scores of gymnasts on two constructs. The first was socially prescribed perfectionism (SPP), which is the tendency to employ excessively high standards. The second was emotionally focused coping, which refers to the tendency to employ emotional rather than problem-focused coping strategies. The researcher created three groups based on participants' perfectionism scores. One group was based on those who scored one standard deviation or more above the mean. A second groups was based on those who scored one standard deviation or more below the mean, and the third was the middle group.

The null hypothesis was that there would be no difference in the mean coping scores of the three groups of gymnasts.

From the **Explore** option the researcher's results included the information in Table 6.7.

Table 6.7

Descriptives

	HILO_SPP		Statistic	Std. Error
EMOTION	High	Mean	2.4107	.1385
		Std. Deviation	.5365	
		Skewness	.590	.580
		Kurtosis	-.351	1.121
	Middle	Mean	3.0800	.1020
		Std. Deviation	.6451	
		Skewness	-.158	.374
		Kurtosis	1.007	.733
	Low	Mean	3.5733	.1142
		Std. Deviation	.4422	
		Skewness	-.471	.580
		Kurtosis	-.855	1.121

The researcher noted that all three means were different and that when these differences were examined in the context of their standard deviations this suggested that there would be little overlap in the distribution of the three sets of scores.

The researcher also calculated that when the skewness and kurtosis values were divided by their respective standard errors the resulting values would all be less than ±1.96, which suggested that none of the three groups would have scores that significantly deviated from normal.

Both these interpretations were supported by the boxplot in Figure 6.2 from the **Explore** option.

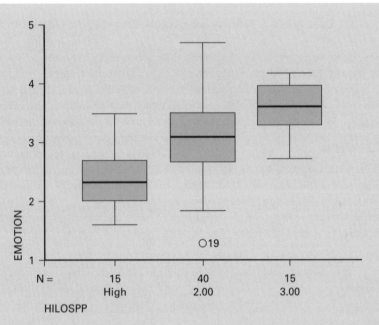

Figure 6.2

Table 6.8 **Test of homogeneity of variances**

EMOTION

Levene Statistic	df1	df2	Sig.
.924	2	67	.402

The researcher observed from the boxplots for all three groups that the medians were approximately in the middle of each of their boxes and there was very little overlap between the three boxes. This suggested support for the alternate rather than the null hypothesis. The researcher also noted that although the whiskers for each box were uneven, these differences were not sufficiently large to suggest that the data was significantly skewed. However, the researcher did notice the outlier in group 2.

From the one-way ANOVA analysis the results included the following.

From Table 6.8 the researcher interpreted that the homogeneity of variance assumption was met as the results suggested that 40 times out of 100 variances as different as those observed in the three groups would be obtained by chance. The researcher therefore went on to examine the results of the ANOVA analysis given in Table 6.9.

As the alpha level ('Sig.') associated with the observed value of F was less than 0.05 the researcher rejected the null hypothesis and concluded that at least one of the three means was significantly different from the other two.

Table 6.9 **ANOVA**

EMOTION

	Sum of Squares	df	Mean Square	F	Sig.
Between Groups	10.271	2	5.136	14.961	.000
Within Groups	22.999	67	.343		
Total	33.270	69			

EXERCISE 6.1 BETWEEN-GROUPS ONE-WAY ANOVA USING SPSS

In a previous independent *t*-test exercise you investigated the amount of pre-performance anxiety in beginners and intermediate scuba divers. You are now going to extend that research to include novice and expert divers.

While conducting the investigation, you are able to obtain access to a group of novice divers who have never been diving before and a group of expert divers. You assess the pre-performance cognitive state anxiety of both these groups and obtain the data listed below. You then combine this additional data with the previous data from beginners and intermediate scuba divers. This means that you now have four groups: novices, beginners, intermediates and experts. Your research question remains

> What is the effect of experience on pre-performance anxiety in scuba diving?

But now you need to write one or more research hypotheses for four groups rather than the previous two.

Hypothesis

....

....

....

1. **Enter the additional data**. Add the data below to the previous example in which you analysed the results of 40 beginners and intermediate scuba divers using a *t*-test. In total you should now have 80 participants so you should have used 80 rows. Don't forget to add additional value labels to the variable you labelled **Exp**. You could use the value 3 for novice and the value 4 for expert.

2. **Check that the data in each group is normally distributed**. You will need to check that the data is normally distributed so follow the instructions from the previous SPSS exercise in Chapter 5 to use the **Explore** option, that is

Novice	Expert
22	13
25	09
24	11
18	13
23	17
29	12
23	06
24	04
20	12
31	07
16	08
18	15
32	16
21	09
23	09
13	11
27	10
26	09
27	14
35	8

Table to show how the data should appear in SPSS, after following the instructions below.

Exp	Anxiety
1	10
1	18
etc.	etc.
2	9
2	10
etc.	etc.
3	22
3	25
3	24
etc.	etc.
4	13
4	9
4	11
etc.	etc.

Analyze
> **Descriptive Statistics**
>> **Explore**
>> Enter 'Anxiety' in the **Dependent List** and 'Exp' in the **Factor List**
>>> Click on the **Plots** box
>>> Deselect **Stem-and-leaf** and select **Histogram**
>>>> **Continue**
>>>> **OK**

3. **Test the null hypothesis using a between-groups one-way ANOVA.** Go to the **Analyze** menu and open the sub-menu **Compare Means**. Because you are now comparing four means on one variable of interest (anxiety), you need to select a **One-way ANOVA** (analysis of variance). Anxiety is the dependent measure and experience is the factor.

Click on the **Post-Hoc** dialog box, select the **Least-significant difference** test, the **Tukey´s b test**, the **Scheffe** test and then **Continue**. Please note that the output this selection produces is explained in the following chapter on analytical comparisons.

Click on the **Options** box, and select **Descriptive Statistics** and **Homogeneity-of-variance.**

Run the analysis and then print the results.

Examine the skewness and kurtosis statistics and explain whether any of the four groups significantly deviate from normal:

Novice   ....

Beginners   ....

Intermediate   ....

Expert   ....

Examine the boxplots and explain whether these suggest:

(a) That any of the four groups significantly deviate from normal:

    Novice   ....

    Beginners   ....

    Intermediate   ....

    Expert   ....

(b) Support for the null or alternate hypothesis.

    ....

    ....

    Look at the means and standard deviations in the table of descriptive sta-
    tistics and explain whether these suggest support for the null or alternate
    hypothesis.

    ....

    ....

    Describe the results of the ANOVA test (i.e. SS, df, MS, F and Sig. F), and
    explain whether you are going to accept or reject the null hypothesis.

    ....

    ....

    To determine which if any of the individual groups differ from any other
    group look at the results of the post-hoc tests you have carried out. Read
    the first two pages of the next chapter and then explain why these post-hoc
    tests produce different results.

    Novice   ....

    Beginners   ....

    Intermediate   ....

    Expert   ....

Write down what you conclude from this analysis.

....

....

References

Keppel, G. (1991) *Design and Analysis: A Researcher's Handbook* (3rd edn).
   Englewood Cliffs, NJ: Prentice Hall.
Tabachnick, B.G. and Fidell, L.S. (1989) *Using Multivariate Statistics* (2nd edn). New York:
   Harper Collins.
Wilcox, R.R. (1987) 'New designs in analysis of variance', *Annual Review of Psychology*,
   38, 29–60.

7   ANALYTICAL COMPARISONS

Purpose

The purpose of the techniques known as analytical comparisons is to determine which group means are significantly different from each other. In a one-way ANOVA the null hypothesis that is tested predicts that the means of the dependent variable scores for each level of the independent variable will not be significantly different. So if, as in the previous chapter, there are three groups A, B and C, then the null hypothesis would predict that the performance scores of the three groups would not be significantly different from each other, that is

$$H_0 \text{ states that } \mu_A = \mu_B = \mu_C$$

If the significance level associated with testing this null hypothesis is less than the alpha level, for example 0.05, then the null hypothesis is rejected. Therefore the decision is made, with a precise level of confidence, that all three means are not equal and as an alternative the experimental hypothesis is accepted. However, for the null hypothesis to be incorrect it is not necessary that all three group means are different from each other; it is only necessary that one group mean be significantly different from one of the other group means. So the researcher is in the position of knowing that all of the group means are not equal but not knowing which of the group means are significantly different from each other. To enable the identification of which means are significantly different analytical comparisons need to be employed. These comparisons can be either unplanned or planned.

Unplanned Comparisons: Post-hoc Tests (Data Snooping)

Unplanned comparisons are comparisons that are conducted after the data is examined. That is, they are not specifically predicted before the start of an investigation. They are used in preference to doing multiple t-tests on various combinations of means because in general they make corrections to avoid increasing the risk of committing a Type I error. These tests differ in how cautious they are in making these corrections. For example, the one termed least significant difference (LSD) is equivalent to executing multiple t-tests across all combinations of pairs of group means without making any correction for the inevitable increased risk of committing a Type I error.

Table 7.1

Examples of post-hoc tests	Power	When to use
Least significant difference	Same as multiple *t*-test	*Don't* as no correction is made
Duncan's multiple range test	(Least conservative)	
Student–Newman–Keul's test	(In between)	
Tukey's HSD test		Pairwise comparisons
Tukey's (b) test		
Scheffe's test	(Most conservative)	Compare all groups

In contrast, Scheffe's test, which can be used for the same purpose as the LSD test, makes corrections of sufficient magnitude that it becomes more difficult for the researcher to reject the null hypothesis.

SPSS includes, for example, the alternative comparisons in the **Post Hoc** options of the **One-Way ANOVA** window (Table 7.1).

The power of a test is inversely related to how conservative it is. Power, you may recall from Chapter 4, refers to a test's ability to detect a significant difference when one truly exists. Therefore, Scheffe's test, being the most conservative, requires larger differences in the means before significance is achieved. If you examine your output from the previous one-way ANOVA exercise you may note that they produce different results. The LSD identifies the most number of significant differences and Scheffe's test the least. Never use the LSD test unless you are going to make a correction for the increased risk of a Type I error. How such a correction can be made is explained later in this chapter. To carry out one of the above post-hoc tests click on the **Post Hoc** box in the **One-Way ANOVA** window and make sure there is a cross in the box of the test you want, and then click on **Continue**.

Each of the above tests is conceptually similar to a *t*-test in that they identify which groups differ from each other but they are calculated in different ways. To illustrate the logic behind them the formula for Scheffe's test is given below. Omit this section if formulae confuse you and turn to example 6.1.

Scheffe's Confidence Interval

If you want to compare all the possible means or groups of means this is the test you should use. It computes an interval size (*I*) which is the minimum difference in means that must exist before significance can be declared. To this end it uses the following formula:

$$I = \sqrt{(k-1)(F_\alpha)(\mathrm{MS_E})\left(\frac{1}{n_1} + \frac{1}{n_2}\right)}$$

where

$$k = \text{number of groups}$$
$$F_\alpha = \text{F-value for chosen alpha level with the appropriate degrees of freedom}$$
$$MS_E = \text{Mean square error from ANOVA}$$
$$n = \text{Number of participants in each group}$$

Scheffe's test makes a conservative correction for increases in Type I error. This results in it calculating an increased probability that the results are due to chance. The consequence of this is that it becomes more difficult for the researcher to reject the null hypothesis.

Applying a Post-hoc Analysis to Example 6.1

In this example of a between-groups one-way ANOVA the researcher was interested in testing the null hypothesis that there would be no difference in the mean coping scores of the three groups of gymnasts.

If you look back to Table 6.9 you will note that as the alpha level ('Sig.') associated with the observed value of F was less than 0.05 the researcher rejected the null hypothesis and concluded that at least one of the three means was significantly different from the other two. However, the researcher did not know where these differences lay so went on to execute a Scheffe post-hoc test. The results of this analysis are shown in Table 7.2.

Table 7.2 **Multiple comparisons**

Dependent Variable: EMOTION
Scheffe

(I) HILOSPP	(J) HILOSPP	Mean Difference (I-J)	Std. Error	Sig.	95% Confidence Interval Lower Bound	Upper Bound
High = 1.00	2.00	-.6693*	.1774	.002	-1.1134	-.2252
	3.00	-1.1627*	.2139	.000	-1.6983	-.6271
Middle = 2.00	1.00	.6693*	.1774	.002	.2252	1.1134
	3.00	-.4933*	.1774	.026	-.9374	-4.9245E-02
Low = 3.00	1.00	1.1627*	.2139	.000	.6271	1.6983
	2.00	.4933*	.1774	.026	4.925E-02	.9374

* The mean difference is significant at the .05 level.

As all of the alpha levels ('Sig.') in this table were below 0.05 the researcher could conclude not only that the null hypothesis should be rejected but also that all three group means were significantly different from each other.

To see if you can execute and interpret such an output work through the following exercise.

EXERCISE 7.1 BETWEEN-GROUPS ONE-WAY ANOVA

A researcher wanted to evaluate the effectiveness of three different teaching methods. The researcher randomly allocated the 15 participants to the three groups where they were taught by one of the three methods. The performance of the participants was then measured by means of a multiple choice examination (Table 7.3).

Table 7.3 **Effects of teaching strategy on performance on a multiple choice test**

	Group 1	Group 2	Group 3
Exam	12	9	6
scores	10	7	7
	11	6	2
	7	9	3
	10	4	2

To use SPSS select **Statistics, Compare Means, One-Way ANOVA**, and then enter the dependent variable into the **Dependent List** box and the grouping variable into the **Factor** box. Click on the **Post Hoc** box and select **Scheffe** test, then click on **Continue** and **OK**.

Your results will include an additional table (Table 7.4).

Having carried out this analysis write down what you can conclude from its results.

Repeat the above exercise but this time, in addition to a Scheffe test, select a Tukey's b test and an LSD. Compare the outputs and consider why they give different results.

A Priori Tests (Planned Comparisons)

Whereas post-hoc tests are carried out after finding a significant F-ratio, a priori tests are 'planned' prior to the experiment. Which group means you compare will depend upon the predictions you have made in your hypotheses. You need to be aware that

Table 7.4 **Multiple comparisons**

Dependent Variable: SCORE
Scheffe

(I) GROUP	(J) GROUP	Mean Difference (I-J)	Std. Error	Sig.	95% Confidence Interval	
					-ower Bound	Upper Bound
1	2	3.00	1.342	.124	-.74	6.74
	3	6.00*	1.342	.003	2.26	9.74
2	1	-3.00	1.342	.124	-6.74	.74
	3	3.00	1.342	.124	-.74	6.74
3	1	-6.00*	1.342	.003	-9.74	-2.26
	2	-3.00	1.342	.124	-6.74	.74

* The mean difference is significant at the .05 level.

in a one-way analysis for k groups, $k-1$ independent group-mean comparisons can be made. This means that if there are four groups then three independent group-mean comparisons can be made.

By independent group-mean comparisons we mean that the answer you get to one comparison has no bearing on the answer you get to any other comparison(s) you make. For example, imagine you wanted to carry out a comparison on the amount of leisure time three different age groups (A, B and C) spent playing computer games. If you discovered that group A spends more time than group B, and group B spends more time that group C, then you know that group A spends more time than group C. Thus, we can see that the comparison of group A with group C is not independent of the comparison of A with B, and B with C. You can of course carry out whatever comparisons you like but if they are not independent then this will increase the risk of committing a Type I error. This increased risk will have implications for the significance level that you adopt. We shall return to this point later when we discuss orthogonal and non-orthogonal comparisons in more detail.

Principle

The way that we actually execute a planned comparison might seem a little obscure. Let us return to the above example concerning groups A, B and C, and imagine that we are interested in testing to see if the mean of group A is different from the mean of group B. If these two means are the same, that is the null hypothesis is correct, then if we subtract the mean of B from the mean of A the product ought to be zero. Of course, we would not expect it to be exactly zero as there will always be a sampling error. This was discussed at the beginning of Chapter 5. You may recall from that chapter that whenever we measure the means of two samples from a single population we will almost always get slightly different values. Therefore, when the mean of B is subtracted from the mean of A the product will deviate from zero. What the planned comparison computes is whether the observed deviation from zero is sufficiently great for us to reject the null hypothesis and accept that the two means are drawn from different populations.

In a paired samples t-test we simply took one mean from the other and divided by the error term. In this example, however, we have three groups, A, B and C, and imagine that we only want to contrast the mean of group A with that of B. We therefore have to think of a way of including all three groups while only comparing groups A and B. To do this we need to recall two simple rules from algebra. The first of these is that if we multiply a number by minus one we simply change its sign from positive to negative or negative to positive. So, for example, minus three times minus one become plus three. The second rule we have to recall is that whenever we multiply any number by zero the product is zero. Now if we want to take the mean of group B from the mean of group A and ignore the mean of group C we could do the following. Multiply the mean of A by 1, multiply the mean of B by −1, multiply the mean of C by 0 and then add them all up. This is expressed algebraically in equation (7.1) below:

$$\text{Difference between } \bar{X}_A \text{ and } \bar{X}_B = \left[1(\bar{X}_A)\right] + \left[-1(\bar{X}_B)\right] + \left[0(\bar{X}_C)\right] \qquad (7.1)$$

The mean of group C is now ignored, because whatever its original value, it now equals zero, and the mean of Group B has had its sign reversed. If the product of this equation is zero then the means of A and B are identical and therefore the null hypothesis is correct. The more the product of this equation tends away from zero the more likely it is that the null hypothesis is incorrect and that the group means are significantly different. The values 1, −1 and 0 that we have multiplied the three group means by are known as weights. If you add these weights together you will note that they sum to zero:

$$(1) + (-1) + (0) = 0$$

If you have understood the argument so far then you will appreciate that if the null hypothesis is to be tested by how far the product of the equation deviates from zero then the weights must also sum to zero. To explain this, imagine that in fact the means of each group were identical and each had a value of 5. Then if we substitute this value into equation (7.1) we get

$$\left[1(5)\right] + \left[-1(5)\right] + \left[0(5)\right] = 0$$

As the product of this equation is zero we accept the null hypothesis. Now let's change the weightings to 1, 1, 0. If we add them up, they sum to 2, and if we substitute them into equation (7.1), we find that the result is no longer zero:

$$\left[1(5)\right] + \left[1(5)\right] + \left[0(5)\right] = 10$$

Given that we test the null hypothesis by seeing if the product of this equation is zero, we can see that even though the means are in fact equal the product of the equation will not equal zero unless the weights sum to zero.

Let's sum up what we have said so far. To compare treatment means one first assigns a weighting factor (ω) to each mean. Weights of zero are assigned to means that are left out of the comparison, whilst weights with opposite signs (positive and negative) are assigned to means that are to be contrasted. So, for example, if there are four groups and one wants to contrast the first and the third groups one would assign the following weights:

$$1 \quad \quad 0 \quad \quad -1 \quad \quad 0$$

(Note that if you add these all together the answer is zero.) Planned contrasts assume that the sum of the weighted group means is equal to zero when the null hypothesis is correct. Hence, the sum of the weights you assign to group means must also sum to zero to allow the null hypothesis to be correct.

To obtain a comparison we multiply the group means by the coefficients, for example

$$\text{Comparison of group means} = \left[1(\bar{x}_1)\right] + \left[0(\bar{x}_2)\right] + \left[-1(\bar{x}_3)\right] + \left[0(\bar{x}_4)\right]$$

In this comparison the second and fourth means are ignored because they are both multiplied by zero. We are left with simply taking the third mean away from the first. If these two means are equal, that is the null hypothesis is correct, then the result will tend towards zero. The more the result deviates from zero the more confidence one has in rejecting the null hypothesis.

Orthogonal and Non-orthogonal Comparisons

Orthogonal contrasts refer to group-mean comparisons where the answer you get to one comparison has no bearing on the answer you get to any other comparison(s) you make. This is also expressed as the contrasts being independent of one another. Non-orthogonal simply means the opposite of this. That is, it refers to group-mean comparisons where the answer you get to one comparison has some bearing on the answer you get to any other comparison(s) you make, that is the contrasts are not independent of one another. For example, if Lisa is taller than Lucy, and Lucy is taller than Hamish, then these two contrasts tell you something about a third potential contrast between Lisa and Hamish: that is, we already know that Lisa is taller than Hamish.

To explore this in more detail let's imagine that we have four groups and we want to undertake three contrasts. We want to contrast the first and third groups, the second and fourth groups, and the average of the first and the third with the average of the second and fourth groups. The appropriate weightings to employ in these planned contrasts are shown in Table 7.5.

Table 7.5 **A set of orthogonal comparisons and coefficients for $K = 4$ groups**

Comparison	Values of coefficients (ω)			
	$\overline{X}_1$	$\overline{X}_2$	$\overline{X}_3$	$\overline{X}_4$
1 vs 3	1	0	−1	0
2 vs 4	0	−1	0	1
1 and 3 vs 2 and 4	−1	1	−1	1

First of all note that if you sum the weights for any of the three contrasts the total will be zero. Remember that this has to be the case if we are going to test the null hypothesis by measuring how far the differences between the means deviate from zero.

Now notice that if you multiply the corresponding weights for any pair of comparisons you will find they sum to zero. For example,

'1 vs 3' and '2 vs 4' $(1)(0) + (0)(-1) + (-1)(0) + (0)(1) = 0$

'1 vs 3' and '1 and 3 vs 2 and 4' $(1)(-1) + (0)(1) + (-1)(-1) + (0)(1) = 0$

This observation is very important because if the sum of the cross-multiplication of the relevant weights equals zero then the comparisons are all orthogonal or, as we termed it earlier, independent of each other. For example, if one of two contrasts demonstrates a significant difference between the relevant group means, then this conclusion has no bearing on whether the other contrast is significant. In fact the number of orthogonal comparisons is the same as the degrees of freedom, that is $(k - 1)$. Therefore, if there are four groups then there are three possible independent planned contrasts.

Of course, there are other comparisons we could have included. For example, we could have compared the mean of the second group with the mean of the third. Here the weights would be as in Table 7.6.

Table 7.6

Comparison	Values of coefficients (ω)			
2 vs 3	0	−1	1	0

However, if we sum the cross-products of this contrast with any of the others, for example the means of the first group against the mean of the third group (Table 7.7), we find the sum is not equal to zero. For example,

Table 7.7

Comparison	Values of coefficients (ϖ)			
2 vs 3	0	−1	1	0
1 vs 3	1	0	−1	0

$$(0)(1) + (-1)(0) + (1)(-1) + (0)(0) = -1$$

This means that the question of whether the mean of the second group differs from that of the third group has some bearing on whether the mean of the first group differs from that of the third group.

Non-orthogonal Comparisons and Type I Error

If one employs only orthogonal comparisons then there is no increase in the risk of committing a Type I error and so the critical F remains the same as for the omnibus ANOVA, that is 0.05. However, if one uses non-orthogonal comparisons, for example more than $(k - 1)$ comparisons, then the probability of committing a Type 1 error will be increased. To understand why this is the case you simply have to recall that a Type 1 error is where you reject the chance explanation when it is in fact correct, and that the probability of doing so will equal the significance level. For example, with a 5% significance level one is prepared to reject the null hypothesis even though 1 time out of 20 it will be correct. So, if you carry out 20 non-orthogonal comparisons on the same sample of data, the probability is that one of them is simply significant as a result of chance. Unfortunately, you will not know which one.

The probability of committing a Type I error is equal to the alpha level. Therefore, to avoid an increased risk of rejecting the null hypothesis when it is in fact true, the size of the significance level on each comparison may be reduced in such a way that the overall alpha will remain at whatever level we want, for example 5%. Usually this is done by employing a Bonferroni-type adjustment that determines the size of the more stringent alpha level to be employed for each of the contrasts. One rather simple but conservative form of this adjustment appropriate for a between-groups design is to divide the required alpha level by the number of contrasts. So, for example, if one has five non-orthogonal contrasts and one desires a 0.05 alpha level, then this can be achieved by dividing the alpha by 5, that is the new alpha level for each comparison is 0.01. If you are quite content to employ this principle with no further explanation then you may skip the next section.

Bonferroni-type Adjustment for Inflated Type I Error on Univariate F-tests

The use of non-orthogonal contrasts will inflate the probability of committing a Type I error for the reason outlined above. To control for this inflated Type I error one should adjust the alpha for each contrast so that the final alpha for the complete set of contrasts does not exceed the significance level one wishes to employ. This can be done by employing the following equation:

$$\alpha = 1 - (1 - \alpha_1)(1 - \alpha_2)...(1 - \alpha_p) \qquad (7.2)$$

From the following equation we can see that this means that if a significance level of 0.05 was employed for an analysis containing six non-orthogonal comparisons, the Type I error rate (α) would be 0.265:

$$\alpha = 1 - (0.95)^6 = 1 - 0.735$$
$$= 0.265$$

This means that if there are p contrasts and one wishes to employ the same significance criterion for each comparison, then the individual value of alpha for each comparison (α_c) can be obtained by solving the following equation:

$$\alpha = 1 - (1 - \alpha_c)^p$$
$$\alpha - 1 = -(1 - \alpha_c)^p$$

If we now multiply both sides by minus one we get

$$1 - \alpha = (1 - \alpha_c)^p$$
$$\sqrt[p]{(1 - \alpha)} = 1 - \alpha_c$$
$$\sqrt[p]{(1 - \alpha)} - 1 = -\alpha_c \qquad\qquad (7.3)$$

So, for example, if there are six comparisons and one wants to employ a common alpha level for each, such that the final decision does not exceed 0.05 significance, then substituting these values into equation (7.3) we find that

$$\sqrt[6]{(1 - 0.05)} - 1 = -\alpha_c$$
$$\sqrt[6]{(0.95)} - 1 = -\alpha_c$$
$$0.9915 - 1 = -\alpha_c$$
$$-0.0085 = -\alpha_c$$
$$\alpha_c = 0.0085$$

This means that when interpreting the significance of any univariate effect for a particular comparison we should employ a significance level of 0.0085 rather than 0.05.

The alpha level does not have to be set at the same level for each comparison. However, when the chosen significance levels are substituted in equation (7.2) the end product must not be greater than the Type I error rate one is prepared to accept.

SPSS Contrast Command

SPSS uses the **Contrast** subcommand to test a priori contrasts using the t-statistic. To select this command click on the **Contrast** box in the **One-Way ANOVA** window, then use the **Coefficients** box to specify the values for the coefficients. For example, if you enter the coefficients

$$-1 \qquad\qquad 0 \qquad\qquad 1$$

this contrasts the first group with the third group, and

$$0.5 \qquad\qquad 0.5 \qquad\qquad -1$$

contrasts the average of the first and second groups with the third group. Enter each coefficient in turn (e.g. −1) and then click on the **Add** box. When you have entered all the coefficients for one comparison, and if you want to carry out a further comparison, then click on the **Next** box and enter the second set of coefficients.

Remember that the coefficients, such as −1, for each comparison should sum to zero. SPSS automatically adds the weights of your coefficients for you and displays the sum on the bottom line. Multiply the corresponding weights for the above pair of comparisons and determine if these two contrasts are orthogonal. To illustrate how this works in practice, Example 7.1 below shows a planned contrast of the data contained on page 102.

Summary

Analytical comparisons are used in conjunction with ANOVA techniques when there are more than two levels of the independent variable to determine which group means are significantly different. There are two sorts of comparisons: those known as post-hoc tests, which are undertaken after the omnibus F-value has led to the rejection of the null hypothesis; and those known as a priori which, as they are specified before any analysis is undertaken, are known as planned contrasts.

To employ a post-hoc test simply click on the **Post Hoc** box in the **ANOVA** window and select the test you want to use. If in doubt about which test to use then select Scheffe's test as it allows you to compare all group means and makes a conservative correction for Type I errors.

Use planned contrasts when you want to test specific null hypotheses that are specified before any analysis is undertaken. Check to see if any contrasts you plan are non-orthogonal. If they are non-othogonal then divide your alpha by the number of planned contrasts and use this new alpha in deciding whether to reject or accept the null hypothesis. Instructions on how to execute a planned contrast are specified in the previous section.

Example 7.1 Output from SPSS for Windows for a Planned Comparison

In this example we are going to look at the output when two planned contrasts have been undertaken. The first contrasts the first group with the second and the

Table 7.8 **Contrast coefficients**

Contrast	Group			
	1	2	3	
1	1	-1	0	*The means of group 1 & group 2 will be contrasted*
2	.5	.5	-1	*The average of the means of group 1 & group 2 will be contrasted with the mean of group 3*

second contrasts the average of the first two groups with the third group. The weights for these two contrasts are shown in Table 7.8.

Before we can interpret the output we must know if these two contrasts are orthogonal. If they are not a Bonferroni adjustment will have to be made for the increased risk of committing a Type I error. To see if the contrasts are orthogonal we cross-multiply the relevant weights:

$$(1 \times 0.5) + (-1 \times 0.5) + (0 \times -1) = 0.5 - 0.5 + 0 = 0$$

As the product of this cross-multiplication is zero we conclude that the two contrasts are orthogonal.

As with an independent t-test, SPSS will produce one set of results based on the homogeneity of variance assumption being met and another set based on the assumption that it is not met. To determine which set of results to look at, Levene's test is used. This tests the null hypothesis that the variances of the three groups are not significantly different. As the 'Sig.' value from this test is greater than 0.05 (Table 7.9) the null hypothesis is accepted and equal variance is assumed.

Table 7.9 **Test of homogeneity of variances**

Levene Statistic	df1	df2	Sig.
.686	2	12	.522

The contrast table (Table 7.10) is interpreted in the same way as the results from the previously discussed t-test. As with the t-test, which row you use will depend upon the similarity of the variances of the group means. As the homogeneity of variance assumption was met the row 'Assume equal variances' should be examined.

As the contrasts are orthogonal no correction has to be made for an increased risk of committing a Type I error. Therefore this table tells us that:

1. There is a significant difference between the means of group 1 and group 2 ($\alpha = 0.045$).
2. There is a significant difference between the average of the means of group 1 and group 2 and the mean of group 3 ($\alpha = 0.002$).

Table 7.10 **Contrast tests**

		Contrast	Value of Contrast	Std. Error	t	df	Sig. (2-tailed)
SCORE	Assume equal variances	1	3.00	1.34	2.236	12	**.045**
		2	4.50	1.16	3.873	12	**.002**
	Does not assume equal variances	1	3.00	1.26	2.372	7.877	.046
		2	4.50	1.22	3.674	6.970	.008

EXERCISE 7.2 PLANNED COMPARISONS

1. What is meant by orthogonal contrasts?
2. Why is it important that a researcher knows if contrasts are orthogonal?
3. If you have four groups, A, B, C and D, write in the weights required to execute the following two contrasts:

	A	B	C	D	Sum of weights
A vs B	...	...	...	...	...
A vs BC	...	...	...	...	...

Show how to determine if these two contrasts are orthogonal.

4. If you have four groups, A, B, C and D, write in the weights required to execute the following three contrasts:

	A	B	C	D	Sum of weights
A vs BCD	...	...	...	...	...
B vs CD	...	...	...	...	...
C vs D	...	...	...	...	...

Show how to determine which of these contrasts are orthogonal.

5. If you wish to adopt an alpha level of 0.05 but the three contrasts that you execute are not orthogonal, what should you do?

EXERCISE 7.3 ONE-WAY ANOVA

You have been employed as a research assistant in the Sport Studies Department at a prestigious institution. You have been asked to help with the data analysis on one of the following three projects.

Project One. This project investigated baseball pitching and attempted to determine the effects of baseball experience on the speed that pitchers can throw a fast-ball pitch. Fifty participants from three separate samples of pitchers (high school, collegiate and major league) were asked to throw 10 fast-ball pitches from the pitcher's mound to a catcher located in the usual position behind home plate. Only the fastest pitch was recorded. The speed of the pitch was measured by a radar gun located behind home plate. The experience level and pitching speed of each athlete were recorded in the second and third columns on the data sheet (Table 7.11).

Project Two. This project investigated individuals' cardio-respiratory fitness and attempted to determine the effects of activity status on VO2 max (maximum oxygen uptake). Fifty participants were selected, representing five different fitness status groups. These were (1) distance runners, (2) physically active adults, (3) sedentary adults, (4) recovered coronary heart disease patients, (5) current coronary heart disease patients. All 50 patients were given a graded exercise test on a treadmill to determine cardio-respiratory fitness, and their VO2 max was recorded. The fitness status and VO2 max of each participant was recorded in the fourth and fifth columns of the data sheet.

Project Three. This project investigated athletes' percentage body fat, and attempted to determine whether male athletes who compete in different sports differ in their percentage body fat. Fifty athletes were selected, representing four different sports (marathon runners, soccer players, rugby players and sumo wrestlers). All athletes' percentage body fat was measured by hydrostatic weighing. The sport and percentage body fat of each athlete were recorded in the sixth and seventh columns of the data sheet.

1. Select one project and identify the research question. Write a brief hypothesis that you can test. Your hypothesis should reflect the expected results of the analysis.
2. Decide upon an appropriate statistical test to answer the research question.
3. Input the data that is printed in Table 7.11, taking care to input the correct data set. Use the previous exercises as a guideline to help set up your data file correctly.
4. Analyse the data. Carry out two planned contrasts and note whether they are orthogonal or not. Don't forget to compute the appropriate descriptive statistics and check that the test's assumptions are met.
5. Write a paragraph explaining the descriptive statistics and outlining your conclusions from the tests employed.

Table 7.11 **Data sheet**

	Experience	Ball speed	Fitness status	V02 max	Sport	% body fat
1	High school	87	Distance run	59	Marathon	6
2	High school	82	Distance run	54	Marathon	7
3	High school	76	Distance run	52	Marathon	9
4	High school	91	Distance run	54	Marathon	6
5	High school	85	Distance run	56	Marathon	7
6	High school	77	Distance run	55	Marathon	7
7	High school	81	Distance run	62	Marathon	7
8	High school	76	Distance run	48	Marathon	5
9	High school	95	Distance run	56	Marathon	7
10	High school	72	Distance run	59	Marathon	8
11	High school	82	Physically active	38	Marathon	8
12	High school	83	Physically active	44	Marathon	6
13	High school	82	Physically active	48	Soccer player	1
14	High school	84	Physically active	32	Soccer player	9
15	High school	80	Physically active	35	Soccer player	11
16	High school	80	Physically active	44	Soccer player	12
17	Collegiate	99	Physically active	46	Soccer player	15
18	Collegiate	98	Physically active	48	Soccer player	8
19	Collegiate	81	Physically active	37	Soccer player	8
20	Collegiate	82	Physically active	38	Soccer player	9
21	Collegiate	95	Sedentary	29	Soccer player	11
22	Collegiate	96	Sedentary	34	Soccer player	11
23	Collegiate	94	Sedentary	32	Soccer player	12
24	Collegiate	97	Sedentary	29	Soccer player	8
25	Collegiate	98	Sedentary	30	Rugby player	14
26	Collegiate	94	Sedentary	31	Rugby player	27
27	Collegiate	92	Sedentary	32	Rugby player	11
28	Collegiate	95	Sedentary	27	Rugby player	8
29	Collegiate	91	Sedentary	31	Rugby player	12
30	Collegiate	96	Sedentary	32	Rugby player	12
31	Collegiate	94	Recovered CHD	21	Rugby player	14
32	Collegiate	88	Recovered CHD	22	Rugby player	16
33	Collegiate	83	Recovered CHD	24	Rugby player	8
34	Major league	99	Recovered CHD	18	Rugby player	18
35	Major league	97	Recovered CHD	19	Rugby player	9
36	Major league	104	Recovered CHD	21	Rugby player	9
37	Major league	101	Recovered CHD	21	Rugby player	21
38	Major league	100	Recovered CHD	28	Sumo wrestler	22
39	Major league	90	Recovered CHD	21	Sumo wrestler	34
40	Major league	88	Recovered CHD	21	Sumo wrestler	22
41	Major league	85	Current CHD	17	Sumo wrestler	23
42	Major league	94	Current CHD	19	Sumo wrestler	25
43	Major league	93	Current CHD	19	Sumo wrestler	26
44	Major league	91	Current CHD	17	Sumo wrestler	36
45	Major league	95	Current CHD	17	Sumo wrestler	32
46	Major league	95	Current CHD	15	Sumo wrestler	31
47	Major league	99	Current CHD	19	Sumo wrestler	38
48	Major league	96	Current CHD	17	Sumo wrestler	24
49	Major league	98	Current CHD	18	Sumo wrestler	26
50	Major league	98	Current CHD	21	Sumo wrestler	26

8

WITHIN-GROUPS ONE-WAY ANOVA

Purpose

The purpose of within-groups one-way ANOVA is the same as that of between-groups one-way ANOVA except that the data is obtained by repeatedly measuring the same participants across the different treatment conditions. The previous ANOVA examples in Chapters 6 and 7 have all employed an independent group design, that is the different treatment groups have been composed of different individuals. Often, however, researchers choose to employ the same participants in the different treatment groups as this is a more effective way of controlling for any individual differences that might confound the results and is more economical in its use of participants. Therefore, the purpose of a within-groups one-way ANOVA is also similar to that of a paired *t*-test, except that it can examine the differences between the means of more than two treatment groups. Because of these similarities with tests that have been previously discussed, you will find that much of the content on this and the following pages is very similar to material introduced earlier.

Research Question

As with a between-groups one-way ANOVA, a within-groups one-way ANOVA is employed to address research questions that focus on the difference in the means of one dependent variable and one independent variable with two or more levels. To illustrate this we will use the same example that was employed in Chapter 6 and then you can compare the differences between the two techniques. Let's imagine that a researcher was interested in the research question: is there a difference in the performance of a group of athletes who have each undergone three distinct training schedules? In this case we have one dependent variable (i.e. performance), and three levels of the independent variable (i.e. training schedules). This experiment used one group of three participants, that is $N = 3$ (Table 8.1).

Null Hypothesis

In a one-way ANOVA the null hypothesis that is tested predicts that the means of the dependent variable scores for each level of the independent variable will not be

Table 8.1 **Performance scores obtained from three training schedules (N = 3)**

	Training schedules		
Partcipant code	A	B	C
f	1	3	7
g	0	5	8
h	2	4	6
$\bar{x}$	1	4	7

significantly different. So in the above example this means that the null hypothesis would predict that the performance scores of the group in treatment conditions A, B and C would not be significantly different from each other. If these three sample means are not significantly different then the three samples are drawn from populations that have the same mean, that is $\mu_A = \mu_B = \mu_C$, and therefore the three samples are drawn from the same population.

Why Not Use Multiple t-tests?

To test the null hypothesis that $\mu_A = \mu_B = \mu_C$, multiple t-tests could be employed. This would involve testing that $\mu_A = \mu_B$, that $\mu_A = \mu_C$ and that $\mu_B = \mu_C$. However, in carrying out three t-tests we would be reanalysing the same data three times, which would increase the probability of committing a Type I error.

To understand why the use of multiple t-tests increases the risk of committing a Type I error you simply have to recall that the probability of committing a Type I error is equal to the significance level. So, if a significance level of 0.05 is employed, this means that each time a t-test is carried out there is a 1 in 20 chance that a Type I error will be committed. It follows that the more t-tests are carried out on the same data, the more likely it is that a Type I error will be committed; that is, that the null hypothesis is rejected when it is in fact true. Employing a single one-way ANOVA circumvents this problem as it only analyses the data once.

Assumptions

As a one-way ANOVA is a parametric test it shares similar assumptions to a t-test. These are that the dependent variable has been measured on an interval scale, that the variances of the groups based on the levels of the independent variable are equal and that the distribution in each group does not significantly deviate from normal. These assumptions were discussed in more detail in Chapter 6.

In addition to the assumptions common to all parametric tests a within-groups design ANOVA makes one additional assumption that is known as the sphericity assumption or the circularity assumption. A discussion of this assumption will be presented later in this chapter.

Principles behind a Within-groups One-way ANOVA

When the same participants are repeatedly measured this is known as a repeated measures or related measures design. The logic of a related design ANOVA is similar to that of an independent design (see Chapter 6). In practice, however, there is a difference in how we compute the value of the F-statistic as we have to make a change to the error term. To understand why this is the case, recall that in an independent design the within-groups variance was used to estimate the degree to which experimental error was responsible for the observed differences among the treatment means:

$$F = \frac{\text{between-groups variance}}{\text{Within groups variance}} = \frac{\text{error} + \text{treatment}}{\text{error}}$$

The within-groups variance is used to estimate what proportion of the between-groups variance is due to error and the rest is then attributed to the treatment effects. You may recall that the error component was considered to be a function of inter-individual variability, intra-individual variability and random fluctuations.

Intra-individual variability and random fluctuations will occur as a source of error for every participant in all conditions. Therefore these sources of error will occur at every point at which data is collected irrespective of the number of participants. For example, in Table 8.1 as there are three participants measured at three different levels of the independent variable, then there will be nine data collection points and hence nine occasions on which these two sources of variance will produce error. This is exactly the same number as in the example from Table 6.1. There nine participants were split into three treatment groups and hence nine data collection points.

Inter-individual variability, on the other hand, is limited by the number of participants. To illustrate this point consider the scores of participant f from Table 8.1. Note that participant f had a performance score of 1 in condition A and 3 in condition B. These differences in scores reflect the effects of treatment and error. However, the error on this occasion is a function of intra-individual variability and random fluctuations. In a within-groups design the differences between these two scores cannot be due to individual differences as they are both the product of the same participant. The same holds true for the typical scores. The differences between the mean scores in the three conditions A, B and C, namely 1, 4 and 7, are not confounded by individual differences as they are the average of the same three participants.

If individual differences do not confound the scores in a within-groups design then it follows that the error term adopted in a between-subjects designs, which would include inter-individual differences, will overestimate the extent to which experimental error influences the performance scores across the three treatment conditions. This is because the sum of the within-groups variances (error) was used to estimate the error variance component of the between-groups variance (error + treatment). Therefore what is needed is a measure of the error variance that does not include any variance due to individual differences. Given that this within-groups variance is a product of intra-individual variability, random fluctuations and individual differences, this means that the component of variance due to individual differences has to be removed from the within-groups variance. When this is done the variance that is left, known as the residual variance, can be used as the estimate of the error in the between-groups variance.

In Chapter 6 it was noted that the within-groups variance was calculated by dividing the sum of squares by the appropriate degrees of freedom. Therefore, the error term $SS_{\text{within-groups}}$ can be divided into one portion that reflects individual differences due to participants (SS_{subjects}) and another portion due to the interaction of the individual differences with the treatment (SS_{residual}), that is

$$SS_{\text{within-groups}} = SS_{\text{subjects}} + SS_{\text{residual}}$$

This sum of squares, known as the **residual sum of squares** (SS_{residual}), reflects the influence of intra-individual variability and random fluctuations. It is computed by taking the sum of squares for each individual participant (SS_{subjects}) away from the within-groups sum of squares. When the SS_{residual} is divided by the appropriate degree of freedom it will produce the MS_{residual} which will be the error term for a within-groups one-way ANOVA:

$$F = \frac{MS_{\text{between-groups}}}{MS_{\text{residual}}}$$

We will now look at how the SS_{residual} is calculated.

Calculating the $SS_{residual}$

To work out the SS_{residual} first compute a value for [S] where this value is the sum of all the squared totals for each participant across the conditions in the experiment divided by the number of treatments, that is

$$[S] = \frac{\sum (s)^2}{k}$$

Table 8.2

		A	B	C	(s)	s^2
Performance		1	3	7	11	121
Score		0	5	8	13	169
		2	4	6	12	144
	Σ	3	12	21	36	434
	$\overline{X}$	1	4	7		

Using the example from Table 8.1 we may construct the results in Table 8.2, where (s) is the sum of the scores in the three groups A, B and C

Therefore

$$[S] = \frac{434}{3} = 144.7$$

Next we compute the **subject sum of squares** $SS_{subjects}$ by using the formula

$$SS_{subjects} = [S] - [T]$$

where

$$[T] = \frac{(T)^2}{k(n)}$$

and

$T =$ total of all scores
$k =$ number of conditions
$n =$ number of participants in each group

Thus

$$[T] = \frac{36^2}{3(3)} = \frac{1296}{9} = 144$$

Therefore

$$SS_{subjects} = 144.7 - 144 = 0.7$$
$$SS_{residual} = SS_{within\text{-}groups} - SS_{subjects}$$

Looking back to p. 83 we can note that the $SS_{within\text{-}groups}$ was calculated to be 6

Therefore

$$SS_{residual} = 6{-}0.7 = 5.3$$

The degrees of freedom for the residual source is obtained by multiplying the degrees of freedom for treatment and participants, that is

$$\begin{aligned}
df_{kn} &= (df_k)\,(df_n) \\
&= (k-1)\,(n-1) \\
&= (3-1)\,(3-1) \\
&= 4
\end{aligned}$$

Therefore

$$F = \frac{MS_{between\text{-}groups}}{MS_{residual}}$$

$$= \frac{27}{5.3/4}$$

$$= \quad 20.4$$

If we compare the within-subjects error term with that produced by the between-subjects design on page 85 we can produce Table 8.3.

Note from this table that in this example $SS_{residual}$ (5.3) is smaller than the sum of the squares in the previous between-subjects design, namely $SS_{within\text{-}groups}$ (6), and also the degrees of freedom in the within-subjects design $(k-1)(n-1)$ gave us the value 4, which is smaller than that for a between-subjects design $k(n-1)$ produced the value 6. Therefore, in the within-subjects design, we find that both the sum of squares and the degrees of freedom are smaller than in the between-groups design. However, if we examine these more closely, we can see that while the degree of freedom is smaller by 30% the corresponding change in the sum of squares is only 11.7%. This means that the error term (i.e. the mean square) is larger for the within-subjects design (1.3) than for the between-subjects design (1). So we find in this example that a between-subjects design produces a value of F equal to 27 whilst a within-subjects design produces a value of F equal to 20.4.

Table 8.3 **Comparing error terms and F in between- and within-subjects design**

Design	SS	df	MS	F
Between-subjects	6	6	1	27
Within-subjects	5.3	4	1.3	20.4

A within-subjects ANOVA will always be more conservative; that is, it becomes more difficult to reject H_0 when there are no consistent individual differences in scores or if there is an interaction between subjects and treatment, where participants respond differently to the treatment.

If we analyse this data using SPSS for Windows then we find it produces the results as shown in Example 8.1 on page 121.

Remember that if we have employed a repeated measures design in collecting the data then we are interested in looking at differences across the conditions **within subjects**. Examine the results from both designs and compare the values obtained with those worked out previously in this textbook.

Additional Assumptions of a Within-subjects Design ANOVA

In the previous chapter it was noted that when undertaking a between-groups design ANOVA it is important to check the assumptions that the data is normally distributed and that the within-groups variances are equal. In undertaking a within-groups design ANOVA one is making an additional assumption that is known as the sphericity assumption or the circularity assumption.

To understand what this involves consider the previous example where we have sets of scores from participants operating under three conditions termed A, B and C. This provides three potential contrasts between pairs of scores, namely AB, AC and BC. Now for each participant find the difference between each pair and then work out the variances of these three sets of differences. The sphericity assumption is that these variances are not significantly different. If this assumption is not met then this can greatly increase the risk of committing a Type I error (Keppel 1991, p. 351).

To see how this works out in practice Table 8.4 displays the variances of the differences between the three conditions in the previous example. The values of 11, 38.7 and 9.7 in this table suggests that the sphericity assumption may not be met. SPSS automatically executes a test known as Mauchly's test when a repeated measures

Table 8.4 **Variances of the differences between the conditions A, B and C**

	Groups			Contrasts between pairs of scores					
	A	B	C	A–B	$(A–B)^2$	A–C	$(A–C)^2$	B–C	$(B–C)^2$
	1	3	7	−2	4	−6	36	−4	16
	0	5	8	−5	25	−8	64	−3	9
	2	4	6	−2	4	−4	16	−2	4
Σ	3	12	21		33		116		29
$\overline{X}$	1	4	7	s^2	**11**		**38.7**		**9.7**

Table 8.5   **Mauchly's test of sphericity**

	Mauchly's W	Approx. Chi-Square	df	Sig.	Epsilon		
Within Subjects Effect					Greenhouse-Geisser	Huynh-Feldt	Lower-bound
TREATMEN	.563	.575	2	**.750**	.696	1.000	.500

Tests the null hypothesis that the error covariance matrix of the orthonormalized transformed dependent variables is proportional to an identity matrix.
a May be used to adjust the degrees of freedom for the averaged tests of significance. Corrected tests are displayed in the Tests of Within-Subjects Effects table.
b Design: Intercept Within Subjects Design: TREATMEN

analysis is undertaken. This tests the sphericity assumption and its output for the data in Table 8.1 is shown in Table 8.5.

As the significance value is greater then 0.05 the null hypothesis is accepted and it is concluded that the spericity assumption is met. Had this not been the case then there are a variety of strategies open to the researcher, but the simplest is to take advantage of the fact that SPSS not only provides a significance value when sphericity is assumed but also provides a value based on the Greenhouse–Geisser correction.

This correction assumes that the variances are as different as they can be and therefore it provides a very conservative significance value. So if the significance associated with Mauchly's test is less than 0.05 examine the row headed 'Greenhouse-Geisser' in the output headed 'Tests of Within-subjects Effects'. An example of this output is shown below in Table 8.6.

Table 8.6   **Tests of Within-subjects Effects**

Source		Type III Sum of Squares	df	Mean Square	F	Sig.
FACTOR1	**Sphericity Assumed**	**54.000**	**2**	**27.000**	**20.250**	**.008**
	Greenhouse-Geisser	54.000	1.391	38.812	20.250	.023
	Huynh-Feldt	54.000	2.000	27.000	20.250	.008
	Lower-bound	54.000	1.000	54.000	20.250	.046
Error (FACTOR1)	**Sphericity Assumed**	**5.333**	**4**	**1.333**		
	Greenhouse-Geisser	5.333	2.783	1.917		
	Huynh-Feldt	5.333	4.000	1.333		
	Lower-bound	5.333	2.000	2.667		

Output from a Within-subjects Design

The 'Sphericity Assumed' row in Table 8.6 provides the least conservative interpretation and therefore will produce the lowest significance value. The F-value is obtained by dividing the mean square value of 27.00 by the appropriate error mean square value of 1.333. (Note that if the sphericity assumption had not been met the 'Greenhouse-Geisser' row ought to be examined. This indicates that the probability that the null hypothesis is correct is 0.023.) If you contrast this value of 0.008 with the value of 0.001 below you can see that the within-groups design has provided the more cautious significance value.

Comparing the Results from a Within- and Between-groups Design

Comparing the results of a within-subjects design shown in Table 8.6 and the between-subjects design shown in Table 8.7 it can been seen that the significance values differ. The 'Sig.' value from the within-subjects design gives a probability of 8 in 1000 while the between-subjects design calculates the significance to be 1 in 1000. In both cases the null hypothesis would be rejected.

Table 8.7

	Sum of Squares	df	Mean Square	F	Sig.
Between Groups	54.000	2	27.000	27.000	.001
Within Groups	6.000	6	1.000		
Total	60.000	8			

Summary

A within-groups one-way ANOVA is used to test the significance of group differences when there is one dependent variable and one independent variable and the data was collected by means of a repeated measures design.

Whereas a t-test can only test the differences between the means of two groups, there is no restriction on the number of groups a within-groups one-way ANOVA can test. Therefore, when we have more than two groups a one-way ANOVA is used in preference to multiple t-tests because it does not increase the risk of committing a Type I error.

A within-groups one-way ANOVA tests the null hypothesis that all the means of the treatment group scores are equal. In computing the value of F an error term known as the mean square residual is used. If the probability associated with the value of F is less than the significance level the null hypothesis is rejected.

In addition to the three assumptions of all parametric tests, a within-subjects design also makes an additional assumption that is known as the sphericity assumption or the circularity assumption. This assumption is automatically tested by SPSS using Mauchly's test of sphericity. If the significance associated with Mauchly's test is less than 0.05 then examine the row headed 'Greenhouse-Geisser' in the output headed 'Tests of Within-Subjects Effects'.

EXERCISE 8.1 WITHIN-GROUPS ONE-WAY ANOVA

Skilled judges rated the performance of five gymnasts on three particular sets of movements (Table 8.8). The gymnasts had been taught each set of movements in a different way. The order in which the gymnasts were taught these sets was varied so as to counterbalance any order effects.

Table 8.8 **Movement scores for five gymnasts taught by three different methods**

Participant	Method 1	Method 2	Method 3
1	12	09	06
2	10	07	07
3	11	06	02
4	07	09	03
5	10	04	02

1. Write out a two-tailed hypothesis for this investigation.
2. Enter the data remembering that this is a repeated measures design and that each row is to contain the data from one participant and each column is for a different variable. Thus you will have five rows and three columns, one for each method.
3. Having entered the data, then as in the previous examples use the **Explore** option to test the assumption that the data is normally distributed. As this is a within-groups design each of the three methods will be entered into the **Dependent list** and as there is no between-subjects effect then no variable will be entered into the **Factor list**. Before you run the **Explore** option click on

Plots

Then in the **Boxplots** section select **Dependents together**

    Continue

      OK

This will produce one graph with three boxplots. This makes it much easier to compare than having three individual boxplots.

4. To carry out a within-groups one-way ANOVA, click on **Analyze**, **General Linear Model**, and then **Repeated Measures**.

5. In the **Within Subject Factor Name** box enter an appropriate name such as 'method', then click on the **Number of Levels** box and enter the number of groups. Click on **Add** and then on **Define**.

6. Enter the three within-subjects variables by highlighting them and click on the appropriate arrow. Next click on the **Options** box and in the **Display** area select **Descriptive Statistics** and then click on **Continue** and finally on **OK**.

7. Examine the skewness and kurtosis statistics and explain whether any of the three groups significantly deviate from normal.

Method 1 ....

Method 2 ....

Method 3 ....

8. Examine the boxplots and explain whether these suggest that any of the three groups significantly deviate from normal.

Method 1 ....

Method 2 ....

Method 3 ....

9. Examine the boxplots and explain whether these suggest support for the null or alternate hypothesis.

....

10. Look at the means and standard deviations in the table of descriptive statistics and explain whether these suggest support for the null or alternate hypothesis.

....

....

11. Next examine the 'Mauchly's Test of Sphericity' and explain whether the sphericity assumption is met.

12. Now look at the 'Test of Within-Subjects Effects'. If you previously decided that the sphericity assumption is met then look at the 'Sphericity Assumed'

the assumption is not met then look at the 'Greenhouse–Geisser' row. Describe the results of the ANOVA test (i.e. SS, df, MS, F and Sig. F), and explain whether you are going to accept or reject the null hypothesis.

....

13.   Write down what you conclude from this analysis.

....

....

Analytical Comparisons for Within-groups ANOVA

You may find it useful to re-read the section on a priori tests in Chapter 7 before continuing with this section.

When discussing analytical comparisons we noted that if the value of F leads us to reject the null hypothesis that all the means are equal, it does not tell us which particular means are significantly different from each other. To address this problem we employed **analytical comparisons** and we noted that these could be either planned or unplanned.

In a within-groups design ANOVA, the unplanned or post-hoc tests are not available to us and, therefore, we have to rely on planned contrasts. SPSS can execute such comparisons in a number of different ways. To illustrate the simplest of these we will return to the data set in the previous exercise.

The sixth instruction told you to click on the **Options** box and in the **Display** area select **Descriptive Statistics**. Now what you need to do is select the name you gave for the within-groups factor and move into the box headed **Displays means for** by means of the little arrowhead pointing to the right. Now select **Compare main effects**. This causes a tick to appear in this little box and the box that displays **LSD (none)** to turn white. Click on the downward-pointing arrowhead to the right of **LSD (none)** and select **Bonferroni**. Finally click on **Continue** and then on **OK**.

The output you produce should now include the details in Table 8.9

The numbers in the first two columns refer to group numbers. These two columns represent the pairs that are being contrasted. Therefore if there is a one in the first column and a two in the second column then the difference between the means of groups 1 and 2 is being tested. The column headed 'Sig.' provides the probability of getting means as different as the observed means by chance. The note at the bottom of the table tells us that a Bonferroni adjustment for multiple comparisons has been made. This adjustment has to be made to avoid increasing the risk of committing a Type I error because these contrasts are not orthogonal. Look at the section on orthogonal and non-orthogonal contrasts in the previous chapter if you are unclear about this point. In this example it appears that the only significant difference lies between groups 1 and 3.

Table 8.9 **Pairwise comparisons**

(I) FACTOR1	(J) FACTOR1	Mean Difference (I-J)	Std. Error	Sig. a
1	2	3.000	1.378	.285
	3	6.000	1.140	.019
2	1	-3.000	1.378	.285
	3	3.000	1.000	.120
3	1	-6.000	1.140	.019
	2	-3.000	1.000	.120

Based on estimated marginal means
* The mean difference is significant at the .05 level.
a Adjustment for multiple comparisons: Bonferroni.

As there are three groups this Bonferroni adjustment has taken the form of multiplying the observed probability by approximately 3. This means that the non-adjusted probability associated with the contrast between groups 1 and 2 would have been 0.285 divided by 3, or 0.095. (You can check this by carrying out a paired samples t-test on the two groups concerned.) This means that there will be occasions when you find that the F-value in the 'Test of Within-Subjects Effects' table leads you to reject the null hypothesis but that the above procedure fails to find a significant difference between any pair of groups. To overcome this problem you can always resort to using some of the pre-set orthogonal contrast available in SPSS.

A list and explanation of what each of these do can be found in the **Help** option of SPSS. The following instructions tell you how to select and execute one such contrast in SPSS known as a Helmert comparison. In this contrast 'Each category of the factor, except the last category, is compared to the mean effect of subsequent categories' (SPSS help file). To explain this imagine that we have four groups A, B, C and D. If you carried out a Helmert comparison on these four groups it would be equivalent to adopting the coefficients in Table 8.10.

If you multiply the corresponding weights for any pair of these comparisons you will find that they sum to zero, that is they are all orthogonal.

Table 8.10

Comparison	$\bar{X}_A$	$\bar{X}_B$	$\bar{X}_C$	$\bar{X}_D$
1 vs 2, 3, 4	-3	1	1	1
2 vs 3, 4	0	-2	1	1
3 vs 4	0	0	-1	1

To illustrate how this works, let us return to Exercise 8.1. After you have completed the fifth instruction click on the **Contrasts** box. Click on the downward-facing arrowhead to the right of the word **None** and select **Helmert**. Now click on **Change**, **Continue** and then on **OK**.

These instructions will add Table 8.11 to your output.

Table 8.11

Tests of Within-Subjects Contrasts

Source	FACTOR1	Type III Sum of Squares	df	Mean Square	F	Sig.
FACTOR1	Level 1 vs. Later	101.250	1	101.250	15.000	.018
FACTOR1	Level 2 vs. Level 3	45.000	1	45.000	9.000	.040
Error(FACTOR1)	Level 1 vs. Later	27.000	4	6.750		
	Level 2 vs. Level 3	20.000	4	5.000		

The row which has 'Level 1 vs. Later' in the second column tests that the mean of the first group is equal to the average of the means of the second and third group. In this case, as the 'Sig.' is less than 0.05, the null hypothesis is rejected. The weightings for this contrast would be

$$1 \quad\quad -0.5 \quad\quad -0.5$$

The row which has 'Level 2 vs. Level 3' in the second column tests that the mean of the second group is the same as the mean of the third group. In this case, as the 'Sig.' is again less than 0.05, the null hypothesis is rejected. The weightings for this contrast would be

$$0 \quad\quad 1 \quad\quad -1$$

Summary

Once the significance value associated with the omnibus F has led to rejection of the null hypothesis you can determine which means are significantly different from each other by two methods. The first of these is to employ a set of pairwise comparisons. However, as these contrasts are not orthogonal they will increase the risk of committing a Type I error unless a Bonferroni-type correction is made. This can result in a situation where the omnibus F leads to the rejection of the null hypothesis but no significant difference can be determined between any of the groups contrasted. The second method, which may overcome this problem, is to employ the pre-set orthogonal contrasts.

9

FACTORIAL ANOVA

Purpose

The purpose of this technique is to test for group-mean differences when there are two or more independent variables. In the previous chapters on ANOVA we have looked at the effect of one independent variable, known as a factor, on one dependent variable. However, researchers may be interested in the effects of more than one independent variable. For example, they may expect that not only will participants who fall into different age groups display different fitness levels, but also males and females will display different fitness levels. In this example there are two factors, age and gender.

Research Question

Thus factorial ANOVA is employed to address research questions that focus on the difference in the means of one dependent variable when there are two or more independent variables. For example, consider the following research question: is there a difference in the fitness levels of men and women who fall into one of three different age groups? In this case we have one dependent variable (i.e. fitness) and two independent variables (i.e. gender and age). The first of these, gender, has two levels (i.e. men and women), and the second, age, has three levels. The appropriate statistical test to address this question is known as 2 by 3 factorial ANOVA, where the numbers 2 and 3 refer to the number of levels in the two independent variables.

Null Hypothesis for Main Effects

Examining the research question in more detail we can see that it has two parts that are each a product of the two independent variables. These are:

> Is there a difference in the fitness levels of men and women?
> Is there a difference in the fitness levels of the three different age groups?

As it is quite possible that the answer to one of these questions is 'yes' and the answer to the other question is 'no', we require a null hypothesis to test each part independently. Each of these null hypotheses will predict that the means of the scores on the dependent variable for each level of the independent variable will not be significantly different. So in the above example this means that one null hypothesis would predict that the fitness scores of men and women would not be significantly different from each other. The other null hypothesis would predict that the fitness scores of the three age groups would not be significantly different from each other. These two null hypotheses may take the form of the following:

> There is no significant difference in the fitness level of men and women.
> There is no significant difference in the fitness level of the three different age groups.

Each of the above two hypotheses are concerned with testing what are known as the main effects. There is always one main effect for each independent variable.

Null Hypothesis for Interaction Effects

In addition to each of these main effects there is a third possible effect, for it is conceivable that whatever the effect of age on fitness it may not be the same for men and women. For example, if fitness tends to decrease with age, it may not do so at the same rate for men and women. Another way of expressing this is to say that there is an interaction between the independent variables in terms of their influence on the dependent variable. To test for such an effect an appropriate null hypothesis needs to be postulated. This might take the form of the following:

> There will be no significant interaction between age and gender on fitness levels.

If there are more than two independent variables then the number of possible interactions can increase dramatically. For example, if a third factor of social class were added to the example above then the four possible interactions would be:

1. age * gender
2. age * social class
3. gender * social class
4. age * gender * social class.

Why Not Use Multiple One-way ANOVAs?

It would be quite possible to get an answer to the two main questions in the above example by carrying out two one-way ANOVAs. One reason that we do not do this is exactly the same as the reason that was given in Chapter 6 for carrying out a one-way ANOVA rather than employing multiple *t*-tests, for to do so would involve analysing in part the same data twice and therefore there may be an increased risk of committing a Type I error. However, there is one additional and very important reason for carrying out a factorial ANOVA in preference to executing multiple one-way ANOVA tests. This reason is that carrying out multiple one-way ANOVAs would not enable the researcher to test for any interactions between the independent variables. Therefore a factorial ANOVA is carried out in preference to multiple one-way ANOVAs to avoid any increased risk in committing a Type I error and to enable both main and interaction effects to be tested.

Assumptions

As a factorial ANOVA is a parametric test it shares similar assumptions to all other parametric tests. These are that the dependent variable has been measured on an interval scale, that the variances of the groups based on the levels of the independent variable are equal and that the distribution in each group does not significantly deviate from normal. These assumptions were discussed in more detail in Chapter 6.

Principle behind a Factorial ANOVA

To illustrate the principle behind this technique consider the data in Table 9.1 in which the letters A, B, C, D, E, F are simply used to identify cells, whilst the numbers in each cell (e.g. 0, 1 and 2 in cell A) are some measure of the dependent variable fitness.

Table 9.1   **Fitness scores of men and women in three age categories (high score = low fitness)**

	Age categories		
	20–29	**30–39**	**40–49**
Male	0,1,2	5,4,6	9,9,9
	A	B	C
Female	2,3,4	8,7,9	9,8,8
	D	E	F

To understand the principles behind a factorial ANOVA it is helpful to reflect on the sources of variance in the scores in the above cells.

Cell A

The variability in the scores in cell A reflects error in our measurement. In Chapter 6 we noted that there were three sources of this error. These were:

1. **Inter-individual variability**. The three scores, 0, 1, 2, are different because they are produced by three different people, that is they reflect individual differences.
2. **Intra-individual variability**. This refers to the potential variability within each person's score. Whenever an individual engages in some behaviour in exactly the same situation on a different occasion there will always be some degree of variability in their behaviour. The individual in group A who scored 0 on this particular occasion might not score 0 if they were to be tested on some other occasion.
3. **Random fluctuations**. By this is meant extraneous variables, such as situational variables, that cannot be controlled.

Cells A and D

The variability in the scores contained across both cells A and D reflects error in our measurement *and* the effect of the independent variable gender. For example, the difference between the score of 1 in cell A and 3 in cell D is due to all of the above three sources of error plus one other factor which is the effect of gender.

Cells A and B

The variability in the scores contained across both cells A and B reflects error in our measurement *and* the effect of the independent variable age. For example, the difference between the score of 1 in cell A and 4 in cell B is due to all of the above three sources of error plus one other factor which is the effect of age.

Cells A and E

Here variability in the scores contained across both cells reflects error in our measurement *and* the effect of both of the independent variables gender and age. For example, the difference between the score of 1 in cell A and 7 in cell E is due to all of the above three sources of error plus two other factors which are the effects of gender and age.

Plotting the Main and Interaction Effects

While the above examination of the sources of variances shows how the independent factors might influence the variance of the scores across the levels of the factors of age and gender, it does not illustrate the effects of any interaction between the two factors. Any such interaction can, however, be illustrated by plotting the mean values for each cell. These values are shown in Table 9.2.

These mean values can now be plotted on a multiple line graph as shown in Figure 9.1. On this graph a line is drawn for each gender group and its mean fitness scores are plotted for each of the three age groups.

Table 9.2 **Mean fitness scores of men and women in three age categories where high scores equal low fitness**

	Age categories		
	20–29	**30–39**	**40–49**
Male	1	5	9
Female	3	8	8.3

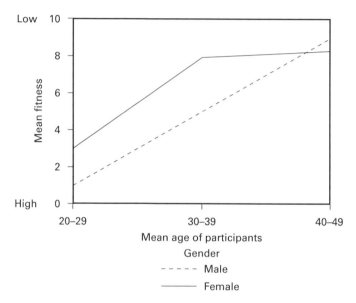

Figure 9.1 **Graph showing mean fitness levels of men and women in three different age groups**

Looking at the graph we can now consider each of the effects in turn.

Main Effect: age

If the fitness for women or men did not change as a consequence of age then the lines would be horizontal. The fact that the two lines are not horizontal suggests that age does influence fitness for both gender groups.

Main Effect: gender

If gender did not influence fitness then the lines for men and women would not be separated. The fact that the two lines are apart suggests that gender influences fitness.

Interaction Effect: age * gender

If the effect of age on fitness is the same for both genders then the two lines will be parallel. The fact that the lines are not parallel suggests that there is an interaction effect.

Although this graph suggests that both main effects and the interaction influence fitness levels of the participants a factorial ANOVA needs to be carried out to test each of the three null hypotheses. The principle behind the calculation of the F-statistic in executing a factorial ANOVA is exactly the same as that in a one-way ANOVA, that is

$$F = \frac{\text{error} + \text{treatment}}{\text{error}}$$

How this works out in practice is best illustrated by working through the example in this chapter. Follow the instructions in the next section and then compare your output with that given below.

Instructions to Execute a Factorial ANOVA Using SPSS

Enter the data in Table 9.1 in the manner shown in Table 9.3. Note that one column must be used to identify the age group of the participant, one column must be used to identify the gender group of the participant, and one column must be used to enter the fitness level of the participant.

Table 9.3

Gender	Age	Fitness		
1	1	0		
1	1	1		
1	1	2		
1	2	5	Note:	
1	2	4		
1	2	6	Gender:	
1	3	9		1 = male
1	3	9		2 = female
1	3	9		
2	1	2	Age	
2	1	3		1 = 20–29 age group
2	1	4		2 = 30–39 age group
2	2	8		3 = 40–49 age group
2	2	7		
2	2	9		
2	3	9		
2	3	8		
2	3	8		

Use the **Explore** option to test that the data is normally distributed. Then, from the **Analyze** menu select **General Linear Model** and then **Univariate**. Enter the name you gave the dependent variable, for example fitness, in the **Dependent** box and both of the independent variables into the **Fixed Factor(s)** box. Click on the **Options** box and select **Homogeneity tests** and then click on **Continue**. Click on the **Plots** box and then enter gender into the **separate lines** space and age into the **Horizontal Axis** space. Click on **Add** and then on **Continue**. Next click on the **Post Box** and select age from the **Factors** box and click on the arrow to enter them in the **Post Hoc tests for** window. From the **Equal variance assumed** selection choose **Bonferroni**. Finally click on **Continue** and then **OK** and this should produce results that include the following.

Edited Output from SPSS

Before carrying out the factorial analysis it is important to check the descriptive statistics (Table 9.4) to see if a one-tailed hypothesis has been postulated that the data is in the predicted direction and to check that the data does not significantly deviate from normal. The descriptive statistics by gender are provided in Table 9.4 and the statistics by age are provided in Table 9.5.

Table 9.4 **Descriptives**

	GENDER		Statistic	Std. Error
FITNESS	male	Mean	5.00	1.18
		Std. Deviation	3.54	
		Skewness	-.087	.717
		Kurtosis	-1.602	1.400
	female	Mean	6.44	.90
		Std. Deviation	2.70	
		Skewness	-.806	.717
		Kurtosis	-1.185	1.400

NORMALITY

If the kurtosis and skewness values are divided by their standard errors it can be seen that none of the values will be greater than ± 1.96. The data therefore does not significantly deviate from a normal distribution.

DIFFERENCES

This data is concerned with testing the following null hypothesis:

There is no significant difference in the fitness level of men and women.

Although there is a difference in mean scores this difference is quite small in the context of the standard deviations suggesting that there will be a large overlap in the two sets of scores. This is confirmed by the boxplot in Figure 9.2 which tends to support the null hypothesis.

NORMALITY
If the kurtosis and skewness values are divided by their standard errors it can be seen that none of the values will be greater than ±1.96. The data therefore does not significantly deviate from a normal distribution.

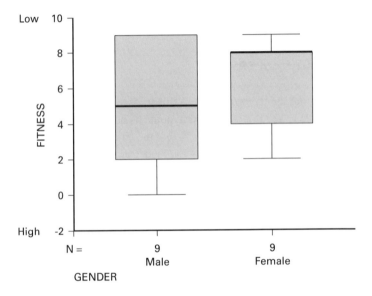

Figure 9.2

Table 9.5 **Descriptives**

	AGE		Statistic	Std. Error
FITNESS	20 - 29	Mean	2.00	.58
		Std. Deviation	1.41	
		Skewness	.000	.845
		Kurtosis	-.300	1.741
	30 - 39	Mean	6.50	.76
		Std. Deviation	1.87	
		Skewness	.000	.845
		Kurtosis	-1.200	1.741
	40 - 49	Mean	8.67	.21
		Std. Deviation	.52	
		Skewness	-.968	.845
		Kurtosis	-1.875	1.741

DIFFERENCES

This data is concerned with testing the following null hypothesis:

> There is no significant difference in the fitness level of the three different age groups.

The differences in mean scores are quite large in the context of the standard deviations suggesting that there will be little overlap in the two sets of scores. This is confirmed by the boxplot in Figure 9.3 which suggests that the null hypothesis will be rejected.

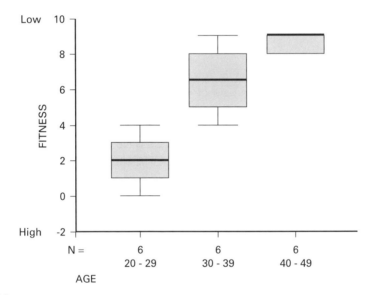

Figure 9.3

Checking the Homogeneity of Variance Assumption

The significance value from Levene's test shown in Table 9.6 is greater than 0.05. Therefore the null hypothesis should be accepted.

Table 9.6 **Levene's test of equality of error variances**

Dependent Variable: FITNESS

F	df1	df2	Sig.
.951	5	12	.484

Tests the null hypothesis that the error variance of the dependent variable is equal across groups.

a Design: Intercept + GENDER + AGE + GENDER * AGE

As the homogeneity of variance assumption was met the results of the factorial ANOVA can be examined without concern for their validity.

Factorial ANOVA

The output from a factorial ANOVA is very similar to that from a one-way ANOVA. Before looking at Table 9.7 it is useful to recall from Chapter 6 that

$$F = \frac{SS_{\text{between-groups}}}{(k-1)} \div \frac{SS_{\text{within-groups}}}{k(n-1)}$$

$$= MS_{\text{between-groups}} \div MS_{\text{within-groups}}$$

So, for example, if you look at the row with 'AGE' in the first column you may note that when the corresponding sum of squares value of 138.778 is divided by the 2 degrees of freedom this produces a mean square value of 69.389.

Now look at the row with 'Error' in the first column and note that when the corresponding sum of squares value of 8.667 is divided by the 12 degrees of freedom this produces a mean square value of 0.722. Note that when the mean square for age (69.389) is divided by the mean square error (0.722) this produces an F-value of 96.077.

Table 9.7 **Tests of between-subjects effects**

Dependent Variable: FITNESS

Source	Type III Sum of Squares	df	Mean Square	F	Sig.
Corrected Model	158.944	5	31.789	44.015	.000
Intercept	589.389	1	589.389	816.077	.000
AGE	138.778	2	69.389	96.077	.000
GENDER	9.389	1	9.389	13.000	.004
AGE * GENDER	10.778	2	5.389	7.462	.008
Error	8.667	12	.722		
Total	757.000	18			
Corrected Total	167.611	17			

a R Squared = .948 (Adjusted R Squared = .927)

Main Effect: 'AGE'

This effect is testing the null hypothesis that there is no significant difference in the mean fitness score of the three age groups. It is important that you understand that in testing this hypothesis the men and women fitness scores are combined in each of the three age groups. So from Table 9.5 above we can see that the question being addressed is: are the means of 2.0, 6.5 and 8.67 significantly different?

Returning to examine the row with 'AGE' in the first column we can note that in the last column the significance is given as '.000'. This means that there is close to zero probability that the overall means of the three age groups are equal; therefore the null hypothesis is rejected, that is the average fitness scores of the three age groups are different.

Main Effect: 'GENDER'

This effect is testing the null hypothesis that there is no significant difference in the mean fitness score of the two gender age groups. Again, it is important that you understand that in testing this hypothesis the three age group fitness scores are combined in each of the two gender groups. So from Table 9.4 we can see that the question being addressed is: are the means of 5.00 and 6.44 significantly different?

Looking at the row with 'GENDER' in the first column note that in the last column the significance is given as '.004'. This means that there is only a 4 in 1000 chance that the overall means of the two gender groups are equal; therefore the null hypothesis is rejected, that is men and women have different mean fitness scores.

Interaction Effect: 'AGE * GENDER'

Looking at the row with 'AGE*GENDER' in the first column note that in the last column the significance is given as '.008'. This means that there is only 8 in 1000 chance that there is no interaction; therefore the null hypothesis is rejected, that is age shows a differential effect on the fitness of men and women.

POST-HOC Tests

While the main effect on 'AGE' led to the rejection of the null hypothesis that there is no significant difference in the mean fitness score of the three age groups, it did not provide any information as to which of the three groups were significantly different. Following the advice in Chapter 7 we can see from Table 9.8 that in fact all three groups are significantly different from each other.

Table 9.8 **Multiple comparisons**

(I) AGE	(J) AGE	Mean Difference (I-J)	Std. Error	Sig.	95% Confidence Interval	
					Lower Bound	Upper Bound
20 - 29	30 - 39	-4.50	.49	**.000**	-5.86	-3.14
	40 - 49	-6.67	.49	**.000**	-8.03	-5.30
30 - 39	20 - 29	4.50	.49	.000	3.14	5.86
	40 - 49	-2.17	.49	**.003**	-3.53	-.80
40 - 49	20 - 29	6.67	.49	.000	5.30	8.03
	30 - 39	2.17	.49	.003	.80	3.53

Summary

A factorial ANOVA is used to test the significance of group differences when there is one dependent variable and two or more independent variables. This can be seen from the tables in Appendix 2.

This technique tests the null hypothesis that all the means of the groups are equal for each main effect. There is always one main effect for each independent variable. In addition, this technique tests for all combinations of interactions between the independent variables. This means that it tests to see if the effect of one independent variable on the dependent variable is dependent upon the level of one or more of the other independent variables. If the probability associated with the value of F for any effect is less than the significance level the null hypothesis is rejected.

A factorial ANOVA is carried out in preference to multiple one-way ANOVAs to avoid any increased risk of committing a Type I error and to enable both main and interaction effects to be tested. Like all parametric tests it assumes that the dependent variable has been measured on an interval scale, that the variances of the groups based on the levels of the independent variable are equal and that the distribution in each group does not significantly deviate from normal.

The data employed in the examples so far has come from an independent groups design and therefore we have carried out a between-groups ANOVA. The principles in testing the main effects are therefore exactly the same as those that were discussed in Chapter 6 on between-groups one-way ANOVA. In Chapter 8 we discussed a within-groups one-way ANOVA design, where the data has been collected by means of a repeated measures design and all that was written there applies to a repeated measures factorial ANOVA. However, factorial ANOVA is not limited to either a within-groups or between-groups design as it is quite possible that one independent variable reflects different groups whilst another reflects different measures of the same participants. This is known as a mixed design and an example is given at the end of this chapter.

EXERCISE 9.1 FACTORIAL ANOVA

You have decided to investigate factors underlying performance satisfaction in competitive sport. After reading some literature on motivation, you decide to look at the effects of motivational orientation and performance outcome on post-game satisfaction in squash players. You first select a sample of competitive squash players from a local club. As luck would have it, when you measure the motivational orientation of your sample, you find that half your sample is task oriented (defines success in terms of personal improvement) and half is ego oriented (defines success in terms of demonstrating greater ability than others).

Your sample of players then engages in a competitive squash match against opponents of equal ability. Once again, as luck would have it, winners and losers are

Table 9.9 **Satisfaction scores**

Task orientation		Ego orientation	
Winners	Losers	Winners	Losers
35	31	37	15
45	37	21	16
30	31	44	32
32	21	29	18
21	26	37	22
27	31	32	10
29	22	26	15
34	23	34	22
21	26	17	21
25	24	40	18

evenly split between task- and ego-oriented players. After recording the outcome of the game, you assess post-game satisfaction utilising a self-report scale. This scale has a maximum possible score of 50 (high satisfaction), and a minimum possible score of 10 (low satisfaction). The data you have obtained is listed in Table 9.9.

The research question you are attempting to answer asks:

Are there differences in performance-related satisfaction as a function of motivational orientation and performance outcome?

1. Enter the data in the following manner. Remember: as you have 40 participants you should use 40 rows. Don't forget to provide value labels for the orientation and outcome variables.

Orient	Outcome	Satisfaction
1	1	35
1	2	31
2	1	37
2	2	15

2. Use the **Explore** option to obtain skewness and kurtosis values for each main effect and to obtain boxplots for each effect.
3. From the **Statistics** menu select **General Linear Model** and then **Univariate**. Enter the name you gave the dependent variable in the **Dependent** box and both of the independent variables into the **Fixed Factor(s)** box.
4. Click on the **Options** box, and in the **Display** area select **Descriptive statistics,** then select **Homogeneity test** and click on **Continue**.
5. Click on **Plots**, enter one factor into the **Horizontal axis** box and the other factor into the **Separate Lines** box, then click on **Add, Continue** and finally on **OK**.
6. Examine the output from **Explore** to test for assumptions of normality and to look for support for the null or alternate hypothesis for each main effect.

7. Examine the descriptive statistics and line graph and comment on what they suggest with respect to the research question.
8. Look at the 'Levene's test of Equality of Variances' table and state whether the assumption of homogeneity of variance is met. (You may find it useful to refer to the section beginning on page 91.)
9. Examine the 'Tests of Between Subjects Effects' and comment on the main effects and interaction.
10. Finally, comment on what you conclude with respect to the research question.

EXERCISE 9.2 MIXED DESIGN FACTORIAL ANOVA

The data that you analysed in the previous exercise was treated as if it came from a random or independent design, that is different participants were used in all four conditions. However, imagine that the data was drawn from only two groups of participants who differed in their motivational orientation. These participants were then measured for the degree of satisfaction they felt after both losing and winning a game. This means that we now have what is termed a mixed design, for we have a between-groups design that reflects motivational orientation and a within-groups design that reflects the outcome of winning and losing.

By using the options in the **Edit** menu, copy and paste the data such that it is displayed in three columns as shown below.

Orientation	Satisfaction after Winning	Satisfaction after Losing
1	35	31
1	45	37
1	30	31
1	32	21
etc.		
2	37	15
2	21	16
2	29	18
2	21	26
etc.		

Don't forget to rename the dependent variables to something such as SatWin and SatLose, and delete the column variable that had previously identified the outcome.

1. Having entered the data you don't need to use the **Explore** option as you can use the output from the previous between-groups design exercise.
2. Click on **Analyze, General Linear Model**, and then **Repeated Measures**.
3. In the **Within Subject Factor Name** box enter an appropriate name such as 'outcome', then click on the **Number of Levels** box and enter the number of groups, that is 2. Click on **Add** and then on **Define**.

4. Enter the two within-subjects variables, winning and losing, by highlighting them and click on the appropriate arrow. Then enter the independent variable labelled 'orientation' on the previous page into the **Between Subjects Factor(s)** box.

5. Click on the **Options** box, and in the **Display** area select **Descriptive statistics**, then select **Homogeneity test** and click on **Continue**.

6. Click on **Plots**, enter one factor into the **Horizontal axis** box and the other factor into the **Separate Lines** box, then click on **Add**, **Continue** and finally on **OK**.

7. At this point you should examine the output from **Explore** to test for assumptions of normality, but you have already done this in the previous exercise.

8. Examine the 'Descriptive Statistics' table and the line graph and explain what implications the means and standard deviation values have for the acceptance of the null hypothesis.

9. Next examine the 'Mauchly's Test of Sphericity' and explain whether the sphericity assumption is met.

10. Now look at the 'Test of Within-Subjects Effects'. If you previously decided that the sphericity assumption is met then look at the 'Sphericity Assumed' row; if the assumption is not met then look at the 'Greenhouse-Geisser' row. Based on the appropriate significant values explain whether you are going to accept or reject the null hypothesis.

11. Look at the 'Levene's Test of Equality of error Variances' table and explain what it is examining and what conclusions you draw from it.

12. Explain what you interpret from the table of 'Tests of Between Subjects Effects'.

13. Write a summary of your findings explaining what you conclude from this analysis.

14. Complete Table 9.10.

Table 9.10

Experimental design		F	Sig. of F
Independent	Orientation		
Mixed	Orientation		
Independent	Outcome		
Mixed	Outcome		
Independent	Orientation by outcome		
Mixed	Orientation by outcome		

15. How do you account for the differences in the significance of F-values produced by the two designs? (You may find it helpful to refer to the last part of the section on repeated measures one-way ANOVA and to compare the relative sum of squares and degrees of freedom values.)

MORE ADVANCED APPLICATIONS IN ANOVA

Testing Simple Effects in Factorial ANOVA

Main Effects and Simple Effects

In Chapter 9 it was explained that a factorial ANOVA is concerned with testing main effects and interactions. Main effects are concerned with testing the null hypotheses that there is no significant difference between the mean scores of the various levels of one independent variable when the scores at the different levels of other independent variables are combined into one group. However, researchers often want to test for significant differences between the various levels of one independent variable for a particular level of the other independent variables. These are known as simple effects.

To illustrate what this means, consider the situation where a researcher has measured the performance of male and female participants before and after some treatment. The structure of the results is shown in Table 10.1. The letter A designates a cell of male performance scores in the pre-test trial, the letter D the female performance scores in the post-test trial, the letter H the mean of males and females in the post-test trial and so on.

Table 10.1

	Trials		
	Pre-test	Post-test	Row means
Male (1)	A	B	E
Female (2)	C	D	F
Column Mean	G	H	

Main Effects

The experimental design that would produce data to fit into Table 10.1 would be a mixed design. This is exactly the same design as in the last exercise from the previous chapter. It is called a mixed design because it has both an independent groups component and a related measures design component. In the language of ANOVA this translates into the independent variable gender being the between-groups design component and trials being the within-groups design component.

In a mixed design factorial ANOVA the main effects test for significance differences in the following manner:

Between groups   Compares row mean E with mean F
Within groups   Compares column mean G with mean H

These main effects test, for example, that there is no significant within-groups difference in the combined means of men's and women's scores in the pre- and post-tests; that is, that the means of cells G and H are not significantly different? However, main effects will not test if there is a significant difference for just the men or for just the women across these two conditions; that is, they will not compare cells A and B or cells C and D. To answer these sorts of questions we need to look at what are termed simple effects. The analysis of simple effects with SPSS requires a different approach to that which we have previously adopted.

SPSS Syntax Window

In our use of SPSS to date we have selected the analysis we wanted to execute through the menu system and then clicked on the OK button to carry out this analysis. In making these selections what we are actually doing is constructing a small batch of instructions from the menu of instructions available. Then, by clicking on the OK button, we command the SPSS program to run this batch of instructions; that is, to execute this set of instructions. Unfortunately, simple effects are not available from the menu system in SPSS. Instead, instructions have to be written in what is known as the syntax window of SPSS and then SPSS is told to run these commands.

This syntax window is nothing more than a simple text editing program that is used to write and edit a batch of instructions. In this window you can still run your batch by simply highlighting the instructions you want SPSS to execute and clicking on the run symbol or choosing **RUN** from the menu available in this window. Instructions written in the syntax window can be saved like any other file by choosing **Save** from the **File** menu.

Example 10.1 An Illustration of Simple Effects

To illustrate what is involved in executing a simple effects analysis using the syntax window imagine the following scenario. A researcher was interested in manipulating the optimism of participants by means of a course of reading. The researcher measured participants' optimism by means of an optimism scale before and after the 12 week reading course. The scores are shown in Table 10.2 so that you can enter the data into SPSS and experiment with the analysis.

Table 10.2

Gender	Pre-test	Post-test
Male	1.00	2.00
Male	1.50	1.00
Male	2.00	1.50
Male	2.50	3.00
Male	3.00	3.50
Male	3.50	2.50
Female	1.00	3.00
Female	1.00	3.50
Female	1.50	3.50
Female	2.00	4.00
Female	2.50	4.00
Female	3.00	4.00

Once the data has been entered exactly as it is shown in Table 10.2, then from the **Analyze** menu click on **Compare Means** and then **Means**. Enter 'Gender' in the **Independent List** and the two other variables in the **Dependent List**. The SPSS output is as shown in Table 10.3.

Table 10.3 **Report**

GENDER		PRE_TEST	POST_TES
Male	Mean	2.2500	2.2500
	Std. Deviation	.9354	.9354
Female	Mean	1.8333	3.6667
	Std. Deviation	.8165	.4082
Total	Mean	2.0417	2.9583
	Std. Deviation	.8649	1.0104

From these results construct by hand Table 10.4.

Table 10.4 **Mean pre- and post-test optimism scores for six male and six female participants**

	Pre-test	Post-test	Row means
Male (1)	2.25	2.25	2.25
Female (2)	1.83	3.67	2.75
Column means	2.04	2.96	

Examine the means in this table and write down what they suggest to you. Then, from the **Analyze** menu select **General Linear Model** and then the **Repeated Measures** option. Use the **Plots** option to produce the graph shown in Figure 10.1.

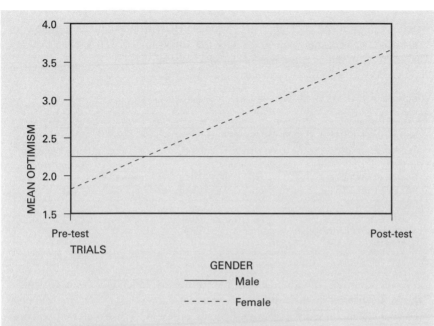

Figure 10.1 **Graph showing change in optimism score**

This graph ought to represent visually what you concluded from examining the means in Table 10.4. That is, while there is no difference in the pre- and post-test scores for males the scores for females do differ. It also suggests one additional interpretation, which is that there is an interaction between the two dependent variables, gender and trials, in their effects on the dependent variable.

FIRST SYNTAX INSTRUCTIONS

Now enter the following commands into the SPSS syntax window and run the analysis. To open a syntax window make the following selection: **File**, **New**, **Syntax**. Enter the following commands exactly, including the full stop:

```
MANOVA
 pre_test post_tes BY gender(1,2)
 /WSFACTORS trials(2)
 /design=mwithin gender(1) mwithin gender(2)
 /ERROR WITHIN+RESIDUAL
 /PRINT
  SIGNIF(MULT AVERF)
 /NOPRINT PARAM(ESTIM).
```

The line **/design=mwithin gender(1) mwithin gender(2)** will test trials within gender. This means that it will test for differences between the pre- and post-test scores for men and then again for women. When you have entered this text, highlight it and click on **RUN** or choose **RUN** from the menu available in this window. This analysis will produce the output in Table 10.5. Note that the explanation in italics is not part of the SPSS output.

Table 10.5

Tests involving 'TRIALS' Within-Subject Effect. Tests of Significance for T2 using UNIQUE sums of squares						*Simple Effects being tested*
Source of Variation	SS	DF	MS	F	Sig. of F	
WITHIN + RESIDUAL	2.17	10	.22			
MWITHIN GENDER(1) BY TRIALS	.00	1	.00	.00	1.000	*2.25 v 2.25*
MWITHIN GENDER(2) BY TRIALS	10.08	1	10.08	46.54	.000	*1.83 v 3.67*

From Table 10.5 it can be noted that for men (Gender 1) there is no significant difference in their pre- and post-test scores. However, for women (Gender 2) these scores are significantly different. These values of F are smaller than those obtained from carrying out a within-groups one-way ANOVA, where, for example, Gender 2 would compute F as 75.625 rather than the value of 46.54 shown in Table 10.5. To check to see that the appropriate analysis is being executed a paired samples t-test could be executed. This analysis would produce a value of t that is the square root of the above F-value of 75.625, that is t would equal 8.7.

The output from the above syntax instructions also includes a test of the between-subjects main effect for gender. From Table 10.4 it can be noted that the mean scores for men were 2.25 and for women 2.75. Table 10.6 shows the probability that means as different as these two values would be obtained by chance.

Table 10.6

******Analysis of Variance - design 2****** Tests of Between-Subjects Effects. Tests of Significance for T1 using UNIQUE sums of squares					
Source of Variation	SS	DF	MS	F	Sig. of F
WITHIN + RESIDUAL	10.75	10	1.07		
GENDER	1.50	1	1.50	1.40	.265

From Table 10.6 it can be noted that 26.5 times out of 100 we would get means as different as 2.25 and 2.75. As this value is greater than 0.05 the null hypothesis is accepted.

The output from the first syntax instructions above also includes a test of the within-subjects main effect of trials and the interaction of gender with trials.

From Table 10.4 it can be noted that the mean scores for pre-test were 2.04 and for post-test 2.96. Table 10.7 shows the probability that means as different as these two values would be obtained by chance.

Table 10.7

******Analysis of Variance - design 2******					
Tests involving 'TRIALS' Within-Subject Effect.					
Tests of Significance for T2 using UNIQUE sums of squares					
Source of Variation	SS	DF	MS	F	Sig. of F
WITHIN+RESIDUAL	2.17	10	.22		
TRIALS	5.04	1	5.04	23.27	.001
GENDER BY TRIALS	5.04	1	5.04	23.27	.001

From Table 10.7 it can be noted that one time in 1000 we would get means as different as 2.04 and 2.96. As this value is less than 0.05 the null hypothesis is rejected. The significance of F associated with the interaction is also 0.001, meaning that there is a significant interaction between gender and trials thus confirming the observation from Figure 10.1.

SECOND SYNTAX INSTRUCTIONS

It is crucially important that syntax instructions are entered in the appropriate manner for the question one wants to answer. To illustrate this enter the following instructions into the SPSS syntax window and run the analysis. You can either add these commands to the existing syntax window or open a new window by making the following selection: **File, New, Syntax**. The commands must be entered exactly as they are written below including the full stop.

```
MANOVA
 pre_test post_tes BY gender(1,2)
 /WSFACTORS trials(2)
 /wsdesign =mwithin trials(1) mwithin trials(2)
 /ERROR WITHIN+RESIDUAL
 /PRINT
  SIGNIF(MULT AVERF)
 /NOPRINT PARAM(ESTIM).
```

The line **/wsdesign=mwithin trials(1) mwithin trials(2)** will test gender within trials. This means that it will test for differences between the pre-test scores for men and women and then again test the post-test scores for both genders. This is different to the first instructions which tested trials within gender, that is pre- against post-test scores for men and then for women.

This analysis will produce the output in Table 10.8. Note that the explanation in italics is not part of the SPSS output. Examine the output and focus on which means are being compared and what you can conclude from this analysis.

Table 10.8

******Analysis of Variance - design 1******						
Tests involving 'MWITHIN TRIALS(1)' Within-Subject Effect.					*(Simple Effects)*	
Tests of Significance for T1 using UNIQUE sums of squares						
Source of Variation	SS	DF	MS	F	Sig. of F	
WITHIN+RESIDUAL	7.71	10	.77			
MWITHIN TRIALS(1)	50.02	1	50.02	64.89	.000	
GENDER BY MWITHIN TRIALS(1)	.52	1	.52	.68	.430	*2.25 against 1.83*

The value of F for the simple effect ($F = 0.68$) is the same as that obtained from carrying out a between-groups one-way ANOVA, where, for example, Trial 1 would compute F as 0.6757. You could also check to see that the appropriate analysis is being executed by carrying out an independent samples t-test which would produce a value of t that was the square root of the above F, that is t would equal 0.82. Based on this analysis the conclusion is that there is no significant difference between men's and women's optimism scores of 2.25 and 1.83 during the pre-test as differences as large as these would be found 43 times out of 100 by chance.

The output from these instructions also tests the null hypothesis that there is no significant difference between men's and women's optimism scores during the post-test. The results of this analysis are show in Table 10.9.

Table 10.9

******Analysis of Variance - design 1******						
Tests involving 'MWITHIN TRIALS(2)' Within-Subject Effect.					*(Simple Effects)*	
Tests of Significance for T2 using UNIQUE sums of squares						
Source of Variation	SS	DF	MS	F	Sig. of F	
WITHIN+RESIDUAL	5.21	10	.52			
MWITHIN TRIALS(2)	105.02	1	105.02	201.64	.000	
GENDER BY MWITHIN TRIALS(2)	6.02	1	6.02	11.56	.007	*2.25 against 3.667*

The values of F for the simple effect ($F = 11.56$) is the same as that obtained from carrying out a between-groups one-way ANOVA, where, for example, Trial 2 would compute F as 11.56. You could also check to see that the appropriate analysis is being executed by carrying out an independent samples t-test which would produce a value of t that was the square root of the above F, that is t would equal 3.4. Based on this analysis the conclusion is that there is a significant difference between men's and women's optimism scores of 2.25 and 3.667 during the post-test as means as different as these would only be found 7 times in 1000 by chance.

The differences in the analyses produced by the two sets of instructions can be illustrated by Table 10.10. Remember that the first instructions tested trials within gender and the second instructions tested gender within trials.

Table 10.10   **Mean pre- and post-test optimism scores for six male and six female participants**

	Pre-test		Post-test	Grand means
Male (1)	2.25 ↑	←trials within gender 1→	2.25 ↑	2.25
	gender within trial 1 ↓		gender within trial 2 ↓	
Female (2)	1.83	←trials with gender 2→	3.67	2.75
Grand means	2.04		2.96	

You may find it useful in the future when carrying out a simple effects analysis to identify the variables whose means you want to compare and then modify the appropriate instructional set given in this example.

When writing the syntax commands you may have noted that the first command was **MANOVA**, which stands for multivariate analysis of variance. MANOVA, as can be seen from Appendix 2, is used to address the same sorts of research questions as ANOVA but it can be used when there is more than one dependent variable. Because MANOVA makes quite stringent assumptions about the data, it is difficult to interpret, and in most cases is less powerful than ANOVA, Tabachnick and Fidell (1989) recommend that MANOVA be avoided except when there is a compelling need to measure several dependent variables.

However, it is very common to test participants on more than one variable and on more than one occasion. This is known as a doubly multivariate repeated measures design and an example of this type of analysis is outlined in the next section.

Summary on Simple Effects Analysis

Simple effects are concerned with testing for significant differences between various levels of one independent variable for a particular level of another independent variable. Tests for simple effects may be employed in a within-groups, between-groups or mixed design factorial ANOVA. For example, in a pre–post design with male and female participants this analysis allows the researcher to test if men and women differ at the pre-treatment stage or the post-treatment stage. It also allows the researcher to determine if either gender differ in their pre- or post-treatment scores.

To analyse simple effects in SPSS the MANOVA command is used. This command is accessed through writing a set of commands using the SPSS syntax option. The values of F obtained for the simple effects will be the same as that produced by carrying out a one-way ANOVA. Therefore appropriate Bonferroni-type corrections, such as those described in Chapter 7, need to be made to adjust for any increased risk of committing a Type I error.

Doubly Multivariate Repeated Measures Design

Doubly multivariate repeated measures design is so called because each subject has multiple variables measured at multiple times. For example, this would be the case if one has a repeated measures design in which there is one or more independent variables and multiple dependent variables. Consider the following example (Table 10.11) where a researcher has measured the anxiety and the confidence levels of 12 participants at two time periods.

To analyse this data, click on **Analyze**, **General Linear Model**, and then **Repeated Measures**.

In the **Within Subject Factor Name** box enter an appropriate name such as 'Trials', then click on the **Number of Levels** box and enter the number of trials, that is 2. Click on **Add** and then on **Measures**.

For each dependent variable enter a name up to eight letters that is not identical to any variable name, for example 'Anx'. Click on **Add**. Repeat this procedure for the other dependent variable using a name such as 'Conf' and then click on **Define**.

Enter the within-subjects variables into their appropriate positions by highlighting them and clicking on the arrowhead pointing towards the right.

Table 10.11 **Anxiety and confidence scores measured at two time periods (T1 and T2)**

	Anx_T1	Anx_T2	Conf_T1	Conf_T2
1	53.00	59.00	56.00	37.00
2	74.00	81.00	58.00	45.00
3	38.00	35.00	47.00	33.00
4	61.00	58.00	50.00	40.00
5	84.00	63.00	46.00	49.00
6	56.00	52.00	48.00	35.00
7	76.00	74.00	34.00	40.00
8	33.00	53.00	46.00	35.00
9	57.00	49.00	42.00	40.00
10	53.00	58.00	38.00	30.00
11	49.00	34.00	45.00	33.00
12	61.00	56.00	35.00	37.00

Next click on the **Options** box and in the **Display** area select **Descriptive Statistics**. Now select the name you gave for the within-groups factor and move it into the box headed **Displays means for** by means of the little arrowhead pointing to the right. Then select **Compare main effects**. This causes a tick to appear in this little box and the box that displays **LSD (none)** to turn white. Click on the downward-pointing arrowhead to the right of **LSD (none)** and select **Bonferroni**. Finally click on **Continue** and then on **OK**.

This analysis will address one multivariate and two univariate questions. (Multivariate just means that there is more than one dependent variable.) These questions are:

1. Is there a difference in a linear combination of the two dependent variables, anxiety and confidence, across the two time periods?
2. Is there a difference in anxiety scores across the two time periods?
3. Is there a difference in confidence scores across the two time periods?

The output from SPSS includes the following tables.

The first table (Table 10.12) simply summarises the design of the analysis.

Table 10.12

Within-Subjects Factors

Measure	TRIALS	Dependent Variable
ANX	1	ANX_T1
	2	ANX_T2
CONF	1	CONF_T1
	2	CONF_T2

The table of descriptive statistics (Table 10.13) allows us to see that question 2 above is asking if 57.9167 is significantly different from 56.0000, while question 3 is asking if 45.4167 is significantly different from 37.8333.

Table 10.13

Descriptive Statistics

	Mean	Std. Deviation	N
ANX_T1	57.9167	14.8780	12
ANX_T2	56.0000	13.5311	12
CONF_T1	45.4167	7.4279	12
CONF_T2	37.8333	5.3570	12

The multivariate test table (Table 10.14) provides an answer to question 1. As the significance value is less than 0.05 we conclude that there is a difference in a linear combination of the two dependent variables across the two time periods.

Table 10.14

Multivariate Tests

	Value	F	Hypothesis df	Error df	Sig.
Pillai's trace	.597	7.416	2.000	10.000	.011
Wilks' lambda	.403	7.416	2.000	10.000	.011
Hotelling's trace	1.483	7.416	2.000	10.000	.011
Roy's largest root	1.483	7.416	2.000	10.000	.011

Because this design involves a repeated measures component the analysis makes the assumption of sphericity. In Chapter 8 it was explained that this assumption is that the variances of the differences between each level of the independent variable are not significantly different. However, as there are only two levels in this example this assumption cannot be tested as there are no degrees of freedom. SPSS will report that as there are no degrees of freedom the sphericity cannot be tested and it will produce the output shown in Table 10.15.

Table 10.15

Mauchly's Test of Sphericity

Within Subjects Effect	Measure	Mauchly's W	Approx. Chi-Square	df	Sig.	Epsilon Greenhouse-Geisser	Huynh-Feldt	Lower-bound
TRIALS	ANX	1.000	.000	0	.	1.000	1.000	1.000
	CONF	1.000	.000	0	.	1.000	1.000	1.000

Tests the null hypothesis that the error covariance matrix of the orthonormalized transformed dependent variables is proportional to an identity matrix.

If the sphericity assumption was not met then the Greenhouse–Geisser statistics should be examined as in Table 10.16. As the significance value for anxiety is 0.547 this table suggests that the null hypothesis should be accepted for question 2. However, for confidence the corresponding value is 0.007 which indicates that the null hypothesis should be rejected for question 3. Therefore it should be concluded that there is not a significant difference in anxiety scores across the two time periods but that there is a significant difference in confidence scores across the two time periods.

Table 10.16

Univariate Tests

Source	Measure		Type III Sum of Squares	df	Mean Square	F	Sig.
TRIALS	ANX	Sphericity Assumed	22.042	1	22.042	.385	.547
		Greenhouse-Geisser	22.042	1.000	22.042	.385	.547
		Huynh-Feldt	22.042	1.000	22.042	.385	.547
		Lower-bound	22.042	1.000	22.042	.385	.547
	CONF	Sphericity Assumed	345.042	1	345.042	11.051	.007
		Greenhouse-Geisser	345.042	1.000	345.042	11.051	.007
		Huynh-Feldt	345.042	1.000	345.042	11.051	.007
		Lower-bound	345.042	1.000	345.042	11.051	.007
Error(TRIALS)	ANX	Sphericity Assumed	629.458	11	57.223		
		Greenhouse-Geisser	629.458	11.000	57.223		
		Huynh-Feldt	629.458	11.000	57.223		
		Lower-bound	629.458	11.000	57.223		
	CONF	Sphericity Assumed	343.458	11	31.223		
		Greenhouse-Geisser	343.458	11.000	31.223		
		Huynh-Feldt	343.458	11.000	31.223		
		Lower-bound	343.458	11.000	31.223		

Table 10.17

Tests of Within-Subjects Contrasts

Source	Measure	TRIALS	Type III Sum of Squares	df	Mean Square	F	Sig.
TRIALS	ANX	Linear	22.042	1	22.042	.385	.547
	CONF	Linear	345.042	1	345.042	11.051	.007
Error(TRIALS)	ANX	Linear	629.458	11	57.223		
	CONF	Linear	343.458	11	31.223		

The next two tables (Tables 10.17 and 10.18) repeat the results from the previous tables. They are produced because **Compare main effects** was selected in the instructions. While this does not make any sense if one only has two conditions, they are included because they would be very useful if there were more than two levels to an independent variable.

These results are the same as would be gained by analysing each dependent variable separately as no adjustment has been made for the fact that two contrasts

Table 10.18

Pairwise Comparisons

Measure	(I) TRIALS	(J) TRIALS	Mean Difference (I-J)	Std. Error	Sig.	95% Confidence Interval for Difference	
						Lower Bound	Upper Bound
ANX	1	2	1.917	3.088	.547	-4.881	8.714
	2	1	-1.917	3.088	.547	-8.714	4.881
CONF	1	2	7.583	2.281	.007	2.562	12.604
	2	1	-7.583	2.281	.007	-12.604	-2.562

Based on estimated marginal means
* The mean difference is significant at the .05 level.
a Adjustment for multiple comparisons: Bonferroni.

have been made. The need to make adjustments for increased risks to committing a Type I error was explained in Chapter 7. To make the appropriate correction, simply divide the significance level by the number of contrasts. In this case the significance level of 0.05 should be divided by 2 and therefore an alpha level of 0.025 should be employed in evaluating the significance of the observed differences.

Summary on Doubly Multivariate Repeated Measures Design

Doubly multivariate repeated measures design is so called because each participant has multiple variables measured at multiple times. For example, this would be the case if one has a repeated measures design in which there is one or more independent variables and multiple dependent variables.

This analysis will address multivariate and univariate questions. These questions are:

1. Is there a difference in a linear combination of the dependent variables across the time periods?
2. Is there a difference in each of the dependent variables across the time periods?

Because this design involves a repeated measures component the analysis makes the assumption of sphericity which was explained in Chapter 8. If the sphericity assumption was not met then the Greenhouse–Geisser statistics should be examined to determine the significance associated with the multivariate null hypothesis.

The results from the univariate analysis are the same as would be gained by analysing each dependent variable separately as no adjustment has been made for the fact that two contrasts have been made. The need to make adjustments for increased risks to committng a Type I error was explained in Chapter 7. To make the appropriate correction, simply divide the significance level by the number of contrasts.

Test for Linear Trend in One-way ANOVA

In the next two chapters the focus will change from statistical techniques that address research questions that focus on differences to techniques that address research questions that focus on relationships. Before that transition is made it is useful to know that the ANOVA that forms the basis of last four chapters can also be employed to look at trends.

To illustrate how ANOVA achieves this, imagine that a leisure researcher wondered whether visitors who travelled different distances to a country park spent different amounts of time visiting the park. To explore this question, the researcher carried out a survey and Table 10.19 shows the results of this survey.

The researcher subjected this data to a one-way ANOVA and found that all the groups differed significantly from each other. The researcher then drew the graph in Figure 10.2.

What struck the researcher about this graph was that there appeared to be a linear relationship between the dependent and independent variables, namely time and distance. Therefore, the researcher decided to test for a linear trend. To do this, the researcher first had to measure the probability that a linear trend existed and then

Table 10.19 **Mean time visitors spent at country park**

Distance travelled	Mean duration of visit (hours)
Up to 5 km	2.1
5 to 10 km	3.2
10 to 15 km	3.9
15 to 20 km	5.0

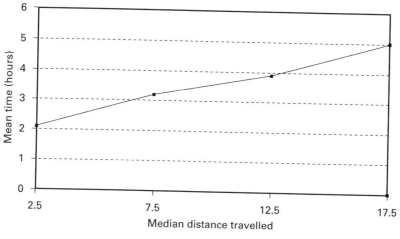

Figure 10.2 **Graph showing mean duration time of visit**

measure the significance of any deviation from a linear trend not accounted for by the linear component.

This analysis for linear trend is relatively simple to carry out if the levels of the independent variable form a series of *equal* steps along an ordered scale, such as distance in this example. If the conditions are not equally spaced, then regression analysis must be employed, which will be discussed in the next chapter.

To illustrate the principles involved, let's consider a design in which *n* different subjects are tested under each of the equally spaced *c* levels of the variable.

First of all we need to calculate the **linear component**. This is assessed by the sums of squares for linear trend: that is, that part of the variability due to the linear trend. If the condition means lie exactly on a straight line then this component will account for all the between-conditions variation.

$$SS_{\text{linear trend}} = \frac{(W_1 T_1 + W_2 T_2 + \cdots + W_c T_c)^2}{n(W_1^2 + W_2^2 + \cdots + W_c^2)}$$

where

T_c = sum of scores in condition *c*

n = number of scores in each condition (assumed equal here)

W_1 = coefficient for first condition (taken from Table 10.20)

Table 10.20 **Linear coefficients of orthogonal polynomials for equally spaced intervals**

Number of conditions	W_1	W_2	W_3	W_4	W_5	W_6
3	−1	0	1			
4	−3	−1	1	3		
5	−2	−1	0	1	2	
6	−5	−3	−1	1	3	5

Next we need to calculate the **mean square for linear trend**

$$MS_{\text{linear trend}} = \frac{SS_{\text{linear trend}}}{df}$$

where df (degrees of freedom) = 1 (this is always 1).

Finally, we need to compute a value of **F for linear trend** by dividing $MS_{\text{linear trend}}$ by the error term $MS_{\text{within-groups}}$:

$$F_{(1,k)\text{df}} = \frac{MS_{\text{linear trend}}}{MS_{\text{within-groups}}}$$

where

$$k = \text{df associated with } MS_{\text{within-groups}}$$

Using the F-tables, the results of this analysis will allow the probability that the data follows a linear trend to be determined. However, even if this result is significant, there will be deviations from the linear trend because all of the scores will not fall on a straight line. It is important to check that these deviations themselves are not significant because it is also possible that the data we have sampled represents part of a quadratic or cubic trend. Tests for quadratic and cubic trends can be carried out by using a different set of coefficients. Examples of these are provided at the end of this chapter (see Table 10.22).

To compute a value of **F for significance of deviations from linear trend** the sum of squares deviations from linearity ($SS_{\text{deviation from linear}}$) has to be calculated. This is obtained by taking the linear sum of squares away from the between-groups sum of squares:

$$SS_{\text{deviation from linear}} = SS_{\text{between-conditions}} - SS_{\text{linear trend}}$$

$$MS_{\text{deviation from linear}} = SS_{\text{deviation from linear}}/\text{df}$$

where

$$\text{df} = \text{number of conditions} - 2 = c - 2$$

$$F_{(c-2,k)} = \frac{MS_{\text{deviation from linear}}}{MS_{\text{within-groups}}}$$

Before testing for a linear trend construct a line graph by making the following selections. Click on **Graph**, then **Line** and make sure that **Summaries of groups of cases** is selected and then click on **Define**. In the **Line Represents** section select **Other summary function** and enter the dependent variable in the **Variable** box and the independent variable in the **Category Axis** box and then click on **OK**. This graph should provide an indication of any trend in the data.

To test for a linear trend in SPSS for Windows click on the **Contrast** box in the **One-Way ANOVA** window. Make sure a cross is showing in the **Polynomial** box and that the appropriate sort of trend (e.g. **Linear**) is showing in the **Degree** box. Now enter the appropriate coefficients for the type of trend analysis you want to carry out for the number of groups that you have. A table of coefficients is given in Table 10.22.

To illustrate how this analysis works the following shows the results from employing the above instructions on the data contained in Table 6.3. In using this data it is recognised that although the weights employed of −1, 0 and 1 assume that the levels of the independent variable form a series of equal steps along an ordered scale, this assumption does not hold for this data.

From the graph in Figure 10.3 the data appears to display a clear linear trend. To confirm this the results displayed in Table 10.21 need to be examined.

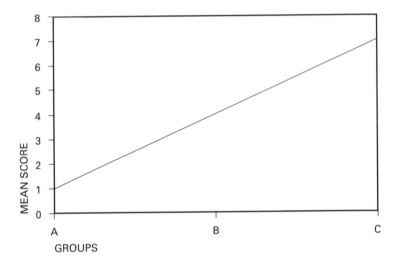

Figure 10.3 **Line graph displaying mean performance scores for three training groups**

Table 10.21 **Oneway**

			Sum of Squares	df	Mean Square	F	Sig.	
Between Groups	(Combined)		54.000	2	27.000	27.000	.001	A
	Linear Term	Contrast	54.000	1	54.000	54.000	.0003	B
		Deviation	.000	1	.000	.000	1.000	C
Within Groups			6.000	6	1.000			
Total			60.000	8				

In Table 10.22 the 'Sig.' column indicates that:

A   There is only a 1 in 1000 chance that H_0 is correct, that is $\mu_1 = \mu_2 = \mu_3$. We therefore reject the null hypothesis and accept that all the means are not equal.

B   We would get this result only 3 times in 10,000 by chance if there was not a linear trend. We therefore accept that there is a linear trend.

C   On 100% of occasions a truly linear trend would produce deviations as large as those observed. We therefore accept that a linear trend is the most appropriate description of the data.

Summary on Test for Linear Trend in One-way ANOVA

Linear trend analysis is a statistical technique that employs ANOVA to look at trends in the relationship between the dependent and independent variables. It assumes that the levels of the independent variable form a series of equal steps along an ordered scale, such as distance. If the conditions are not equally spaced, then regression analysis should be employed.

To employ this analysis a set of weights are used. Which weights are employed depends upon whether the trend is thought to be linear, quadratic or cubic. These weights are used to determine how much of the variability is due to the trend. If this trend component accounts for a significant portion of the between-condition variability then the conclusion is drawn that the trend describes the nature of the relationship between the independent and dependent variable.

References

Tabachnich, B.G. and Fidell, L.S. (1989) *Using Multivariable Statistics* (2nd edn). New York: Harper Collins.

Table 10.22 **Coefficients of orthogonal polynomials for equally spaced intervals**

k	Comparison	1	2	3	4	5	6	7	8	9	10	$\Sigma\alpha^2$
3	Linear	−1	0	1								2
	Quadratic	1	−2	1								6
4	Linear	−3	−1	1	3							20
	Quadratic	1	−1	−1	1							4
	Cubic	−1	3	−3	1							20
5	Linear	−2	−1	0	1	2						10
	Quadratic	2	−1	−2	−1	2						14
	Cubic	−1	2	0	−2	1						10
	Quartic	1	−4	6	−4	1						70
6	Linear	−5	−3	−1	1	3	5					70
	Quadratic	5	−1	−4	−4	−1	5					84
	Cubic	−5	7	4	−4	−7	5					180
	Quartic	1	−3	2	2	−3	1					28
7	Linear	−3	−2	−1	0	1	2	3				28
	Quadratic	5	0	−3	−4	−3	0	5				84
	Cubic	−1	1	1	0	−1	−1	1				6
	Quartic	3	−7	1	6	1	−7	3				154
8	Linear	−7	−5	−3	−1	1	3	5	7			168
	Quadratic	7	1	−3	−5	−5	−3	1	7			168
	Cubic	−7	5	7	3	−3	−7	−5	7			264
	Quartic	7	−13	−3	9	9	−3	−13	7			616
9	Linear	−4	−3	−2	−1	0	1	2	3	4		60
	Quadratic	28	7	−8	−17	−20	−17	−8	7	28		2772
	Cubic	−14	7	13	9	0	−9	−13	−7	14		990
	Quartic	14	−21	−11	9	18	9	−11	−21	14		2002
10	Linear	−9	−7	−5	−3	−1	1	3	5	7	9	330
	Quadratic	6	2	−1	−3	−4	−4	−3	−1	2	6	132
	Cubic	−42	14	35	31	12	−12	−31	−35	−14	42	8580
	Quartic	18	−22	−17	3	18	18	3	−17	−22	18	2860

Note that the coefficients in each row sum to zero.

The sum of the products of the coefficients for any two degrees of curvature is also zero (therefore orthogonal)

$$\sum\alpha^2 = \text{the sum of the squared coefficients in the row}$$

The value for a comparison is obtained by multiplying the group sums by the coefficients for the comparison. For example, in a linear comparison of three groups:

$$C_{linear} = -1\sum X_1 + 0\sum X_2 + 1\sum X_3$$

11

LINEAR REGRESSION

Correlational Research

In the previous chapters the focus was on identifying significant differences between two or more sets of scores. In this chapter the focus is on the linear relationship between two variables. It is important to distinguish between research questions that focus on differences and those that focus on relationships as the type of question has a direct influence on the statistical analysis employed by the researcher. Furthermore in an experiment the researcher manipulates the independent variable and measures the changes in the dependent variable. Holding all other variables constant, the researcher infers that any changes in the dependent variables are caused by the manipulations of the independent variable.

In contrast, a researcher may be interested in the relationship between two variables. The researcher simply measures both variables and observes the relationship between them. If a strong relationship is found the researcher cannot immediately infer a causal relationship as it is not known which is the cause and which is the effect. For example, there may be a strong relationship between performance and self-confidence. However, simply by measuring the variables and the linear relationship between them does not tell the researcher whether performance causes a change in self-confidence, or self-confidence produces a change in performance. In addition, it is always possible that any observed relationship between two variables could be the product of a third variable. Moreover, it needs to be stressed that a causal relationship cannot exist between two variables unless they are correlated. Thus, a correlation is a necessary, but not a sufficient factor for us to infer a causal relationship.

Purpose

The purpose of regression analysis is to test the degree of linear relationship between two variables.

Research Question

Linear regression is appropriate for research questions where the direction and magnitude of the linear relationship between two variables is of interest. The relationship between the two variables may then be used for predictive purposes. For example, if there is a relationship between scores in an entrance test and subsequent performance on a university course, then a prediction of an applicant's future performance may be made on the basis of his/her score on the admission test.

Null Hypothesis Tested

In linear regression and correlation the null hypothesis states that there is not a significant linear relationship between two variables. For example, there will be no significant linear relationship between hat size and intelligence.

Linear Regression

To illustrate the principles behind linear regression, consider the following example. A sports scientist was interested in the question of whether confidence was related to performance. The scientist measured the confidence of participants to perform a familiar task and then measured their performance. The results are shown in Table 11.1.

Table 11.1

	Self-confidence X	Performance Y
	3	5
	5	5
	4	6
	2	3
	3	3
	4	4
	5	6
	2	4
Σ	28	36

To get an indication of how self-confidence and performance are related, the scores on the data may be plotted on a graph known as a scattergram. This is done by plotting each individual's performance score against their self-confidence score (Figure 11.1).

This scattergram displays a trend for the two sets of scores to change in the same direction. That is, there appears to be a positive relationship between the two variables, with performance tending to increase as self-confidence increases.

If changes of a certain magnitude on one dimension always produced changes of a consistent magnitude on another dimension then the data points on the scattergram would produce a straight line. That is, a perfect linear relationship would exist between the two variables.

Although all the points do not fall on a straight line in this case, a clearer picture of the relationship emerges when a line that is equidistant from all the plotted points is drawn (Figure 11.2). In this case the line would be drawn from R to R on the graph. This line is called the regression line.

Figure 11.1 **Scattergram of performance with self-confidence**

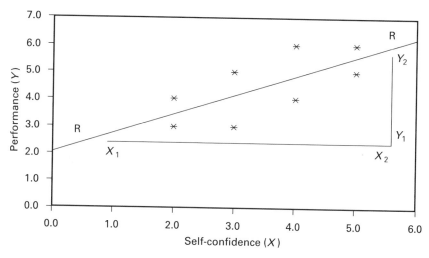

Figure 11.2 **Regression line showing the relationship of performance plotted against self-confidence**

Regression Lines

The regression line may be defined by two key characteristics. The first is the slope of the line. The slope of the line reflects the change in Y (performance) that is accompanied by a change in X (self-confidence). A steep slope means that a small change in X is accompanied by a large change in Y. A shallow slope means that a large change in X is accompanied by a small change in Y. It is quite simple to produce a value that reflects the slope of a line. To do this, consider the convention that is adopted in road traffic signs. Traffic signs previously indicated the gradient of a hill by presenting a ratio such as 1 in 10. This ratio meant that for every 10 metres travelled forward one climbs 1 metre in height. The more recent system presents this information as a percentage. In this case, the 1 in 10 sign is replaced with one that states 10%. This means that for every 100 metres travelled forward one climbs 10 metres in height. If the same convention is applied in the context of the regression line in Figure 11.2, the formula for the slope becomes

$$\text{Slope}_{(b_y)} = \frac{\text{rate of change in } Y}{\text{rate of change in } X} = \frac{Y_2 - Y_1}{X_2 - X_1}$$

The second defining characteristic of the regression line is the point at which it crosses the vertical (Y) axis, that is the value of Y when X equals zero. The point where the regression line crosses the Y-axis is known as the **Y-intercept** (a_y). In Figure 11.2, the regression line crosses the Y-axis at a value close to 2. This means that if a person has a self-confidence score of 0 we would expect their performance score to be approximately 2.

Once the slope and intercept have been identified, a straight line can be defined according to the following formula:

$$Y = a_y + (b_y)(x)$$

where a is the Y-intercept and b the slope. Therefore,

$$\text{Performance} = \text{intercept} + (\text{slope of the line} \times \text{self-confidence score})$$

If the values for the intercept and the slope of the line are known, any value for X may be entered into the equation and the corresponding value of Y calculated. In the current example, this means that if an athlete's self-confidence score is known, then their performance level may be predicted using the regression equation.

In this example, the researcher found that the scattergram did not produce a straight line; that is, there is not a perfect relationship between the two variables confidence and performance. Instead the points tended to be scattered around the regression line. This means that knowing someone's self-confidence (X) only allows an **estimation** of their performance level (Y) to be made. To show that the result of the calculation is an estimation of performance we use the notation Y' (termed Y prime) rather than Y.

Estimating the Slope

This estimation of Y' will be based on the estimation of the slope and intercept of the regression line. The formula for calculating the slope will be presented first as it is a component of the formula for estimating the intercept.

The slope takes into account how the two sets of scores X and Y vary together divided by the variation in X. In this example,

$$\text{Slope } b_y = \frac{\text{how self-confidence } (X) \text{ and performace } (Y) \text{ vary together}}{\text{variance in self-confidence}}$$

$$= \frac{\text{covariation of } X \text{ and } Y}{\text{variation of } X}$$

Covariation of X and Y refers to the degree to which the two variables covary, that is vary together. So if

$$\text{Variance of } (X) = \frac{\sum (x - \bar{x})^2}{df} = \frac{SS_x}{df}$$

and

$$\text{Variance of } (Y) = \frac{\sum (y - \bar{y})^2}{df} = \frac{SS_y}{df}$$

then

$$\text{covariance}(X, Y) = \frac{\sum (x - \bar{x})(y - \bar{y})}{df}$$

The numerator (i.e. the top line) in this equation is the sum of the products of the corresponding deviations on the X and Y variables; thus it is known as the **sum of products** or SP_{xy}.
    Therefore,

$$\text{covariance}(X, Y) = \frac{SP_{xy}}{df}$$

Remember that the slope

$$b_y = \frac{\text{covariation of } X \text{ and } Y}{\text{variation of } X}$$

Therefore

$$b_y = \frac{\text{covariance}(X, Y)}{\text{variance}(X)} = \frac{SP_{xy}/df}{SS_x/df}$$

However, because the degrees of freedom for both the numerator and the denominator are the same they cancel out. Hence

$$b_y = \frac{SP_{xy}}{SS_x}$$

Estimating the Intercept

In addition to the slope, an estimation of the Y-intercept (a_y), the point at which the regression line cuts across the Y-axis, is required. For example, this is the level of performance expected when self-confidence is zero. To calculate the intercept, the means of X and Y are substituted into the following formula:

$$a_y = \bar{Y} - (b_y)(\bar{X})$$

that is

Intercept = mean performance score − (slope × mean self-confidence score)

To illustrate using the previous example concerning self-confidence (X) and performance (Y), first work out the slope of the regression line b_y (Table 11.2).
    The mean self-confidence score $(\bar{X}) = 3.5$ and the mean performance score $(\bar{Y}) = 4.5$. Therefore

$$\text{Slope } b_y = \frac{SP_{xy}}{SS_x} = \frac{7.0}{10} = 0.70$$

Table 11.2

Self-confidence			Performance		
X	$(X-\bar{X})$	$(X-\bar{X})^2$	Y	$(Y-\bar{Y})$	$(X-\bar{X})(Y-\bar{Y})$
3	−0.5	0.25	5	0.5	−0.25
5	1.5	2.25	5	0.5	0.75
4	0.5	0.25	6	1.5	0.75
2	−1.5	2.25	3	−1.5	2.25
3	−0.5	0.25	3	−1.5	0.75
4	0.5	0.25	4	−0.5	−0.25
5	1.5	2.25	6	1.5	2.25
2	−1.5	2.25	4	−0.5	0.75
Σ 28		$(SS_x) = 10.0$	36		$(SP_{xy}) = 7.00$

This means that, on average, every single-point increase in self-confidence is accompanied by a 0.70-point increase in performance score.

Now the intercept is calculated as follows:

$$a_y = \bar{Y} - (b_y)(\bar{X}) = 4.5 - (0.70)(3.5) = 2.05$$

This means that when self-confidence measures zero, the predicted performance score is 2.05. Returning to the original scattergram for the data, it is apparent that this value is approximately where the extrapolated line cuts through the Y-axis.

Predicting from the Regression Line

Recall that once the slope and the intercept are identified, the regression line can be defined according to the following formula:

$$Y = a_y + (b_y)(X)$$

Having calculated a_y and b_y above, any value for X may be entered into the equation and the corresponding value of Y estimated. For example, if $X = 3$ then

$$Y' = 2.05 + (0.70)(3)$$

$$= 2.05 + 2.1 = 4.15$$

This means that if someone's self-confidence score is 3, their predicted performance score would be 4.15.

The accuracy of this estimation will depend on how far the scores are dispersed around the regression line. If the relationship is perfect, all the scores will fall exactly on the line. Under these conditions, the prediction would be 100% accurate. However, as the scores become more widely dispersed around the regression line, that is the relationship becomes weaker, the predictive accuracy of the line is reduced.

Correlation Coefficients

To assess the predictive value of the regression line a measure of the strength of the relationship between the two variables is necessary. The nature of the relationship between two variables is represented by a **correlation coefficient** (r).

The following presents one way of obtaining a measure of r:

$$r = \frac{\text{covariance}(X, Y)}{\sqrt{[\text{variance}(X)][\text{variance}(Y)]}}$$

$$= \frac{SP_{xy}}{\sqrt{(SS_x)(SS_y)}}$$

Using the figures from the previous example this gives us

$$r = \frac{7.0}{\sqrt{(10)(10)}} = \frac{7.0}{10} = 0.70$$

Therefore, the correlation coefficient between self-confidence and performance is 0.70.

Interpreting Correlation Coefficients

The above computation will always produce a value for the correlation coefficient between −1 and +1. The positive and negative signs indicate the direction of the relationship. A positive sign indicates that the two variables covary in the same direction. For example, the relationship between height and weight is positive. In general, taller people tend to weigh more than shorter people. Of course there are exceptions; thus the relationship is less than perfect, that is $r < 1$. On the other hand, a negative r-value suggests that the two variables covary in opposite directions. For example, the relationship between the amount of alcohol consumed and driving performance is negative. As alcohol consumption increases, driving skill decreases. The strength of the relationship is indicated by the magnitude of the r-value. If the value of the coefficient is 0 this means that there is no **linear** relationship between the two variables. If, on the other hand, the absolute value of the coefficient is 1 then there is a perfect linear relationship between the two variables.

The scattergrams presented in Figure 11.3 illustrate the approximate dispersion of data points for relationships of varying strength and direction. It is apparent from the scattergrams that the pattern of data points represents a straight line for very

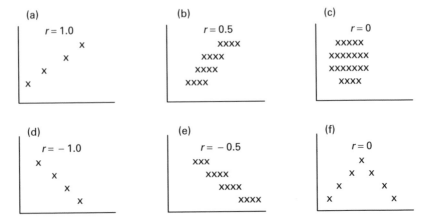

Figure 11.3 **Hypothetical scattergrams illustrating approximate relationships of varying magnitude and direction**

strong linear relationships and tends to deviate further from a straight line as the linear relationship weakens.

From the graphs in Figure 11.3 it can be noted that:

1. As the correlation becomes weaker, it becomes more difficult to predict a person's score on one variable from a knowledge of the score on the other variable.
2. Although graph (f) shows a curvilinear relationship between the two variables, this data still produces a coefficient of zero. It is for this reason that it is important to draw a scattergram before one calculates the correlation coefficient.

Reliability of *r*

One way of interpreting the reliability of an r-value is to look up its significance level in the appropriate tables. To do this one needs to know the degrees of freedom, which is always equal to the number of participants minus two ($N - 2$). In the preceding example, the critical r-value for the 5% significance level with a one-tailed hypothesis and 6 degrees of freedom is 0.62. This means that a correlation of 0.62 or greater must be observed before one can be 95% confident that the observed relationship was not obtained by chance. Note from Table 11.3 that if there were 100 participants in the study, then a correlation coefficient of 0.1638 would be statistically significant, although it may be of no practical significance because of its predictive weakness.

Table 11.3 **Critical values of the Pearson correlation coefficient**

df	$\alpha = 0.05$
1	0.9877
5	0.6694
10	0.4973
30	0.2960
100	0.1638

To illustrate what is meant by 'practical significance' it is useful to calculate and interpret the **coefficient of determination**.

Coefficient of Determination

One way of rendering a correlation coefficient more meaningful is to compute the coefficient of determination. This coefficient expresses the amount of the variance on one dimension that can be explained or accounted for by the variance on the other dimension. To compute this coefficient one simply squares the value of r and multiplies it by 100 to convert it to a percentage. So in the above example:

$$\text{Coefficient of determination} = 0.70 \times 0.70 \times 100 = 49.0\%$$

This means that 49.0% of the variance in performance scores (Y) can be explained by the variance in self-confidence scores (X). Of course, this leaves 51% of the variance in performance scores unexplained by the variance in self-confidence scores. The amount of unexplained variance provides an indication of the error involved in the prediction, that is it reflects the difference between Y and Y'.

The coefficient of determination highlights two key points:

1. That a correlation of 0.71 is required before half of the variance on one variable can be explained by changes in the other.
2. That for a correlation of 0.9 the coefficient of determination is 81%, but for a correlation of 0.3 the coefficient of determination is only 9%. This means that while a correlation of 0.9 is three times larger than a correlation of 0.3, the strength of the relationship it reflects is nine times larger as the amount of variance accounted for is nine times greater.

SPSS not only computes a value for r square but it also provides a value for what is termed the adjusted r square. This adjusted r square is the estimate of the proportion of overlapping variance that will be found in the population that the sample is drawn from. An example can be found in Table 11.5.

Pearson's Product Moment Coefficient of Correlation (r)

Correlation coefficients are commonly calculated in one of two ways depending on the level of data collected. If the data is ordinal a Spearman's rank correlation is appropriate. If the data is on an interval scale, a Pearson's product moment correlation is required. In keeping with the theme of the book, only the parametric test, Pearson's product moment correlation, will be presented. This parametric test assumes that the data is on an interval scale. It is also assumed that the scores on the two variables are normally distributed. Pearson's product moment can be computed in a variety of ways, for example

$$r = \frac{N \sum (XY) - (\sum X)(\sum Y)}{\sqrt{[N \sum X^2 - (\sum X)^2][N \sum Y^2 - (\sum Y)^2]}}$$

To use this formula one simply:

1. Totals each set of scores.
2. Squares each set of scores and sums the total.
3. Multiplies each pair of scores and sums the total.

How this works out in practice can be seen from the following exercise.

EXERCISE 11.1

Consider the values given in Table 11.4.

Table 11.4

Self-confidence X	Performance Y	X^2	Y^2	XY
3	5	9	25	15
5	5	25	25	25
4	6	16	36	24
2	3	4	9	6
3	3	9	9	9
4	4	16	16	16
5	6	25	36	30
2	4	4	16	8
Σ 28	36	108	172	133

Thus

$$r = \frac{\text{covariance}(X, Y)}{\sqrt{[\text{variance}(X)][\text{variance}(Y)]}}$$

$$= \frac{\text{SP}_{xy}}{\sqrt{(\text{SS}_x)(\text{SS}_y)}}$$

$$= \frac{N \sum(XY) - (\sum X)(\sum Y)}{\sqrt{[N \sum X^2 - (\sum X)^2][N \sum Y^2 - (\sum Y)^2]}}$$

$$= \frac{(8 \times 133) - (28 \times 36)}{\sqrt{[(8 \times 108) - 28^2][(8 \times 172) - 36^2]}}$$

$$= \frac{1064 - 1008}{\sqrt{(864 - 784)(1376 - 1296)}}$$

$$= \frac{56}{\sqrt{6400}}$$

$$= \frac{56}{80}$$

$$= 0.70$$

What does this value of r tell you about the relationship between self-confidence and performance?

....

....

What is the coefficient of determination associated with this value of r?

....

What can you conclude from this particular coefficient of determination?

....

....

Summary

Linear regression is used when a researcher is interested in the linear relationship between two variables. A plot of the subjects' scores on the two variables is called a scattergram. The line of best fit through the data points is termed the regression line. The regression line may be defined by the equation $Y = a + bX$. In this equation, a is the Y-intercept and b is the slope of the line. If one knows the intercept and slope of the regression line, one may predict the value of Y for any value of X.

The accuracy of the prediction depends on the strength of the relationship between the two variables. The stronger the relationship, the more accurate the prediction. The strength of the relationship between two variables may be determined by calculating the correlation coefficient or r. Correlation coefficients have a possible range from -1 to $+1$. The null hypothesis for a correlation states that there will be no significant relationship between the two variables (i.e. $r = 0$). As the r-value approaches ± 1 the strength of the relationship increases. A positive correlation indicates that the two variables covary in the same direction. A negative sign indicates covariation in the opposite direction. To make the correlation coefficient more meaningful, the coefficient of determination may be calculated. The coefficient of determination is simply $r^2 \times 100$ and is expressed as a percentage. This value indicates the percentage of variance in one variable that is accounted for by the variance in the other variable.

Example 11.1 Linear Regression Output Using SPSS on in Table 11.1 Data Set

Table 11.5

Model Summary

Model	R	R Square	Adjusted R Square	Std. Error of the Estimate
1	.700	.490	.405	.92

a Predictors: (Constant), SELF_CON

Table 11.5 shows that:

- The correlation coefficient between the two variables is 0.7.
- The coefficient of determination for the sample is 49%.
- The estimated coefficient of determination for the population is 40.5%.

Table 11.6

ANOVA

Model		Sum of Squares	df	Mean Square	F	Sig.
1	Regression	4.900	1	4.900	5.765	.053
	Residual	5.100	6	.850		
	Total	10.000	7			

a Predictors: (Constant), SELF_CON
b Dependent Variable: PERFORM

The F-value in Table 11.6 can be used to test the null hypothesis that there is no linear relationship between the independent and dependent variables. F is the ratio of the mean square for regression to the mean square for the residual. As the significance level associated with the observed value of F is 0.05 the null hypothesis cannot be rejected. Although 49% of the variance in performance was accounted for by self-confidence, this percentage was not statistically significant.

Table 11.7

Coefficients

Model		Unstandardized Coefficients		Standardized Coefficients	t	Sig.
		B	Std. Error	Beta		
1	(Constant)	2.050	1.071		1.914	.104
	SELF_CON	.700	.292	.700	2.401	.053

a Dependent Variable: PERFORM

In Table 11.7, the intercept (A) is termed the constant and has the value 2.050. The slope of the line (B) has the value .700. The column headed 'Std. Error' displays the standard errors of the intercept and slope values. If the intercept and slope value are divided by their respective standard errors the values displayed in the column headed 't' will be produced. For example, .700 divided by .292 results in 2.401. This t value is testing the null hypothesis that there is no linear relationship between the two variables performance and self-confidence. As the associated probability of .053 shown in the column headed 'Sig.' is greater than 0.05 the null hypothesis cannot be rejected. In the same way this *t* test is used to test the null hypothesis that the value of the intercept is zero in the population. As 2.050 divided by 1.071 results in a *t* value of 1.914, which has an associated probability of .104, so once again the null hypothesis is accepted. Finally, the column headed 'Standardized Coefficients' can be ignored for the moment as its importance will be explained in the next chapter.

Substituting these values for the intercept and the slope into the equation $Y = A + BX$ results in:

$$Performance = 2.05 + (0.700 \times the\ self\text{-}confidence\ score)$$

EXERCISE 11.2 CORRELATION AND LINEAR REGRESSION USING SPSS FOR WINDOWS

A researcher in education wanted to determine whether there is any relationship between various student activities and academic performance.

A sample of 30 sport science students from a local university were selected, and the students assessed on the following variables by means of a short questionnaire:

1. Hours spent in the pub each week.
2. Hours spent studying outside of class each week.
3. Number of pints of beer consumed each week.
4. Number of classes missed each week.
5. Average academic grade at the end of the year.
6. Average practical grade at the end of the year.

1. For three pairs of variables, state a testable hypothesis which predicts the specific expected relationship, for example: *There will be a positive relationship between 'Beer Consumed' and 'Hours in Pub'.*

   (a) ....

   (b) ....

   (c) ....

2. For each of the first four variables, state a testable hypothesis predicting the specific relationship expected between each variable and students' academic grade, for example: *There will be a negative relationship between 'Classes Missed' and 'Av. Ac. Grade'.*

   (d) ....

   (e) ....

   (f) ....

   (g) ....

3. To test a hypothesis about whether a linear relationship exists between two variables, one needs to obtain the correlation coefficient. In order to test each of the hypotheses formulated, enter the data in Table 11.8. Use the previous exercises as a guide. Remember that variables are to be listed in each column, and each participant's scores are entered on a separate row.

4. Use the **Explore** option to test for deviations from normality in each variable.

5. Choose **Correlate** from the **Analyze** menu, and click on **Bivariate**. Enter all of the variables under the **Variables** command. Click on the **Options** box, and highlight **means and standard deviations**. Then click on **Continue**.

   Make sure the **Pearson Correlation Coefficient** is highlighted and click on **OK** to run the analysis.

6. Examine the printout of the correlation matrix and then complete Table 11.9.

7. The next stage of the analysis involves predicting students' academic grades from knowledge about the time they spend studying each week. In order to make this prediction, a linear regression analysis is required.

   Choose **Regression** from the **Analyze** menu and select **Linear**. Insert **Academic grade** as the **Dependent measure**, and **Study hours** as the **Independent measure** and then click on **OK** to run the analysis.

Table 11.8

Hours in Pub	Study Hours	Beer Consumed	Classes Missed	Av. Ac. Grade	Av. Prac. Grade
26	10	50	10	42	70
15	14	12	2	54	68
3	40	14	0	66	67
14	12	10	1	64	67
21	8	0	0	44	76
10	20	14	2	58	56
5	35	2	0	72	76
6	24	12	0	60	68
14	12	26	1	60	59
12	18	30	1	67	67
6	22	12	0	70	81
18	4	18	2	57	56
22	12	11	2	59	68
35	5	50	4	40	66
30	6	24	4	41	54
1	34	12	0	74	59
0	25	5	0	70	67
2	18	0	0	61	67
6	18	0	0	65	69
10	22	12	1	69	74
8	25	0	1	70	48
6	10	10	0	55	66
20	10	30	3	50	57
15	15	22	2	49	69
15	20	12	3	60	63
12	18	10	2	54	54
6	14	0	1	58	52
1	18	0	0	59	60
0	12	10	0	72	40
10	7	12	1	45	40

Table 11.9

Hypotheses	Variables	Hyp. one or two tailed?	Correlation coefficient	Sig.	Accept or reject H_0?
(a)					
(b)					
(c)					
(d)					
(e)					
(f)					
(g)					

To obtain a scatterplot of the data, choose **Scatter** from the **Graphs** menu. Click on **Simple**. Then click on **Define**, and insert **Academic Grade** on the Y axis and **Study Hours** on the X axis. Click on **OK** to produce the scatterplot.

8. Print a copy of your results by selecting **Print** from the **File** menu.
9. To draw the regression line (the line of best fit) through the data points that graphically represent the relationship between hours studying and academic grade, solve the regression equation

$$Y' = a + bx$$

where:

a = the point where the regression line crosses the Y-axis
b = the slope of the regression line
x = the raw scores for any value of the study hours variable

These values can be obtained from the printout of the regression analysis.

The values for a and b are listed in the column headed 'Unstandardized coefficients' and then 'B'. The first value down after the 'B' is the value of a, which is reported as a constant. The next value down is the value of b and is associated with the study hours variable. Choose any values of x and you should be able to solve the equation for the corresponding Y'-value.

10. Explain what you understand from the above equation.

....

....

....

11. What is the value of r^2?   ....
12. What does the value of r^2 tell you?

....

....

Finally, using the example of SPSS output in Example 11.1 annotate your output explaining what you understand from each table and the graph.

12

MULTIPLE REGRESSION

Purpose

The previous chapter introduced linear regression as a technique for examining the relationship between two variables. Multiple regression is an extension of linear regression. This technique is used when one is interested in the linear relationship between a set of independent variables and one dependent variable. In multiple regression the independent variables are sometimes referred to as predictor variables and the dependent variable as the criterion variable.

Research Question

Multiple regression is appropriate for research questions where the relationship between two or more independent variables and one dependent variable is of interest. Multiple regression allows the researcher to make predictions of the dependent variable based on several independent variables. For example, a researcher may be interested in predicting athletic performance based upon measures of self-confidence and achievement motivation. Conclusions regarding the relative importance of the various independent variables may be drawn.

Assumptions Underlying Multiple Regression

Multiple regression is a very versatile statistical technique as the independent variables can be continuous (i.e. interval) or categorical in nature. If categorical data is used then it needs to be dummy coded (e.g. 1 for a male and 2 for a female). Scores on the dependent variable must be interval in scale.

As multiple regression is merely an extension of bivariate linear regression, only the linear relationships between the independent variables and the dependent variables are tested. If a scatterplot suggests the relationship is curvilinear then it may be possible to transform the data to a linear relationship through the use of a log transformation procedure. Multiple regression analysis assumes that the data is normally distributed.

Null Hypothesis

The null hypothesis for a regression analysis is that there will be no significant linear relationship between the set of predictors and the dependent variable. Separate null hypotheses may also be tested for the linear relationship between each independent variable and the dependent variable.

An Extension of Bivariate Regression

To illustrate the principles behind multiple regression it is simplest to start by presenting a bivariate example. Imagine that a leisure researcher was interested in the way that various features of a landscape contributed to its overall attractiveness to visitors. To investigate this the researcher carried out a pilot study in which the number of trees within eight areas of countryside 1 kilometre square were counted and then a group of participants came to a consensus on the subjective rating of attractiveness of each of the squares. The results were as shown in Table 12.1.

Table 12.1

	Number of trees (X)	Attractiveness (Y)
	3	5
	5	5
	4	6
	2	3
	3	3
	4	4
	5	6
	2	4
Σ	28	36

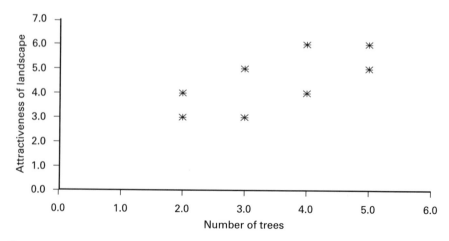

Figure 12.1 **Scattergram of attractiveness and the number of trees**

From the scattergram in Figure 12.1 drawn from this data the researcher noted a trend for the two sets of scores to change in the same direction; that is, there appears to be a positive relationship between the number of trees and the subjective ratings of attractiveness.

In this simple study, there is one independent variable (number of trees), and one dependent variable (attractiveness). This is known as bivariate regression and, as presented in the previous chapter, this analysis allows one to define the nature of this relationship in the form of a regression line. However, the researcher thought it most unlikely that the attractiveness of an area is only related to just one variable. Instead, the researcher expected that attractiveness would relate to a number of different variables, such as the area of water, the length of roads, the area of industry, the length of hedgerows, etc.

If the researcher wants to predict one dependent variable (DV) from several independent variables (IVs), multiple regression is the most appropriate analysis. Multiple regression simply involves an extension of the bivariate regression equation for a straight line.

Recall from the previous chapter that the bivariate regression equation is

$$Y' = a_y + (b_y)x$$

that is,

$$\text{Attractiveness} = \text{intercept} + (\text{slope of the regression line} \times \text{number of trees})$$

The multiple regression equation is simply an extension of this and takes the form

$$Y' = a_y + b_1x_1 + b_2x_2 + \ldots + b_kx_k$$

where

$$
\begin{aligned}
a_y &= \text{the value of the intercept} \\
b_1 &= \text{the slope (weighting) of the first variable} \\
b_2 &= \text{the slope (weighting) of the second variable} \\
b_k &= \text{the slope of the } k\text{th variable}
\end{aligned}
$$

Thus, Y' equals the value of the intercept (a_y) plus the slope of the first variable multiplied by its corresponding value, plus the slope of the second variable multiplied by its corresponding value, and so on for each IV.

The goal of multiple regression is to arrive at the set of values for b_k, called regression coefficients, that bring the Y'-values predicted from the equation as close as possible to the actual Y-values obtained by measurement. To understand the ways in which it does this the different types of multiple regression need to be considered.

There are three broad types of multiple regression:

1. standard multiple regression
2. hierarchical regression
3. statistical (stepwise and setwise) regression.

These methods differ in how they deal with overlapping variability due to correlated IVs and in how they determine the order of entry of IVs into the equation. To illustrate the idea of overlapping variability due to correlated IVs, consider the following which extends the example introduced in the previous chapter. A researcher is interested in predicting athletic performance based on self-confidence and now with the addition of achievement motivation as a second IV. A bivariate linear relationship exists between each of the IVs and performance. Also, there is a linear relationship between the two IVs. In order to identify the contribution of self-confidence and achievement motivation to performance, the researcher must take into account the fact that the two predictors share some overlapping variability.

The way in which this overlapping variance is statistically taken into account is by partial and semi-partial correlation. An understanding of partial and semi-partial correlation is useful, but not essential, for conducting multiple regression analyses. The same basic principles are illustrated graphically through the use of the Venn diagram later in this chapter.

Partial Correlation

The correlation between any two variables may be the result of their common dependence on some third variable. In the above example, some part of the correlation between achievement motivation and performance may be the result of their common relationship with self-confidence. The process of excluding the influence of this third variable before establishing the relationship between the first two is known as partialing out the effect of the third variable. This is written as

$r_{12.3}$ = correlation between variables 1 and 2 (r_{12}) with variable 3 held constant

The general formula for this is

$$r_{12.3} = \frac{r_{12} - r_{13}r_{23}}{\sqrt{1 - r_{13}^2}\sqrt{1 - r_{23}^2}}$$

Imagine that the correlation coefficients among the three variables in the example are as shown in Figure 12.2. AM, PE and SC represent achievement motivation, performance and self-confidence respectively.

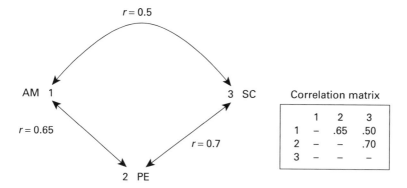

Figure 12.2 Correlation coefficients between achievement motivation, performance and self-confidence

Entering the appropriate values from the correlation matrix into the equation, the calculation of the correlation between variables 1 and 2 with variable 3 partialed out would proceed as follows:

$$r_{12.3} = \frac{0.65 - (0.50 \times 0.70)}{\sqrt{1 - 0.50^2}\sqrt{1 - 0.7^2}}$$

$$= \frac{0.65 - 0.35}{\sqrt{1 - 0.25}\sqrt{1 - 0.49}}$$

$$= \frac{0.30}{\sqrt{0.75}\sqrt{0.51}}$$

$$= \frac{0.30}{0.866 \times 0.714}$$

$$= \frac{0.30}{0.618} = 0.485$$

The correlation between variables 1 and 2 when variable 3 is held constant is 0.485. Note that this value is less than the value of 0.65 as shown in the correlation matrix. The difference between the two correlation values reflects the amount of overlap in variables 1 and 2 that was due to their common relationship with variable 3.

When only one variable is held constant, as in the above example, this is known as a **first-order partial correlation**. When two variables are held constant, this is known as a **second-order partial correlation**. To calculate the correlation that would occur between variables 1 and 2 with the effects of variables 3 and 4 eliminated, the general formula is

$$r_{12.34} = \frac{r_{12.3} - r_{14.3}r_{24.3}}{\sqrt{1 - r_{14.3}^2}\sqrt{1 - r_{24.3}^2}}$$

To solve this equation one must first solve the three first-order partial correlation coefficients, namely $r_{12.3}$, $r_{14.3}$, $r_{24.3}$.

To summarise, partial correlation is a useful statistical technique that allows a researcher to identify the relationship between two variables when the influence of one or more other variables is controlled.

Semi-partial Correlation

In partial correlation, the contribution of the third variable is removed from both key variables of interest. Sometimes it is useful to partial out the influence of a third variable on only one of the two key variables. This is known as a semi-partial correlation. Returning to the previous example of athletic performance semi-partial correlation would allow the researcher to remove the influence of self-confidence on achievement motivation whilst maintaining the influence of self-confidence on performance.

$r_{1(2\,3)}$ = relationship between variables 1 and 2 after relationship between variables 3 and 2 is partialed out

Semi-partial correlation coefficients are used in multiple regression analysis to provide a measure of the strength of the unique relationship between an IV and the DV. This is achieved by taking the square root of the change in R^2 that results from adding a new variable to the equation.

Overlapping Variance

It is not necessary to fully understand partial and semi-partial correlation to undertake multiple regression analysis. The problem addressed by these statistical techniques is graphically illustrated by considering the Venn diagram in Figure 12.3. In this example there are three IVs and one DV. A circle represents each variable. The area of the circle can be considered to represent all of the variance within that variable. The common area shared by each IV and the DV represents the variance in the DV accounted for by that IV. Thus, the total area of the DV overlapping with all the IVs is the total amount of variance in the DV explained by the set of IVs. The area of overlap in the respective IVs represents the degree to which each IV shares a common variance with another IV.

From the diagram it is apparent that IV1 and IV3 both overlap with the DV but do not overlap each other; therefore each makes a separate contribution to our understanding of the variance within the DV. IV3 also overlaps IV2 and this suggests that these two variables are associated with each other, that is changes in one

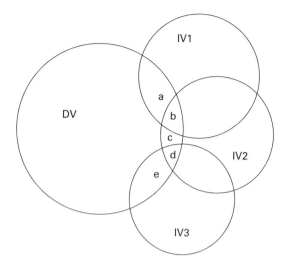

Figure 12.3 **Venn diagram illustrating overlapping variance**

are associated with changes in the other. However, some difficulty is caused by the fact that IV3's overlap with IV2 includes parts of IV2 that overlap the DV, that is area 'd'. This means that both explain a common variance in the DV. Where the same area of the DV is covered by more than one IV it is difficult to attribute this portion of the variance to any one variable. The following section presents different methods for dealing with this overlapping variance.

Standard Multiple Regression (known as Enter in SPSS)

In standard multiple regression, all of the IVs are entered into the regression model at the same time. However, each IV is assessed as if it had entered the equation after all other IVs had been entered. Each is assessed in terms of what it adds to the prediction of the DV that is different from that already covered by the other IVs. In other words, the relationship between each IV and the DV is established with the contributions of the other IVs partialed out. Thus, this type of multiple regression analysis is an elaborate application of the semi-partial correlation technique introduced earlier. Areas of the DV that are overlapped by more than one IV are taken into account in the total variance explained by the set of IVs, but not assigned to any one particular IV.

Thus, in terms of the diagram in Figure 12.3, IV1 is credited with explaining 'a', IV2 with 'c' and IV3 with 'e'; 'b' and 'd' are accounted for with the total variance explained, but are not attributed to any particular IV.

Hierarchical Multiple Regression

In hierarchical regression, IVs enter the equation in an order specified by the researcher. From Figure 12.3 note that the importance of each IV will depend upon the order in which it is entered into the equation. The researcher normally assigns the order of variable entry according to logical or theoretical considerations.

In Figure 12.3, if theoretical considerations were to suggest that the variables should be entered in the order 1, 2, 3, we would find that IV1 is credited with explaining 'a' and 'b', IV2 with 'c' and 'd', and IV3 with 'e'. Compared with standard multiple regression, the total amount of variance explained remains the same but the relative contribution of the IVs changes.

Statistical Regression

In statistical regression (generically called stepwise) the order of variable entry is based solely on statistical criteria. There are three types of statistical regression: forward selection, backward deletion and stepwise regression.

In forward selection, IVs are entered in the order of the magnitude of their bivariate correlation with the DV. The IV with the highest correlation with the DV is entered first. Then the next highest is entered and so on. The analysis is stopped when the addition of new variables no longer makes a significant improvement in the prediction of the DV. In backward deletion, all IVs are entered initially and then they are deleted one at a time if they do not contribute significantly to the regression equation. In stepwise regression, IVs are added one at a time according to the statistical criteria but they may also be deleted at any step when they no longer contribute significantly to the regression.

In applying stepwise regression to the problem of overlapping variance illustrated in the Venn diagram, note that IV1 is credited with explaining 'a' and 'b', but then as this would reduce the contribution of IV2, IV3 would be entered next and credited with 'e' and 'd'. Finally IV2 would be entered and credited with 'c'. Again, the total amount of variance explained in the DV is the same as that under the other two methods presented earlier, but the relative contribution of each IV changes. For ease of comparison, Table 12.2 presents the relative contribution of each IV produced by the three different regression procedures.

Table 12.2 **Portion of variance explained by each IV using three different regression procedures**

IV	Portion of DV explained by each IV		
	Standard	**Hierarchical**	**Stepwise**
IV1	a	a and b	a and b
IV2	c	c and d	c
IV3	e	e	d and e

Ratio of Cases to IVs

Recall from Chapter 10 that the significance of a correlation coefficient is highly dependent upon the sample size. With small samples, a very strong correlation is necessary in order to reach statistical significance, whilst with a very large sample, very small correlation coefficients may be statistically significant. These facts have implications for the ratio of cases (participants) to IVs in multiple regression.

Tabachnick and Fidell (1996) provide guidelines for the minimum number of cases to IVs. With either standard or hierarchical regression, they suggest a minimum of 50 cases plus 8 cases for each IV. For example, in a study with five IVs, the minimum sample size would be $50 + (8 \times 5)$, or 90. In stepwise regression, a ratio of 40 to 1 is recommended.

Type I and Type II Errors in Multiple Regression

When previously discussing planned contrasts within ANOVA models, concern was expressed about the increased risk of committing a Type I error when multiple contrasts were conducted. In the same way, when a multiple regression analysis is carried out, multiple tests of R are executed. This problem becomes more acute when a stepwise method is employed as a whole series of repeated tests are undertaken. Whilst a number of well-documented procedures exist for addressing this concern in ANOVA models, this topic is less fully discussed within the literature for multiple regression analyses. Cohen and Cohen (1983) argue that the potential risk of committing Type 1 errors should initially be minimised by reducing the number of IVs. They write that 'having more variables when fewer are possible increases the risks of both finding things that are not so and failing to find things that are' (page 170). Researchers should be guided by theory in their selection of the IVs and employ reliable and valid measures that display a minimum amount of inter-relationships between the independent measures (collinearity). Cohen and Cohen conclude by stating that a 'general principle in research inference is succinctly stated: "less is more" – more statistical test validity, more power, and more clarity in the meaning of results.'

Grouping the IVs according to their importance to the research question can further refine this approach of rationalising the number of IVs. Then, by employing a hierarchical regression analysis, those that are most central can be entered first, whilst those that are less important can be entered later with an increased risk of a Type I error. The results from the IVs that are not central provide the basis for future research hypotheses rather than conclusions.

Cohen and Cohen go on to suggest that the strategy employed in ANOVA analysis of examining the omnibus F before looking at the individual effects should be copied in multiple regression. Recall from Example 11.1 that the overall F indicates whether a significant relationship exists between the predictor(s) and the DV. This means that the role of individual predictors should only be examined after the overall F for the multiple regression analysis is found to be statistically significant. This prevents the comparison on 95% of the occasions when the overall null hypothesis is true. By following this procedure, they state that 'the t tests are protected from the mounting up of small per-comparison α to large experiment-wise error rates' (page 174). The use of **Backwards** regression in SPSS conforms to the suggestions made by Cohen and Cohen. The **Backwards** method first executes a standard (**Enter**) method and then removes non-significant predictors in a stepwise fashion. If the initial inclusion of all variables in the model does not provide a significant overall F then there is no need to examine the individual predictors.

The following is a simple example of a backwards multiple regression analysis. Read through this analysis and note the explanatory comments. The understanding gained from this reading should then make the subsequent section more meaningful.

Example 12.1 SPSS Multiple Regression Output from the data presented in Table 12.1

A researcher was interested in the contribution of three landscape features to the overall rating of a land's attractiveness. To this end, 10 areas of countryside 1 kilometre square were surveyed for the area of trees, water and length of hedgerows (Table 12.3). A group of participants then came to a consensus on the subjective rating of attractiveness of each of the squares.

Table 12.3 **Survey Results of six areas of countryside 1 kilometre square**

Attractiveness rating	Area of trees	Area of water	Length of hedges
18	19	19	8
9	8	11	5
8	14	10	4
8	10	7	6
5	8	9	4
12	9	11	6
15	13	16	6
3	2	4	2
6	4	7	4
7	8	8	5

A multiple regression analysis was carried out to determine the contribution of each of the landscape features towards the attractiveness rating of the areas surveyed. The results from SPSS and a scattergram of the data (Figure 12.4), which displays the three regression lines, are shown below.

A backward regression method was adopted for this analysis. First, all the IVs are entered at once and then those variables with significance levels below the default criterion of 0.1 are removed (Table 12.4).

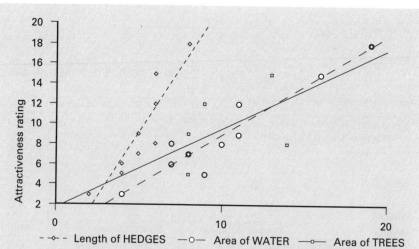

Figure 12.4 **Scattergram of attractiveness against the three predictor variables**

The numbers in the column headed 'Model' refer to steps. So from Table 12.4 it is apparent that on step 1 all three predictors were entered and then on step 2 the variable TREES was removed.

Table 12.4

Variables Entered/Removed

Model	Variables Entered	Variables Removed	Method
1	HEDGES, TREES, WATER	.	Enter
2	.	TREES	Backward (criterion: Probability of F-to-remove >= .100).

a All requested variables entered.
b Dependent Variable: ATTRACT

Table 12.5 shows that R^2 was 0.950 when all three predictors were included on step 1. This means that 95% of the variance in attractiveness is associated with changes in the variables of hedges, trees and water for this sample. The estimated coefficient of determination for the population (i.e. adjusted R^2) is 92.4%. In step 2 in the table, when the variable TREES is removed, then there was a very slight reduction in both these figures.

In Table 12.6 ANOVA tests the null hypothesis that there is no linear relationship between the predictors and the DV. F is the ratio of the mean square for regression to the mean square for the residual. For model 1, when all three predictors are entered, the significance level associated with the observed value

Table 12.5

Model Summary

Model	R	R Square	Adjusted R Square	Std. Error of the Estimate
1	.974	.950	.924	1.2724
2	.974	.948	.934	1.1938

a Predictors: (Constant), HEDGES, TREES, WATER
b Predictors: (Constant), HEDGES, WATER

Table 12.6

ANOVA

Model		Sum of Squares	df	Mean Square	F	Sig.
1	Regression	183.187	3	61.062	37.719	.000
	Residual	9.713	6	1.619		
	Total	192.900	9			
2	Regression	182.924	2	91.462	64.179	.000
	Residual	9.976	7	1.425		
	Total	192.900	9			
	Total	192.900	9			

a Predictors: (Constant), HEDGES, TREES, WATER
b Predictors: (Constant), HEDGES, WATER
c Dependent Variable: ATTRACT

of F is 0.000. Thus, the null hypothesis can be rejected and we may conclude that there is a significant linear relationship between the set of IVs and the DV. Note the increase in the F-value in model 2 when the variable TREES is removed. The F-value increases as there is little change in the sum of squares, but df is reduced from 3 to 2.

Table 12.7 displays the values of the coefficients in the regression equation and measures the probability that a linear relationship exists between each predictor variable and the DV. In this table 'B' is the slope of the line. 'SE B' is the standard error of 'B'. 'Beta' is the standardised regression coefficient. 'Sig'. is the significance level for the test of the null hypothesis that the value of a coefficient is zero in the population. In model 1, the 'Sig'. value for trees is greater than 0.05 (0.7012). Therefore, the null hypothesis that there is no linear relationship between this predictor and attractiveness cannot be rejected. As a result, the variable TREES is removed in model 2. All of the remaining variables in model 2 have significance values less than the criterion of 0.1. Thus, the null hypothesis for water and hedges may be rejected. Significant linear relationships exist between water and attractiveness and hedges and attractiveness.

Table 12.7

Coefficients

Model		Unstandardized Coefficients			Standardized Coefficients	t	Sig.
		B	Std. Error		Beta		
1	(Constant)	-3.165	1.403			-2.256	.065
	TREES	-7.215E-02	.179		-.076	-.403	.701
	WATER	.730	.207		.700	3.519	.013
	HEDGES	1.101	.467		.388	2.356	.057
2	(Constant)	-3.037	1.282			-2.369	.050
	WATER	.679	.153		.651	4.423	.003
	HEDGES	1.043	.417		.368	2.500	.041

a Dependent Variable: ATTRACT

The final table (Table 12.8) provides the coefficients for the excluded variable TREES.

Table 12.8

Excluded Variables

Model		Beta In	t	Sig.	Partial Correlation	Collinearity Statistics
						Tolerance
2	TREES	-.076	-.403	.701	-.162	.233

a Predictors in the Model: (Constant), HEDGES, WATER
b Dependent Variable: ATTRACT

The resulting regression equation is

$$\text{Attractiveness} = -3.165 + 0.679(\text{WATER}) + 1.043(\text{HEDGES})$$

This equation estimates that for the sample surveyed 94.8% of the variance in the DV (*attractiveness*) is explained by the area of water and the length of the hedgerows contained in the ten selected one-kilometre squares.

Terms and Concepts Displayed in Example 12.1

Multiple R

This coefficient reflects the strength of the relationship between the DV and the combination of IVs which have been weighted according to the regression equation (i.e. $Y' = a_y + b_1x_1 + b_2x_2 + \ldots + b_kx_k$). R-values have a potential range of zero to one. An R-value of 0 indicates no linear relationship between the set of predictors and the DV. The higher the R-value, the stronger the linear relationship between the set of predictors and the DV.

R Square

It was noted in the previous chapter that one way of rendering a correlation coefficient more meaningful is to compute the coefficient of determination (R^2). In multiple regression analysis, this coefficient expresses the amount of the variance in the DV that is shared by the combination of the weighted IVs. As with R, R^2 will have a value that falls between 0 and 1. Multiplying R^2 by 100 allows the amount of variance to be stated as a percentage. To work out the proportion of the variance that is not shared, and hence not predicted by the IVs, simply take the value of R^2 away from 1. For example, an R of 0.7 would produce an R^2 of 0.49. This suggests that 0.49 (49%) of the variance in the DV is shared by the predictor variables; therefore 0.51 (51%) is not shared. Thus, R^2 can be considered a measure of the goodness of fit of the model produced by the regression equation.

Standard Error

The regression equation allows one to compute predicted values for each participant on the DV and then compare these with the actual score. Unless the model is perfect (i.e. R^2 has a value of 1), then there will be a difference between the predicted and observed scores. These differences reflect errors in the model and are known as error scores or residual scores. Chapter 2 discussed the utility of describing a data set in terms of its dispersion. In the same way, a description of the dispersion of error scores may be obtained by computing their standard deviation. This standard deviation of the error scores is known as the standard error and it provides a general indication of the average error in the prediction. Therefore, a model that has a high goodness of fit would produce a low standard error. There will be a relatively good match between the predicted and observed values of the DV.

B (Slope of the Regression Line)

B is the partial regression coefficient. As discussed in Chapter 10, the regression coefficient defines the direction and magnitude of the slope of the regression line. For example, a B-value of -1.5 means that with every increase of one unit of the IV the equation predicts a decrease of 1.5 units of the DV. The use of the term partial means that this effect is predicted after the influence of all the other IVs has been statistically controlled.

'Beta' (Standardized Slope of the Regression Line)

The slope, indicated by the value of B, is influenced by the scale upon which the IV was measured. As different IVs may be measured on scales of very different units, it is very difficult to compare their relative influence. The use of standardised scores may overcome this difficulty. Recall from Chapter 2 that standardised scores are calculated by finding the difference between a score and the mean in units of standard deviation. That is, subtract the mean from each score and divide by the standard deviation. Regression analysis based on standardised scores for both the IVs and the DV would produce identical B and 'Beta' values. This would allow comparison of the effects of different IVs by comparing their B values. However, there is a simpler strategy, and to illustrate this consider the situation where there is one IV called W and one DV called Y. If the slope B for W is multiplied by the ratio of the standard deviation of W divided by the standard deviation of the Y this will produce the standardised regression coefficient 'Beta'. That is:

$$\text{'Beta'}_W = B_W \left(\frac{S_W}{S_Y} \right)$$

Thus, if 'Beta' for a particular IV equals 0.5 this means that a one standard deviation increase in the IV predicts 0.5 of a standard deviation increase in the DV. 'Beta' values allow meaningful comparisons regarding the degree of predicted change on the DV associated with changes in a number of IVs. The variable with the largest 'Beta' will have the most relative influence on the DV. One should be cautious when interpreting the 'Beta' values as they are not absolute but depend upon the other IVs in the equation.

R^2 Change

As variables are added to a regression analysis they will cause an increase in R^2. This does not mean that there is an increase in the goodness of fit for the regression equation. In fact, the standard error may actually increase. In evaluating the consequences of adding new variables, one takes into account the change in R^2 produced by the addition of the new variable. R^2 change is simply the difference in the value of R^2 before and after adding the new variable.

A measure of the strength of the independent relationship between the new IV and the DV can be obtained by taking the square root of the change in R^2. This is known as the semi-partial correlation coefficient. Its value will usually be smaller than the simple bivariate correlation between this IV and the DV as all the linear effects of the previous IVs have been removed. The direction of this relationship can be found from the corresponding partial regression coefficient.

Multicollinearity

Collinearity refers to the correlations among IVs. This can be assessed by examining a correlation matrix for the IVs. If there is a high degree of collinearity between two or more IVs, for example $r > 0.7$, then this raises two issues.

The first issue refers to the question of whether the variables are actually measuring different constructs. The purpose of multiple regression is to produce the most parsimonious explanation of the changes in the DV based on two or more predictors. Therefore, it makes little sense to include IVs that are highly correlated as they would not be making a unique contribution to the regression equation. The ideal equation includes a small number of IVs, each of which makes a unique and significant contribution to the overall prediction of the DV.

The second issue is concerned with the difficulty of separating the individual contribution made by each IV to the prediction of changes in the DV. Recall from the previous discussion of the different multiple regression methods (e.g. stepwise, Enter, etc.), the issue of crediting the shared variance to the IVs. This shared variance, which is known as redundant variance, could be the product of any one variable or it may be the product of two or more. This difficulty is the Achilles' heel of multiple regression analysis. However, rather than looking for a statistical solution, the researcher should be guided by the theoretical foundations that originally led to the research question. This theoretical framework may suggest the order in which the IVs should be entered through a hierarchical method and so determine the allocation of the predicted variance.

Summary

Multiple regression is used to examine the relationship between a set of two or more IVs and one DV. The overall strength of the relationship between the set of IVs and the DV is reflected by the multiple R statistic. The coefficient of determination (R^2) provides an indication of the proportion of variance in the DV that is accounted for by the set of IVs. Multiple regression provides the information necessary to make predictions of the DV based on several IVs. To do so, the bivariate equation introduced earlier in this chapter is extended to $Y' = a_y + b_1x_1 + b_2x_2 + \dots + b_kx_k$. The regression coefficients (b) reflect the direction and magnitude of change in Y associated with each change in x. As the size of b is a function of the scale on which it was measured, standardised regression coefficients (Betas values) are interpreted to determine the relative influence of the various IVs. Three different types of multiple regression analyses were discussed: standard multiple regression, hierarchical multiple regression, and statistical (stepwise and setwise) multiple regression. Each method differs in the way that it deals with the problem of overlapping variance among the IVs.

EXERCISE 12.1 MULTIPLE REGRESSION I

In Exercise 11.2 you produced a correlation matrix which indicated the linear relationship between the following variables: (1) hours per week spent in a pub; (2) hours per week spent studying outside of class; (3) beer consumption in pints per week; (4) number of classes missed per week; (5) academic grade; and (6) practical grade.

From the correlation matrix one was able to test specific hypotheses concerning the bivariate relationship between the various student activities and academic performance. To investigate this topic further one might ask:

What student activities are the best predictors of academic success?

The answer to this question may be found through the use of multiple regression. This technique is designed to determine the relationships between variables, but unlike a correlation coefficient which indicates the linear relationship between two variables, multiple regression analysis determines the relationship between two or more predictor variables (e.g. hours in pub and study hours) and one criterion variable (e.g. academic performance).

As can be seen in the correlation matrix produced from the exercise, all variables are related to each other in some way. Multiple regression accounts for this fact in determining which are the best predictors of academic grade.

To conduct this multiple regression exercise, retrieve the data entered from Exercise 11.2. Usually one would use the **Explore** option to test for normality but this was already done for the previous exercise.

1. Click on **Regression** in the **Analyze** menu, and select **Linear**.
2. Select **Academic Grade** as the **dependent variable**, and insert hours per week spent in a pub, hours per week spent studying outside of class, beer consumption in pints per week and the number of classes missed per week as the **independent variables**.
3. Click on **Statistics** and make sure that **descriptives** is highlighted.
4. Select **Backward** as the method of analysis.
5. Click on **OK** to run the analysis.
6. Complete Table 12.9.

Table 12.9

Correlation Coefficients with Average Academic Grade

IVs	R	R Square	Rank Order Based on Value of R
STUD_HRS			
PUB_HRS			
BEER			
CLASS_MS			
	TOTAL		

7. What is 'R Square' a measure of?

   ....

8. What does it mean if the total of the 'R Square' values is greater than 1?

   ....

   ....

9. Which two predictor variables have the strongest relationship to each other?

   ....

10. Which predictor variable has the weakest relationship with the dependent variable?

   ....

11. Which predictor variable was removed first by the **Backward** selection procedure?

   ....

12. In the 'Model Summary' table, what happens to the value of 'R Square' as predictor variables are removed and why does this occur?

   ....

   ....

13. In the 'ANOVA' table, what happens to the value of F and its associated significance as predictor variables are removed and why does this occur?

   ....

   ....

   ....

14. In the 'Coefficients' table what are the t-values a measure of?

   ....

15. Using the values in the 'Coefficients' table specify the final regression equation that predicts academic grade?

   ....

16. In the 'Coefficients' table what do the 'Beta' values measure?

   ....

   ....

17. What can be concluded from this analysis?

   ....

   ....

   ....

Table 12.10

Motive	Entrance	FirstYr	Grade
35	21	54	60
24	16	61	50
40	17	70	66
42	14	56	66
45	22	42	68
25	17	60	41
20	15	45	39
18	18	40	42
36	19	60	54
34	14	56	52
39	14	58	61
34	16	52	58
44	14	62	73
42	17	73	50
34	19	70	55
20	22	63	61
18	13	48	22
43	20	55	64
38	18	60	72
26	16	58	60

EXERCISE 12.2 MULTIPLE REGRESSION II

In order to supplement your income, you have been employed by the university administrators to determine how well we can predict academic performance in the final year (Grade). This prediction is to be made from: (a) a measure of motivation assessed in the first year (Motive), (b) entrance exam performance (Entrance), and (c) performance in the first-year exams (FirstYr) (see Table 12.10).

1. Write a hypothesis indicating the degree to which you think each of the stated variables will predict academic performance in the final year.
2. To test your hypothesis using multiple regression analysis, follow the instructions from the previous exercise.
3. Examine your printout and write a sentence or two explaining whether or not your hypotheses were supported. Indicate which were the best predictors of academic performance in the final year.

References

Cohen, J. and Cohen, P. (1983) *Applied Multivariate regression/Correlation Analysis for the Behavioral Sciences* (2nd edn). New York: Erlbaum.

Tabachnick, B.G. and Fidell, L.S. (1996) *Using Multivariate Statistics* (3rd edn). New York: Harper Collins College Publishers.

13

TWO FINAL EXERCISES

EXERCISE 13.1 HYPOTHESIS WRITING AND TEST SELECTION

The following tasks describe a series of research investigations. For each task you are to:

1. Write a research question
2. Write appropriate null and alternate hypotheses
3. Identify the number of independent variables
4. Identify the number of dependent variables
5. Recommend an appropriate statistical analysis (with reasons for choice)
6. Outline the assumptions that the chosen statistical technique makes (e.g. type of data, distribution of data).

In completing this first exercise you may find it helpful to look at the data that is presented in exercise 13.2 on data analysis.

Scenario One

A physiotherapist has experience of treating a large number of lower body injuries in athletes who have visited her clinic. The physiotherapist's curiosity leads her towards attempting to discover whether the number of lower body injuries sustained is a function of the particular sport in which the athletes engage. She obtains a sample of elite athletes from four different sports (rugby, soccer, hockey, track and field) and examines the athletes' injury records which have been supplied by sports medicine staff associated with each athlete's home club. From this data, she is able to measure the number of lower body injuries each athlete has sustained over the last year.

Scenario Two

A smoker, sceptical about information that has been disseminated by the medical community warning against the dangers of smoking, decides to conduct a personal investigation to determine whether cigarette smoking influences longevity in his home town. He wrote to the local authority and obtained both the age of local residents at the time of death and average number of cigarettes smoked per day over the course of a lifetime.

Scenario Three

A leisure researcher was interested in determining whether age and sex had any bearing upon the amount of time adults engaged in leisure activities. After obtaining data on the average amount of time individuals engaged in leisure activities each week from a representative sample of the population, she divided the sample according to sex, and further subdivided the sample into young adults, middle-aged adults and older adults.

Scenario Four

A cardiologist, worried about the risks of coronary heart disease in his patients, decided to investigate the effects of putting the patients on a low-fat diet in conjunction with regular physical exercise. As the accumulation of cholesterol deposits in the arteries accounted for 50% of the deaths in the USA in 1986, he decided to measure the LDL/HDL ratio (low-density lipoproteins to high-density lipoproteins) in his patients before initiating a plan of diet and exercise, then again after six months of adherence to the diet and exercise regime.

Scenario Five

A researcher was interested in the extent to which heart disease in the form of the amount of atherosclerosis (i.e. a hardening of the arteries) could be predicted by: advancing age, elevated levels of serum cholesterol, obesity, inactivity and Type A Behaviour Pattern. She collected data from a sample of patients on all of these variables. On each scale the higher the value the more of the variable they displayed.

Scenario Six

A researcher was interested in the influence of arousal on attentional breadth. He believed that as arousal increased, the attentional span of an individual would decrease. In addition, he argued that if participants were given a primary task and secondary task to complete at the same time, known as a dual-task paradigm, the influence of arousal would be most notable on the performance of the secondary task.

To test this argument he first of all divided his participants into two groups according to whether they were experts or novices at performing the primary task. He then measured half of the participants' performance on both tasks over a 5 minute period when they displayed low levels of arousal. This situation was then repeated when these participants' arousal levels had been experimentally manipulated to a high level. These two procedures were then reversed for the remaining half of the participants in an attempt to counterbalance for order effects.

EXERCISE 13.2 DATA ANALYSIS

In the previous exercise you determined the research questions being asked by the investigators, devised testable hypotheses, and established the most appropriate statistical analyses in order to obtain answers to the research questions. For each of the tasks, you must now enter the corresponding data, extract the most useful descriptive statistics, and conduct the analysis that you previously suggested as the most appropriate.

Once you have analysed the data, and obtained a printout of the results for each task, you should the answer the following six questions:

1. What do you interpret from the descriptive statistics?
2. What do you interpret from the graphical representations?
3. Are the assumptions of the statistical technique met?
4. What should be inferred from the statistical test employed?
5. Which hypotheses do you accept and which do you reject?
6. What do you conclude with respect to the research question?

Scenario One

A physiotherapist has experience of treating a large number of lower body injuries in athletes who have visited her clinic. The physiotherapist's curiosity leads her toward attempting to discover whether the number of lower body injuries sustained is a function of the particular sport in which the athletes engage. She obtains a sample of elite athletes from four different sports (rugby, soccer, hockey, track and field) and examines the athletes' injury records that have been supplied by sports medicine staff associated with each athlete's home club. From this data, she is able to measure the number of lower body injuries each athlete has sustained over the last year. The data given in Table 13.1 was obtained.

Table 13.1 **Sports injury data**

Rugby	Soccer	Hockey	Track and field
3	9	2	8
4	12	1	4
2	15	3	7
0	10	7	9
8	13	1	6
4	12	4	8
0	8	2	7
6	4	1	9
4	10	6	10
7	7	0	4

Scenario Two

A smoker, sceptical about information that has been disseminated by the medical community warning against the dangers of smoking, decides to conduct a personal investigation to determine whether cigarette smoking influences longevity in his home town. He wrote to the local authority and obtained both the age of local residents at the time of death and the average number of cigarettes smoked per day over the course of a lifetime. The data given in Table 13.2 was obtained.

Table 13.2 **Smoking and longevity data**

Cigarettes/day	Age at death	Cigarettes/day	Age at death
0	85	4	61
10	66	25	62
5	70	30	58
12	64	0	79
1	82	0	78
0	88	0	90
0	94	2	69
2	73	0	79
25	57	40	47
20	60	20	58
30	48	10	66
6	69	0	70
0	85	0	59
0	82	1	66
1	75	2	72

Scenario Three

A leisure researcher was interested in determining whether age and sex had any bearing upon the amount of time adults engaged in leisure activities. After obtaining data on the average amount of time individuals engaged in leisure activities each week from a representative sample of the population, she divided the sample according to sex, and further subdivided the sample into young adults, middle-aged adults and older adults. The data in Table 13.3 was obtained.

Table 13.3 **Leisure data**

Male			Female		
Young	Mid age	Old	Young	Mid age	Old
24	12	16	26	4	8
20	10	14	20	2	2
16	6	20	16	8	4
12	6	22	20	6	4
28	4	20	15	4	12
24	8	18	18	6	16
22	8	12	24	8	2
18	6	16	22	2	8
19	12	24	19	2	6
22	2	22	18	8	8

Scenario Four

A cardiologist, worried about the risks of coronary heart disease in his patients, decided to investigate the effects of putting the patients on a low-fat diet in conjunction with regular physical exercise. As the accumulation of cholesterol deposits in the arteries accounted for 50% of the deaths in the USA in 1986, he decided to measure the LDL/HDL ratio (low-density lipoproteins to high-density lipoproteins) in his patients before initiating a plan of diet and exercise, then again after six months of adherence to the diet and exercise regime. The data in Table 13.4 was obtained.

Table 13.4 **Cholesterol data**

LDL/HDL pre	LDL/HDL post
6.1	4.2
5.6	5.2
4.7	3.1
4.9	4.0
6.7	5.1
5.6	5.0
6.3	4.5
5.2	4.1
6.3	4.8
5.7	4.5
5.4	4.4
5.3	5.0
4.6	4.0
4.9	4.2
4.2	3.8
4.8	4.2
5.8	4.2
5.2	5.0
6.1	4.4
5.8	4.6

Scenario Five

A researcher was interested in the extent to which heart disease in the form of the amount of atherosclerosis (i.e. a hardening of the arteries) could be predicted by: advancing age, elevated levels of serum cholesterol, obesity, inactivity and Type A Behaviour Pattern. She collected data from a sample of patients on all of these variables. On each scale the higher the value the more of the variable they displayed. The data in Table 13.5 was obtained.

Scenario Six

A researcher was interested in the influence of arousal on attentional breadth. He believed that as arousal increased, the attentional span of an individual would

Table 13.5

Age	Cholesterol	Obesity	Inactivity	Type A	Atherosclerosis
30	13	15	5	15	4
55	16	12	7	14	6
48	14	12	7	17	7
72	9	11	5	12	5
65	12	14	6	15	7
45	13	15	7	18	8
67	16	17	9	15	9
53	9	12	4	20	8
57	12	10	6	16	7
70	10	10	7	15	9
38	16	8	8	14	6
56	13	15	8	12	4
63	15	17	7	15	5
56	18	14	9	16	7
49	19	18	9	18	9

decrease. In addition, he argued that if participants were given a primary task and secondary task to complete at the same time, known as a dual-task paradigm, the influence of arousal would be most notable on the performance of the secondary task.

To test this argument he first of all divided his participants into two groups according to whether they were experts or novices at performing the primary task. He then measured half of the participants' performance on both tasks over a 5 minute period when they displayed low levels of arousal. This situation was then repeated when these participants' arousal levels had been experimentally manipulated to a high level. These two procedures were then reversed for the remaining half of the participants in an attempt to counterbalance for order effects.

When comparing the results on the primary task, the researcher found no difference in performance across the two levels of arousal. He found the results in Table 13.6 for performance on the secondary task.

Table 13.6 **Performance scores on secondary task**

Low arousal		High arousal	
Novices	Experts	Novices	Experts
4	6	2	4
5	7	3	5
6	8	4	6
7	9	3	7
8	10	4	8
7	9	3	7
6	8	2	6
5	7	3	5
4	6	3	4
7	8	4	6

Appendix 1
GLOSSARY

Terms

Alternate/experimental hypothesis   This hypothesis states that any observed differences or relationships between sets of data are *not* a product of chance. If the null hypothesis is rejected then this hypothesis is accepted as the alternative explanation.

Boxplot   A graph that displays the actual distribution of the data around the median value that is represented by a horizontal bar. This bar is surrounded by a box that contains 50% of the scores. Extending from this box are whiskers. These whiskers show the highest and lowest value that are not outliers. Outliers that are more than 1.5 box-lengths from the 25th or 75th percentile are displayed by a circle and those that are more than 4 box-lengths away are shown by an asterisk.

Causal relationship   A relationship in which changes in the independent variable(s) cause changes in the dependent variable(s).

Central tendency   A collective term for the statistical measures (mean, median, mode) which aim to provide the value of a typical score.

Chi square   A test that requires nominal data, and compares the difference between the observed and the expected results.

Class boundary   The value that marks the dividing point between two classes.

Class limits   The smallest and largest values that are permitted in each class.

Class mark   The point half-way between the class limits.

Coefficient of determination (r^2)   The amount of variance in the dependent variable accounted for by the independent variable(s).

Confounding variable   A variable that produces systematic error in its influence of the dependent variable.

Control group   A group of participants in an experiment which is used for comparison with the experimental group. The control group experiences exactly the same conditions as the experimental group except for the treatment level of the independent variable. By comparing the results of the two groups, the effects of the independent variable can be observed.

Correlational research   Research that explores the relationship between variables and is restricted in its ability to infer cause and effect.

Counterbalancing   A strategy used in the design of an experiment in which the order of the presentation of the conditions could affect the result, for example practice effects or fatigue effects in a repeated measures design. Counterbalancing involves systematically varying the order of presentation of the conditions: for example, half the participants would have condition A followed by condition B, the other half would have condition B followed by condition A.

Degrees of freedom   A concept that refers to how data is free to vary. For example, in estimating the variance of a population from a sample the degrees of freedom are one less than the sample size.

Demand characteristics   Those features of an investigation which bring about unusual forms of behaviour from the subjects, for example a desire by the participant to give the investigator the results he/she wants.

Dependent variable   The factor which is observed or measured by the investigator, the outcome of the study. If the alternate/experimental hypothesis is correct the value of this factor will depend upon the independent variable.

Descriptive statistics   A branch of statistics that involves describing or displaying data and includes the calculation of measures of central tendency and dispersion.

Dispersion   A collective term for the measures (e.g. range, standard deviation, variance) which describe the spread of a set of scores.

Error bar   A graph that displays the estimated distribution of the data around the mean. This distribution can be confidence intervals, standard errors or standard deviations.

Experimental group   A group of participants which all receive the same experimental condition. When there is only one experimental condition the group is compared with a control group. Sometimes there are several experimental groups, each receiving a different condition.

Experimental research   Research in which the independent variables are manipulated and attempts are made to hold all other variables constant. It aims to establish causal relationships.

Experimenter effects   Problems producing a biased result brought about by the influence of the experimenter, for example an unconscious bias that is transmitted to the participants and brings about a 'self-fulfilling prophecy'.

Extraneous variable A factor that could influence the dependent variable but that is not controlled by the experimental design.

Histogram A barchart of a frequency distribution.

Hypothesis A testable statement, usually derived from theory or observation, which predicts the nature of the relationship between variables, or the nature of differences between treatment results.

Independent variable The factor that is chosen or manipulated by the experimenter in order to discover the effect on the dependent variable.

Inferential statistics A branch of statistics that involves drawing inferences about the population from which the data set was sampled.

Intercept The point where the regression line crosses the Y-axis. It is termed the constant when its value is included in a regression equation.

Interquartile range A measure of dispersion that is usually used with the median. Scores are put into size order and then the value of the score that comes one-quarter of the way along is subtracted from the score that comes three-quarters of the way along. Unlike the range, it is not affected by extreme scores.

Interval scale A scale in which equal differences between pairs of points on the scale are represented by equal intervals, but the zero point is arbitrary.

Kurtosis A measure that indicates whether the arc of a curve is peaked or flat.

Matching The procedure which attempts to ensure that two sets of experimental materials or participants are identical in all important respects.

Mean A measure of central tendency calculated by adding all the scores and dividing by the number of scores. Its advantage over alternative measures of central tendency is that it uses all the scores; its disadvantage is that it is influenced by extreme scores. It should only be used with interval or ratio levels of measurement.

Median A measure of central tendency that is the middle score of a set of scores placed in size order. Its advantage over alternative measures of central tendency is that it is not influenced by the values of extreme scores; its disadvantage is that it does not use the arithmetic values of the intervals between the scores. It requires at least an ordinal level of measurement and should be used instead of the mean when the distribution of data on an interval scale is skewed.

Mode A measure of central tendency which is the most frequently occurring score in a distribution.

Nominal scale   A scale which sorts examples according to categories, for example sorting cars according to make. Every example should belong to one, and only one, category.

Non-parametric tests   Tests that make no assumptions about the distribution of the data.

Normal distribution   A theoretical distribution that is symmetrical and which the distribution of data is described by z-tables. For example, approximately 68% of the population lie within ± 1 standard deviation of the mean, 95% of the population lie within ± 2 standard deviations of the mean and 99.7% of the population lie within ± 3 standard deviations of the mean.

Null hypothesis   This hypothesis states that any observed differences or relationships between sets of data are a product of chance. The probability that this hypothesis is correct is statistically determined.

One-tailed hypothesis   An alternate hypothesis in which the direction of the difference or relationship is predicted. For example, the experimental groups will have significantly *higher* scores than the control group.

Ordinal scale   A scale where the data is ranked in order from the smallest to the largest but where the intervals between each pair of scores may be unequal. For example, the finishing positions in a race are on an ordinal scale as the difference in time between the first and second runners crossing the finishing line may not be the same as that between the second and third runners.

Parametric tests   Tests which use the sample data to estimate the population parameters. They require at least interval data, equal variance and a normal distribution.

Population   All the members of a group defined according to key characteristics.

Post-hoc tests   Tests made after obtaining significant differences in ANOVA to identify differences among levels of the IV(s).

Power (β)   Measures the probability of rejecting the null hypothesis when it is false.

Range   The simplest measure of dispersion; measures the difference between the highest and the lowest scores. Sometimes the value 1 is added to this difference to reflect that the range is inclusive of the end points.

Regression coefficient (B)   The slope of the regression line that reflects the amount of change in Y' associated with each unit change in X.

Regression line   A straight line drawn through the points on a scatterplot that shows the predicted values of one variable for values of the other variable(s).

Sample   A group of participants selected from a population.

Significance level   The probability that one is prepared to accept that the result was obtained by chance and yet still reject H_0. Usually set at 0.05 (5%).

Skewed distribution   A non-symmetrical distribution in which the mean is distorted by the existence of extreme scores that lie to one side of the median.

Sphericity assumption   In a within-subjects ANOVA it is assumed that the variances of the differences between each pair of scores are not significantly different. If this assumption is not met there is an increased risk of committing a Type I error.

Standard deviation   The square root of the variance. It measures the dispersion of the scores around the mean in a normal distribution.

Standard error   The amount of error in the estimation of the population parameters from the sample data. It is equal to the square root of the variance divided by the degrees of freedom.

Sum of squares (SS)   The sum of the square of the mean subtracted from each score.

Symmetrical distribution   A distribution in which the mean, median and mode all have the same value.

Two-tailed hypothesis   An experimental/alternate hypothesis that does not predict the direction of the difference or relationship.

Type I Error   Rejection of H_0 when it is in fact true.

Type II Error   Acceptance of H_0 when it is in fact false.

Variance   A measure of dispersion that is equal to the sum of the squares divided by the degrees of freedom.

Symbols

$\approx$	approximately equal to
$>$	greater than
$<$	less than
$\neq$	not equal to
$\sqrt{9}$	square root of 9 (i.e. the number multiplied by itself which will result in the value 9)
α	alpha – the measure of the internal consistency of a scale or the significance level at which H_0 is rejected

β beta – the regression coefficients when all the variables are standardised to a mean of zero and a standard deviation of one

μ mu – mean of the population

$\sum$ summation – add up all the scores

σ sigma – standard deviation of the population

ω omega – weighting coefficient

a the symbol for the Y-intercept in a regression equation $Y = a + B(x)$

B regression coefficient that reflects the slope of the line in the above equation

BX the value of B multiplied by the value of X

df degrees of freedom

DV dependent variable

f frequency

F cumulative frequency

F test statistic from ANOVA

H_0 null hypothesis

IV independent variable

j number of rows

k number of columns

K number of groups

MS mean square (equals SS/df)

n_1 size of the sample in the first group

N total size of the sample

r bivariate correlation coefficient

r^2 proportion of the variance in one variable that is explained by the variance in the other variable; when multiplied by 100 this provides the coefficient of determination

R multiple correlation coefficient

R^2 proportion of the variance in the DV that is associated with changes in a linear combination of multiple independent/predictor variables

s standard deviation of the sample

s^2 variance of the sample

se standard error

SS sum of squares

t test statistic from t-test

$\bar{X}$ mean of X

Y' predicted value of Y

z the z-score is the distance of a point from the mean measured in units of standard deviation

TEST SELECTION TABLE

Selecting a statistical test

The statistical test one employs to analyse the data depends upon four major factors:

1. What is the research question (i.e. are you looking at relationships between variables or group differences)?
2. How many dependent and independent variables are there?
3. Was the data gathered by means of an independent, related or mixed design?
4. What scale of measurement was used to measure the variables?

Table A2.1 **Factors influencing choice of statistical technique**

Research question	Number of dependent variables (DVs)	Number of independent variables (IVs)	Analytical technique	Goal of analysis
Degree of relationship among variables	One	One	Bivariate r	Create a linear combination
	One	Multiple	Multiple R	of IVs to predict DV optimally
Significance of group differences	One	One	One-way ANOVA or t-test	
	One	Multiple	Factorial ANOVA	
	Multiple	One	One-way MANOVA	Create a linear combination
	Multiple	Multiple	Factorial MANOVA	of DVs to maximise group differences

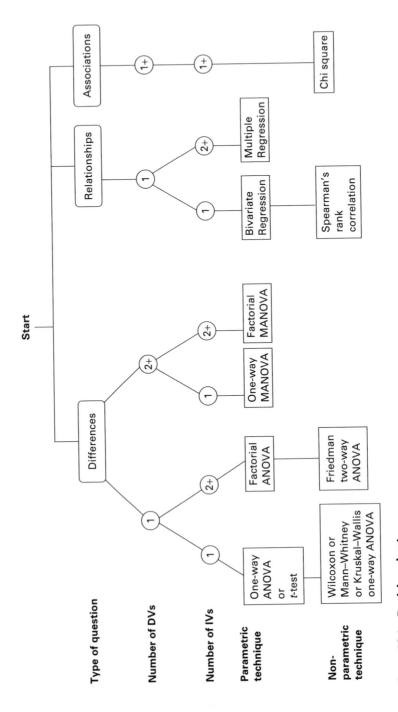

Figure A2.1   **Decision chart**

Appendix 3

ANSWERS TO THE EXERCISES

Exercise 2.1

High Sound Group

<u>Question 1</u>

Frequency Distribution for High Sound Group

Class	Class limits	Class frequency (f)
1	1–2	3
2	3–4	7
3	5–6	9
4	7–8	5
5	9–10	1
	Total	25

<u>Question 2</u>

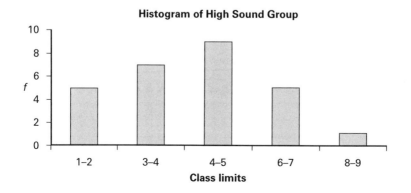

Question 3

Descriptive Statistics for High Sound Group

Mean	5.0
Median	5.0
Mode	5
Variance	4.17
Std. deviation	2.04

Low Sound Group

Question 1

Frequency Distribution for Low Sound Group

Class	Class limits	Class frequency (f)
1	1–2	3
2	3–4	4
3	5–6	5
4	7–8	2
	Total	14

Question 2

Histogram of Low Sound Group

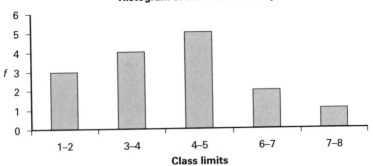

Question 3

Descriptive Statistics for Low Sound Group

Mean	4.2
Median	4.5
Mode	5
Variance	4.03
Std. deviation	2.01

Exercise 2.2

1. Data = Laundry detergents: Nominal scale.
2. Data = Temperature: Interval.
3. Data = SES: If the occupations are categorised on some scale (e.g. ranging from unskilled manual to professional) then the data is on an ordinal scale. If the occupations are arbitrarily categorised (e.g. 1 for a plumber, 2 for a doctor and 3 for an electrician) then the data is on a nominal scale.
4. Data = Attacking capability: Ordinal.
5. Data = Perceived success: Ordinal.
6. Data = Type of sport: Nominal.
   Data = Severity of injury: Interval.
7. Data = Athletes: Ordinal.

Exercise 3.2 Using descriptive statistics using SPSS for windows

Descriptive Statistics

Professor		**Student**	
Median	55.0000	Median	59.0000
Mean	55.0000	Mean	58.5455
Standard Deviation	15.5961	Standard Deviation	7.0355

Boxplot

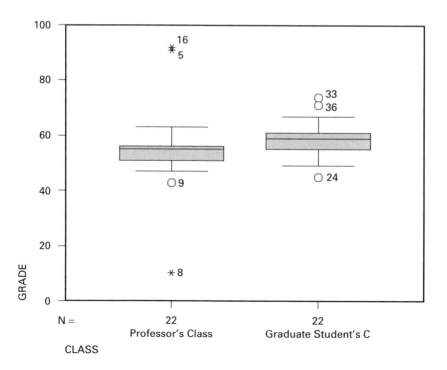

Is the median in the middle of the box?	Yes/No	Yes/No
Are the whiskers the same length?	Yes/No	Yes/No
Are there any outliers?	Yes/No	Yes/No

What do you conclude about the normality of the distributions of each set of scores from the boxplots?

Professor: The narrow box suggests that except for two extreme values and one outlier, the scores are narrowly distributed. This means that although the median is not in the middle of the box and the whiskers are of uneven length the data are unlikely to be significantly skewed. The existence of the two extreme values indicated by an asterisk suggests that the data will not be normally distributed

Student: The narrow box suggests that except for three outliers, the scores are narrowly distributed. The median is closer to the middle of this box and the whiskers are almost equal in length. This suggests that the data are unlikely to be significantly skewed. The existence of the three outliers does not alter the overall impression that the data approximate to a normal distribution.

Is this interpretation supported by the histograms for:

Professor: Yes, the distribution of the data is reasonably symmetrical but does not closely approximate to a normal distribution.

Histogram

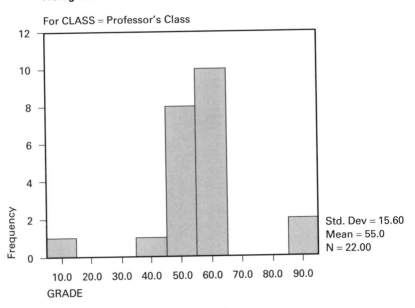

For CLASS = Professor's Class

Std. Dev = 15.60
Mean = 55.0
N = 22.00

GRADE

Histogram

For CLASS = Graduate Student's Class

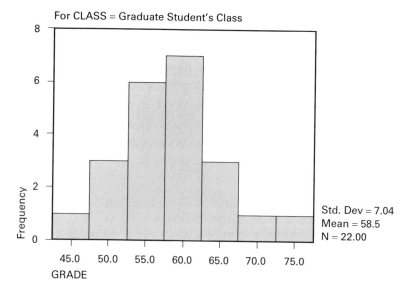

Std. Dev = 7.04
Mean = 58.5
N = 22.00

GRADE

Student: Yes, the distribution of the data is reasonably symmetrical and also approximates to a normal distribution

From comparing the means in the context of the standard deviations and looking at the boxplots, do you think there is practical difference in the final grades of the students in the two classes?

The difference in the means is 3.56 and the standard deviations range from 7.04 to 15.60. This suggests that there will be a large overlap in the two distribution of the sets of data. This observation is confirmed in the two boxplots that overlap a great deal. This suggests that there is not a practical difference in the final grades of the students in the two classes

Exercise 4.1

1.
    A.   First and second division players are different individuals and therefore the data can be considered to be collected from an independent design.
    B.   The scale of measurement is interval as the difference between one goal and two goals is the same as the difference between seven and eight goals.
    Test selected from Table 4.1 is a *t*-test for independent samples.

2.
    A.   The geographical area is the same in both years and therefore the data can be considered to be collected from a repeated measures design.

   B.   Rainfall is measured in millimetres and therefore the scale of measure-
        ment is interval.
   Test selected from Table 4.1 is a *t*-test for paired samples.

3.
   A.   The same woodlice are used in both conditions which are counter-
        balanced and therefore the data can be considered to be collected from
        a repeated measures design.
   B.   Foraging is measured in minutes and seconds and therefore the scale of
        measurement is interval.
   Test selected from Table 4.1 is a *t*-test for paired samples.

4.
   A.   The political choices and religious affiliations expressed are from
        different individuals and therefore the data can be considered to be
        collected from an independent groups design.
   B.   The data is just in the form of a tally sheet and therefore can be con-
        sidered to be on a nominal scale.
   Test selected from Table 4.1 is a chi-square test.

5.
   A.   The random allocation to the two conditions means that the data can
        be considered to be collected from an independent groups design.
   B.   The data is on a subjective scale of 1 to 10 in which it is unlikely all of
        the intervals are equal and therefore the data can be considered to be
        on an ordinal scale.
   Test selected from Table 4.1 is a Mann–Whitney test.

6.
   A.   The two groups of children are independent of one another and there-
        fore the data can be considered to be collected from an independent
        groups design.
   B.   The aspirations are ordered on a scale but the intervals may not be
        equal and therefore a cautious decision would be that the data can be
        considered to be on an ordinal scale.
   Test selected from Table. 4.1 is a Mann–Whitney test.

7.
   A.   The data can be considered to be collected from an independent groups
        design as it is produced by two independent varieties of apple trees.
   B.   The data collected will be on some metric of weight such as kilograms
        and therefore can be considered to be at least on an ordinal scale.
   Test selected from Table 4.1 is an independent samples *t*-test.

8.
   A.   As the two sources of data are matched on what are considered to be
        the important variables a matched pair design has been used.
   B.   The data collected will be measured on an interval scale.
   Test selected from Table 4.1 is a paired samples *t*-test.

9.
   A.   As the two sources of data are from different genders the data can be considered to be collected from an independent groups design.
   B.   The data collected is simply a tally of those who have and have not given up smoking and can be considered to be on a nominal scale.
   Test selected from Table 4.1 is a chi-square test.

10.
   A.   As the same students are used in both the before and after conditions the data can be considered to be collected from a repeated measures design.
   B.   The attitude data is probably measured on a subjective scale of 1 to 7 in which it is unlikely that all of the intervals are equal and therefore the data can be considered to be on an ordinal scale.
   Test selected from Table 4.1 is a Wilcoxon test.

Exercise 4.2

1a 0.99% of students consume more than 22 pints per week.
1b 75% of students drink more than 12.09 pints of beer.
1c 0.39% of students consume less than 7 pints per week.
1d The percentage drinking between 10 and 20 pints is 90.3%.
2a The average amount of time spent reading is 18.5 hours.
2b 2.74% of students fulfill the university reading requirement.
3a The number graduating with debts greater than £10,000 is 2,806 students.
3b The number graduating with debts less than £1,000 is 92 students.
3c The number graduating with debts between £4,000 and £8,000 is 51,865 students.

Exercise 7.2 (numerical components)

3.   For the four groups:

	A	B	C	D	Sum of weights
A vs B	1	−1	0	0	0
A vs BC	2	−1	−1	0	0

The weights shown above are only one of many possible solutions. For example, the following would also be correct:

	A	B	C	D	
A vs B	−1	1	0	0	0
A vs BC	−2	1	1	0	0

To determine if these two contrasts are orthogonal:

$$(1 \times 2) + (-1 \times -1) + (0 \times -1) + (0 \times 0) = 2 + 1 + 0 + 0 = 3$$

As the sum of these cross-multiplied weights does not equal zero the contrasts are not orthogonal and therefore a correction has to be made for the
increased risk of committing a Type I error.

4. For the four groups:

Contrast number		A	B	C	D	Sum of weights
1	A vs BCD	3	−1	−1	−1	0
2	B vs CD	0	2	−1	−1	0
3	C vs D	0	0	−1	1	0

Again, the weights shown above are only one of many possible solutions.
To determine which of these contrasts are orthogonal:

Contrasts 1 and 2 $(3 \times 0) + (-1 \times 2) + (-1 \times -1) + (-1 \times -1)$
$= 0 - 2 + 1 + 1 = 0$
Contrasts 1 and 3 $(3 \times 0) + (-1 \times 0) + (-1 \times -1) + (-1 \times 1)$
$= 0 + 0 + 1 - 1 = 0$
Contrasts 2 and 3 $(0 \times 0) + (2 \times 0) + (-1 \times -1) + (-1 \times 1)$
$= 0 + 0 + 1 - 1 = 0$

As the sum of all of these cross-multiplied weights equals zero all of the contrasts are orthogonal and therefore no correction has to be made for an
increased risk of committing a Type I error.

5. Divide the desired significance level, for example 0.05, by 3 and use the
result as the significance level to be employed in deciding whether to accept
or reject the null hypothesis.

Exercise 13.1

Scenario One

1. **Research question**
   Are the number of lower body injuries sustained a function of the particular
   sport in which athletes engage?

2. **Null and alternate hypotheses**
   H_0 There will be no significant difference in the number of lower body
   injuries sustained in the four different sports
   H_1 There will be a significant difference in the number of lower body injuries
   sustained in the four different sports

3. **Number of independent variables**
   One   Type of sport   Four levels: rugby, soccer, hockey, track and field

4. **Number of dependent variables**
   One   Number of lower body injuries

5. **Recommended statistical analyses**
   Between-subjects one-way ANOVA as the research question is focusing on
   differences and there is only one IV and one DV. Analytical comparisons,
   either post-hoc or planned contrast, to determine where any differences lie.

6. **Assumptions that statistical technique makes**
    Number of lower body injuries is measured on an interval scale.
    Number of lower body injuries is normally distributed.
    The variance of the number of lower body injuries within all the groups is equal.

Scenario Two

1. **Research question**
    Does cigarette smoking influence longevity?
2. **Null and alternate hypotheses**
    H_0 There will be no significant linear relationship between the number of cigarettes smoked and age at the time of death
    H_1 There will be a significant negative linear relationship between the number of cigarettes smoked and age at the time of death
3. **Number of independent variables**
    One predictor variable   Number of cigarettes smoked per day
4. **Number of dependent variables**
    One dependent (criterion) variable   Age at time of death
5. **Recommended statistical analyses**
    Bivariate regression analysis
6. **Assumptions that statistical technique makes**
    Age at time of death is measured on an interval scale.
    Age at time of death is normally distributed.

Scenario Three

1. **Research question**
    Do age and sex have any bearing upon the amount of time adults engage in leisure activities?
2. **Null and alternate hypotheses**
    H_0 There will be no significant difference in the time engaged in leisure activities by adult men and women
    H_0 There will be no significant difference in the time engaged in leisure activities by young adults, middle-aged adults and older adults
    H_0 Age will not show a differential effect upon the amount of time engaged in leisure activities for adult men and women
    H_1 There will be a significant difference in the time engaged in leisure activities by adult men and women
    H_2 There will be a significant difference in the time engaged in leisure activities by young adults, middle-aged adults and older adults
    H_3 Age will show a differential effect upon the amount of time engaged in leisure activities for adult men and women
3. **Number of independent variables**
    Two independent variables:
        Age   Three levels: young adults, middle-aged adults and older adults
        Gender   Two levels: male and female
4. **Number of dependent variables**
    One dependent variable   Time engaged in leisure activities

5. **Recommended statistical analyses**
   Between-subjects factorial ANOVA as the research question is focusing on differences and there is more than one IV.

6. **Assumptions that statistical technique makes**
   Time engaged in leisure activities is measured on an interval scale.
   Time engaged in leisure activities is normally distributed.
   Equal variance in time engaged in leisure activities across the three age groups.
   Equal variance in time engaged in leisure activities across the two gender groups.

Scenario Four

1. **Research question**
   What is the effect of a low-fat diet, in conjunction with regular physical activity, on cholesterol levels?

2. **Null and alternate hypotheses**
   H_0 There is no significant difference in the cholesterol level (LDL/HDL ratio) of patients prior to, and following, a diet and exercise programme
   H_1 Participants' mean cholesterol levels will be significantly lower after the diet and exercise programme with their pre-diet and exercise mean cholesterol levels.

3. **Number of independent variables**
   One independent variable   Diet and exercise programme   Two levels: pre and post

4. **Number of dependent variables**
   One dependent variable   Cholesterol level (LDL/HDL ratio)

5. **Recommended statistical analyses**
   Repeated measures (paired) t-test or one-way within-subjects ANOVA as the research question focuses on differences and there is only one IV.

6. **Assumptions that statistical technique makes**
   Cholesterol level is measured on an interval scale.
   Cholesterol level is normally distributed.
   As there are only two groups neither the homogeneity of variance assumption for the t-test nor the sphericity assumption for the within-subjects ANOVA analysis are relevant.

Scenario Five

1. **Research question**
   How much of the variance in atherosclerosis can be explained by the combination of advancing age, serum cholesterol, obesity, inactivity and Type A Behaviour Pattern?

2. **Null and alternate hypotheses**
   H_0 There will be no significant linear relationship between the dependent variable (atherosclerosis) and the predictor variables (age, serum cholesterol, obesity, inactivity and Type A Behaviour Pattern)
   H_1 There will be a significant linear relationship between atherosclerosis and age, serum cholesterol, obesity, inactivity and Type A Behaviour Pattern

3. **Number of independent variables**
   Five predictor variables: age, serum cholesterol, obesity, inactivity, Type A Behaviour Pattern

4. **Number of dependent variables**
   One dependent (criterion) variable   Atherosclerosis

5. **Recommended statistical analyses**
   Multiple regression analysis employing the backward method. Research question focuses on linear relationship, the prediction of one DV (criterion) (atherosclerosis) from five predictor variables (age, serum cholesterol, obesity, inactivity, Type A).

6. **Assumptions that statistical technique makes**
   Atherosclerosis is measured on an interval scale.
   Age, serum cholesterol, obesity, inactivity, Type A and atherosclerosis are normally distributed.
   Age, serum cholesterol, obesity, inactivity, Type A are linearly related to atherosclerosis.

Scenario Six

1. **Research question**
   Do experience at a primary task and arousal level influence participants' performance score on a secondary task?

2. **Null and alternate hypotheses**
   H_0 There will be no significant difference between experts and novices in performance scores on the secondary task
   H_0 There will be no significant difference in performance scores on the secondary task between low and high arousal conditions
   H_0 There will be no significant interaction between experience and arousal in their effect on performance scores on the secondary task
   H_1 There will be a significant difference between experts and novices in performance scores on the secondary task
   H_2 Participants will perform significantly better in the low arousal condition compared with the high arousal condition
   H_3 There will be a significant interaction between experience and arousal in their effect on performance scores on the secondary task

3. **Number of independent variables**
   Two independent variables:
   Experience on primary task (two levels)   Arousal (two levels)

4. **Number of dependent variables**
   One dependent variable   Performance score on the secondary task

5. **Recommended statistical analyses**
   Mixed design 2×2 factorial ANOVA.
   The research question focuses on differences; there is one DV and two IVs, one of which is a within-subjects (or repeated measures) factor, the other a between-subjects factor.

6. **Assumptions that statistical technique makes**
   Performance score on the secondary task is measured on an interval scale.
   Performance score on the secondary task is normally distributed.

The variance of performance scores on the secondary task within experience groups (between-subjects factor) is equal.
The variance of performance scores on the secondary task within arousal groups (within-subjects factor) is equal.
The sphericity assumption cannot be tested as there are only two within-groups conditions.

Exercise 13.2

What follows is an indication of what should have been included in the completion of the analysis of the data for each of the six scenarios. A complete example is given in Appendix 4.

Scenario One

1. **Presentation and interpretation from descriptive statistics**
   Means and standard deviations for each group should have been presented. Comments, with explanations, should have been made as to whether the above values suggest support for each hypothesis.

2. **Presentation and interpretation from graphical representations**
   An appropriate boxplot should be presented. This graph should have a title and clearly labelled axes. Comments should be made as to what is interpreted from this graph, especially with respect to the null hypothesis.

3. **Presentation and interpretation on whether test assumptions are met**
   Checks should have been made that the data does not significantly deviate from normal by computing z-values for skewness and kurtosis and checking that these z-values fall between plus and minus 1.97.

   The results from Levene's test for equality of error variance should have been presented. Also an explanation of whether the assumption of homogeneity is met and an outline of what implications this decision has for the ANOVA analysis.

4. **Presentation of what is inferred from the one-way between-subjects ANOVA and analytical comparisons (i.e. post-hoc or planned contrasts)**
   The F-value, the degrees of freedom and the significance value from the ANOVA should have been presented. A comment should have been made on what the significance of F means.

   A description of the analytical comparisons conducted and any significant group differences. t-values and significance value from the comparisons should have been presented. A comment should have been made on what the findings mean.

5. **Clear statement, with reasons, of which hypothesis is accepted and which is rejected**

6. **Clear statement, with reasons, of what you concluded with respect to the research question**

Scenario Two

1. **Presentation and interpretation from descriptive statistics**
    Means and standard deviations for each variable should have been presented.

2. **Presentation and interpretation from graphical representations**
    An appropriate scattergram should be presented. This graph should have a title, clearly labelled axes, a legend, and a regression line (line of best fit). Comments should be made as to what is interpreted from this graph, especially with respect to the hypothesis.

3. **Presentation and interpretation on whether test assumptions are met**
    Checks should have been made that the data does not significantly deviate from normal by computing z-values for skewness and kurtosis and checking that these z-values fall between plus and minus 1.97.

4. **Presentation of what is inferred from the bivariate regression**
    The R-value, R^2-value, the F-value and significance value from the ANOVA should have been presented. A comment should have been made on what the significance of F means and what the R^2-value means.

    The constant and B-value should have been used to represent the regression equation (i.e. $Y = a + Bx$).

5. **Clear statement, with reasons, of which hypothesis is accepted and which is rejected**

6. **Clear statement, with reasons, of what you concluded with respect to the research question**

Scenario Three

1. **Presentation and interpretation from descriptive statistics**
    Means, standard deviations and group sizes for each main effect and the interaction should have been presented.

    Comments, with explanations, should have been made as to whether the above values suggest support for each hypothesis.

2. **Presentation and interpretation from graphical representations**
    An appropriate line graph should be presented. This graph should have a title, clearly labelled axes and a legend. Comments should be made as to what is interpreted from this graph, especially with respect to the hypothesis concerning the interaction between the factors.

3. **Presentation and interpretation on whether test assumptions are met**
    Checks should have been made that the data does not significantly deviate from normal by computing z-values for skewness and kurtosis and checking that these z-values fall between plus and minus 1.97.

    The results from Levene's test for equality of error variance should have been presented. Also an explanation of whether the assumption of homogeneity is met and an outline of what implications this decision has for the ANOVA analysis.

4. **Presentation of what is inferred from the factorial ANOVA**
    The F-values, the degrees of freedom, the significance values for each of the main effects and the interaction should have been presented. A

comment should have been made on what the significance of F means in each case.

5. **Clear statement, with reasons, of which hypotheses were accepted and which were rejected**

6. **Clear statement, with reasons, of what you concluded with respect to the research question**

Scenario Four

1. **Presentation and interpretation from descriptive statistics**
   Means and standard deviations for each group should have been presented.

   Comments, with explanations, should have been made as to whether the above values suggest support for each hypothesis.

2. **Presentation and interpretation from graphical representations**
   An appropriate boxplot or error bar should be presented. This graph should have a title and clearly labelled axes. Comments should be made as to what is interpreted from this graph, especially with respect to the hypothesis.

3. **Presentation and interpretation on whether test assumptions are met**
   Checks should have been made that the data does not significantly deviate from normal by computing z-values for skewness and kurtosis and checking that these z-values fall between plus and minus 1.97.

   If a within-subjects ANOVA was used, the results from Mauchly's test of sphericity should have been presented. Also an explanation of the implications this decision has for the within-subjects ANOVA analysis. That is, if the significance value is not computed or less than 0.05 then the Greenhouse–Geisser results should be used, whilst if the value is above 0.05 then the sphericity assumption results should be employed.

4. **Presentation of what is inferred from the t-test or within-subjects ANOVA**
   Paired t-test: t-value, the degrees of freedom and the significance value from the t-test should have been presented. A comment should have been made on what the significance of t means.

   Within-subjects ANOVA: the F-value, the degrees of freedom and the significance value from the ANOVA should have been presented. A comment should have been made on what the significance of F means.

5. **Clear statement, with reasons, of which hypothesis is accepted and which is rejected**

6. **Clear statement, with reasons, of what you concluded with respect to the research question**

Scenario Five

1. **Presentation and interpretation from descriptive statistics**
   A correlation matrix should have been presented. For each predictor variable comments should have been made as to the direction, strength and significance of their relationship with the dependent variable.

An examination of the correlations between the predictor variables should have been made to see if this suggests problems of multicollinearity.

Credit was given if a scattergram was included with appropriate regression lines and interpretative comments. However, the inclusion of the regression lines was not essential to gain full marks.

2. **Presentation of what is inferred from the multiple regression**
   The simplest method would have been to select a backward method but the same result could have been achieved by employing an **Enter** method and then a stepwise method. The results would have been the same but there would theoretically be an increased risk of committing a Type I error.

   If an **Enter** method analysis was executed first then the following should have been presented and interpreted for the first model containing all of the predictor variables:

   R, R Square
   F, Sig. F
   B, Beta, t and Sig. t

   The results of the final model of the stepwise or backward method should then have been included but the interpretation may be restricted to the final model. These should include all of the above, namely

   R, R Square
   F, Sig. F
   B, Beta, t and Sig. t

   In addition the final regression equation should be presented:

   Atherosclerosis = .069Age + .418Inactivity + .646Type_A - 9.961

   An explanation of what this equation means should have been given.

3. **Clear statement, with reasons, of which hypotheses were accepted and which were rejected**

4. **Clear statement, with reasons, of what you concluded with respect to the research**

Scenario Six

1. **Presentation and interpretation from descriptive statistics**
   Means, standard deviations and group sizes for each main effect and the interaction should have been presented.

   Comments, with explanations, should have been made as to whether the above values suggest support for each hypothesis.

2. **Presentation and interpretation from graphical representations**
   An appropriate line graph should be presented. This graph should have a title, clearly labelled axes and a legend. Comments should be made as to

what is interpreted from this graph, especially with respect to the hypothesis concerning the interaction between the factors.

3. **Presentation and interpretation on whether test assumptions are met**
Checks should have been made that the data does not significantly deviate from normal by computing z-values for skewness and kurtosis and checking that these z-values fall between plus and minus 1.97.

The results from Levene's test for equality of error variance are not very useful as they are comparing the variance of the experts and novices in each of the levels of arousal. It would be easier to simply run one of the **Descriptive Statistics** options (e.g. **Explore**) to compute the variances. This would have meant you could have compared the variances for the expert group (combining both high and low arousal groups) and the novice group (combining both high and low arousal groups) to see if the variances were sufficiently different to have implications for Type I error. You could then have compared the variances of the low arousal group (combining both experts and novice groups) with the high arousal group (combining both experts and novice groups). Had you done this you could then have presented an explanation of whether the assumption of homogeneity is met and what the implications are of this for the ANOVA analysis and the interpretation of the significance values.

4. **Presentation of what is inferred from the factorial ANOVA**
The relevant results from the 'Tests of Within-Subjects Contrasts' have been pasted into the answer. These should have included the F-values, the degrees of freedom and the significance values for each of the main effects and the interaction should have been presented. A comment should have been made on what the significance of F means in each case. This should then have been repeated for the 'Tests of Between-Subjects Effects' table.

5. **Clear statement, with reasons, of which hypotheses were accepted and which were rejected**

6. **Clear statement, with reasons, of what you concluded with respect to the research question**

Appendix 4

ILLUSTRATION OF HOW CHAPTER 13 MIGHT BE COMPLETED USING THE DATA ON PAGE 74

Research Question

What is the effect of experience on pre-performance anxiety in scuba divers?

The null hypothesis to be tested is as follows:

H_0 There is no significant difference in the mean anxiety scores of beginners and intermediate scuba divers

As an alternative to this null hypothesis the following one-tailed experimental hypothesis was postulated:

H_1 Beginner scuba divers will have higher mean anxiety scores than intermediate divers

1. Interpretation from Descriptive Statistics

From Table A4.1 it can be noted that the results are in agreement with the experimental hypothesis as the beginners group have a mean anxiety score that is 1.45 points higher than that obtained from the intermediate group.

However, Table A4.1 also indicates that the standard deviation values are quite large in comparison with the mean difference. This will result in a large overlap in the distribution of the two groups of scores, suggesting that the observed difference in the two means is unlikely to prove to be statistically significant.

Table A4.1 **Descriptive statistics**

	Mean	**Standard deviation**	**Variance**
ALL	17.25	6.37	40.59
Beginners	18.15	5.06	25.61
Intermediate	16.70	6.18	38.22

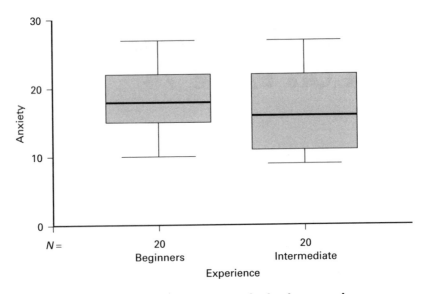

Figure A4.1 **Boxplot displaying anxiety scores for beginners and intermediate scuba divers**

2. Interpretation from Graphical Representations

This interpretation is confirmed by the boxplot in Figure A4.1 that displays a small difference in the medians and a large overlap in the two sets of scores.

In the boxplot for the beginners it can be seen that the median is in the middle of the box and the 'whiskers' are of approximately equal length. This suggests that this data is symmetrically distributed. The boxplot for the intermediate group is very similar except that the two whiskers are of slightly different length. This suggests that the data will be slightly, but probably not significantly, skewed. As the two boxplots overlap a great deal on the anxiety dimension this offers support for the null hypothesis.

3. Comments on Whether Test Assumptions Are Met

To measure the probability of finding a mean difference as large as 1.45 by chance a *t*-test for independent samples was selected. This test was chosen to

Table A4.2 **Kurtosis and skewness values**

Beginners	Kurtosis	S.E. Kurt	K/S.E.K.	Skewness	S.E. Skew	S/S.E.S.
	-.74	.99	-.75	-.06	.5120	-.12
Intermediate	Kurtosis	S.E. Kurt	K/S.E.K.	Skewness	S.E. Skew	S/S.E.S.
	-1.30	.99	-1.34	.31	.51	.61

detect the difference as the hypothesis was concerned with differences and there was only one independent variable, namely experience, and one dependent variable, namely anxiety.

In employing this test we are making three assumptions. These are that anxiety is measured on an interval scale, that anxiety is normally distributed and that the variances of the two groups are equal

3(a) INTERVAL DATA
It is assumed that the anxiety scale employed produces interval data.

3(b) NORMAL DISTRIBUTION
To see if the data is normally distributed the kurtosis and skewness values were computed and are shown in Table A4.2.

To measure the probability that the scores displayed significant kurtosis or skewness the values of each attribute were divided by their standard error. As none of these values are greater than 1.97 we conclude that the data does not significantly ($p > 0.05$) depart from a normal distribution.

3(c) EQUAL VARIANCE
To see if the assumption of homogeneity of variance was met the variances of the two groups were inspected in Table A4.1. From this table we can note that the variances do not appear to be very different as they have values of approximately 25 and 38. As the data was considered to be normally distributed, Levene's test was used to confirm this observation; that is, to test the null hypothesis that there is no significant difference in the variances of the two samples. This test produced the statistics in Table A4.3.

As the probability of getting a value of F of 1.517 by chance is 22.6% we accept the null hypothesis and conclude that the variances are not significantly different.

As the assumptions of normality and equal variance were met a t-test was employed and this produced the results in Table A4.4.

Table A4.3

Levene's Test for Equality of Variances	$F = 1.517$	$P = .226$

Table A4.4   **t-tests for independent samples for mean difference of 1.45**

Variances	t-value df	Two-tail significance		SE of differences
Equal	**0.81**	**38**	**0.422**	**1.786**
Unequal	0.81	36.6	0.422	1.786

4. WHAT YOU INFER FROM THE STATISTICAL TESTS EMPLOYED

As the variances were not considered to be significantly different, the row headed 'Equal' in Table A4.4 was examined. When the mean difference of 1.45 was divided by the standard error of 1.786 this produced a value of t that equalled 0.81. The two-tailed significance associated with this value of t with 38 degrees of freedom was 0.422. However, as the experimental hypothesis was one-tailed this value has to be divided by 2 to produce a probability of 0.211. Therefore 21 times out of 100 a mean difference of 1.45 would be obtained from drawing two samples of 20 from the same population.

5. Which Hypotheses You Accept and Reject

As this probability is greater than the 5% significance criterion to be employed, the null hypothesis is accepted and therefore the alternate hypothesis is rejected.

6. What You Conclude with Respect to the Research Question

Therefore we conclude that there is no significant difference in the anxiety scores of beginner and intermediate scuba divers.

INDEX